A HISTORY OF
LATE NINETEENTH
CENTURY DRAMA
1850–1900

IN TWO VOLUMES

VOLUME I

A HISTORY OF
LATE NINETEENTH
CENTURY DRAMA
1850–1900

BY

ALLARDYCE NICOLL

PROFESSOR OF ENGLISH LANGUAGE AND LITERATURE
IN THE UNIVERSITY OF BIRMINGHAM

VOLUME I

CAMBRIDGE
AT THE UNIVERSITY PRESS
1949

PUBLISHED BY
THE SYNDICS OF THE CAMBRIDGE UNIVERSITY PRESS

London Office: Bentley House, N.W. I
American Branch: New York

Agents for Canada, India, and Pakistan: Macmillan

First Edition 1946
Reprinted 1949

Printed in Great Britain at the University Press, Cambridge
(Brooke Crutchley, University Printer)

To
MY FORMER COLLEAGUES & STUDENTS
AT YALE UNIVERSITY

PREFACE

WITH these two volumes is brought to an end the general history of the English drama from the year when Charles II was restored to the throne down to the conclusion of the Victorian epoch. Although *A History of Restoration Drama* was published in 1923 as a separate volume, it was originally planned as the first of the series of studies which now reaches completion.

Each of these studies has been concerned with a characteristic and distinct manifestation of theatrical activity. Beginning with a thoroughly aristocratic heroic tragedy and comedy of manners, the theatre passed, during the first half of the eighteenth century, into new hands which turned out ballad-operas and comedies of a growing sentimental flavour. By the middle of the century, the stage had become definitely bourgeois and extreme forms of sentimentalism flourished alongside incipient romanticism. Once more, in the first half of the nineteenth century, the scene changed; during this time the playhouses became essentially "popular", with noisy audiences taking vivid enjoyment in melodramas and various forms of extravaganza.

Now, in the period 1850–1900, we return to a theatrical atmosphere which is not so markedly restricted to particular classes within the community and which hence exhibits something of that breadth of spirit and wider vision which once animated the stage during the reign of Queen Elizabeth. If the Victorian drama did not succeed in reaching the heights attained three centuries before, the failure is to be traced, not to lack of universality in appeal, but rather to the prevailing materialism of the age—a materialism that restricted the scope of the playwrights and effectively prohibited that larger utterance from which the characters and themes of Shakespeare may not be separated. Tom Robertson is, in a way, the Christopher Marlowe of the Victorian stage, and this very comparison indicates, by the spiritual contrast between the two men, the measure of difference separating the new from the old.

For us the interest of these fifty years lies in the fact that in this period were born and established the conventions and conditions of our own stage. From Shakespeare's time down to the time of Robertson the stock-company tradition had ruled supreme. Signs of its coming disintegration become apparent in the early eighteen hundreds when histrionic stars assumed ever greater prominence, but before 1850 these remained as signs merely. It was in the latter years of the century that the old system broke and disappeared, giving place to a new theatrical world and calling for fresh adjustments. In order to understand our own stage aright, it is imperative that we should understand the basic innovations which effectually put a great chasm between a Burbage and an Irving, between a Shakespeare and a Shaw.

Naturally, with the increase in theatres resultant from an increase in the playgoing public and with the accompanying break-down of the repertory system, dramatic productivity in these fifty years proceeded to surpass in quantity that of any corresponding period of the past—and this fact calls for something in the nature of an apology so far as the two present volumes are concerned. Unquestionably a book that is about two-thirds devoted to a hand-list of plays may be deemed ill-balanced, yet these proportions were inevitable. When I prepared *Restoration Drama*, I found that no one had attempted to list all the dramatic productions of this time and consequently it seemed to me that one of the most useful things I could do was to append to my text a catalogue of plays produced between 1660 and 1700. Although the compiling of this list was somewhat complicated by uncertainties

and problems regarding dates and published texts, the task
was simplified by the relatively small number of tragedies
and comedies written for the delectation of the exclusive
courtly audience of this period. Having once established the
principle of providing a hand-list and finding that catalogues
of productions after 1700 were also lacking, I naturally was
forced to prepare similar hand-lists in ensuing volumes.

Unfortunately, the total number of plays increased rapidly
as the years passed by. From about 2,000 between 1700 and
1750, it grew to some 3,200 for the latter half of the eighteenth
century. Swelled by the throngs of early nineteenth-century
melodramas and farces, it continued to assume ever larger
proportions, until for the period with which we are now concerned, 1850 to 1900, I have found myself burdened with
more than 20,000 titles. I am fully aware of the fact that such
a hand-list as is given here, with no adequate guides for
assistance, must inevitably have errors and omissions—yet it
has seemed to me that, worthless though many of the dramas
are and though the hand-list may be imperfect, such an
attempt at a cataloguing of the total dramatic productivity of
the time was necessary to serve as the guide that I myself
found lacking and to enable others working on this period
to have at least some general conspectus of the entire field.
This having been done, later workers may fill in such gaps
as I have left and correct mistakes.

It may, perhaps, be proper to record that most of the work
of compilation was undertaken before 1933, and that the
entire study was put into proof in 1938 and 1939. As a
result, references given in the text to books and articles are
not as up-to-date as I could have wished. Had there been
opportunity, for example, allusion would certainly have
been made to the scholarly and suggestive studies recently
published by Dr E. I. West on the histrionic styles of the
period.

To the publishers, and particularly to the Secretary of the Syndics, Mr S. C. Roberts, I wish to tender sincerest thanks for their co-operation in the production of these volumes. To the courtesy of the Right Honourable the Earl of Cromer I am indebted for permission to consult the invaluable collection of dramatic texts in the custody of the Lord Chamberlain. In the labour of cataloguing these Dr Clifford Leech gave me considerable aid.

ALLARDYCE NICOLL

THE UNIVERSITY OF BIRMINGHAM
February 1946

CONTENTS

VOL. I

Chapter Six

JONES AND PINERO: PLAYS OF THE EIGHTIES

Chapter Seven

WILDE AND SHAW: PLAYS OF THE NINETIES

Appendix A

THE THEATRES, 1850–1900

VOL. II

Appendix B

HAND-LIST OF PLAYS PRODUCED BETWEEN 1850
AND 1900

CHAPTER I

THE THEATRE

1. *Introductory*

WITHIN the half-century covered by this survey the modern drama, with all its essential conditions and conventions, was born. The theatre of the eighteen-fifties, even although it may be vaguely within human memory, seems far distant from the theatre of the nineteen-thirties; the theatre of the nineties—and that not only in matter of time—appears to be part of ourselves. In 1850 Tom Robertson was as yet only a touring actor, dreaming perhaps, like Arthur Gower in *Trelawney of the "Wells"*, of dramatic work to come, but still thoroughly immersed in the older stock traditions; Charles Kean was just starting his extraordinary antiquarian experiments at the Princess's; the popular playhouses were rejoicing in eminently moral, but aesthetically unadventuresome, "domestic dramas", of which maybe the titles—*Adam Winter; or, Dark Deeds of Old London* (Brit. 1850), *Pure as Driven Snow; or, Tempted in Vain* (Brit. 1869) and *Faithful under Peril; or, A Father's Dishonour and a Daughter's Shame* (Pav. 1873)—sufficiently illustrate the calibre. When we step into the world of the nineties we seem to have traversed countless ages. Sir Arthur Pinero and Henry Arthur Jones have now definitely established themselves; men are talking freely of, and animatedly discussing, the work of Ibsen, whose *Ghosts* and *A Doll's House* make Robertson's once realistic *Caste* and *School* seem artificial and antiquated; Oscar Wilde is rousing London society by the effervescent play of his wit; and George Bernard Shaw is stepping from the ranks of the musical and theatrical critics to prove himself the dramatic force of the century.

Not often are contemporaries enabled to trace with any surety of appreciation the changing tastes and tendencies of their own age, but the theatrical current was running so strong during those years that none could escape an awareness of its force. A veritable revolution occurred between 1850 and 1900; some deplored it and others praised, but all were conscious of the fact, and the intensity of the revolution may perhaps best be realised by the way in which it stamped itself thus upon the consciousness both of those who in that period were merely spectators and of those who were actively immersed in the practical business of the theatre.

The revolution gathered impetus as it advanced through the decades. From 1850 to 1870 its movement, though sure, was comparatively slight, and in the year 1871 a writer in *The Saturday Review* was reluctantly forced to cast a melancholy eye over the dramatic prospect. Many new theatres, he saw, had been erected in London, but in his opinion these had "been built beyond the possibilities of finding either plays to act in them or audiences to witness the performances". When he wrote, adaptations from the novels of Charles Dickens were still the rage, but "What", he enquired dismally, "What will become of the English stage when the public has grown weary, if it ever does grow weary, of dramatic versions of the stories of the late Mr Dickens? The number of new theatres increases, but the number of these stories must always remain the same."[1]

A bare seventeen years later in the same journal another critic was writing on the same theme, and "Undoubtedly", he said,

the theatres today fill a more important place in the national life, at any rate in London, than ever. Their number has of late years multiplied some three-fold, and plans for still further increasing them are constantly reaching us. The popular interest in the stage is no longer content with the criticisms on plays and players furnished by such daily and weekly papers as deal with general news, but has called into existence numerous publications, of which the drama, either alone or in conjunction with sport, is the *raison d'être*. The monthly magazines have caught the infection, and deal largely in theatrical topics, while even in the *Annual*

[1] xxxi, Jan. 14, 1871, 50–1.

Register, which used to restrict its notice of the contemporary stage to at most a few lines, we now find ample reference, not only to the pieces running from night to night in the London theatres, but even to the more notable of those produced at special matinée performances.

There is no denying the fact that the stage has become more fashionable and more popular.[1]

And by 1895 *The Era* could definitely pronounce its judgment:

The drama in England never was in a better condition than at the present time. The tone of criticism, the ideals of the actor and the actress, and the aims of the dramatist, have all been elevated.... The drama is taking its proper place amongst the arts; and we may expect in the next ten or twenty years to find our progress even more gratifying and astonishing than that which we have made since the fifties.[2]

The preceding paragraphs may perhaps give the impression that all was accomplished within a brief space of thirty years, but such an assumption would be far from the truth. That the movement which led through Tom Robertson to Sir Arthur Pinero, H. A. Jones and G. B. Shaw was not without its embryonic beginnings in the period 1800–50 has been sufficiently indicated in the volumes of this history devoted to that time.[3] Indeed, it may well be correct to state that the theatre of 1900 represents the final and assured culmination of an organic growth which may be traced back at least to the stage of the Restoration. The picture-frame stage is the last achievement of a desire at which we have seen men vaguely grasping for two centuries, and the realistic problem-play is the ultimate realisation of something which has similarly been adumbrated for generations. This essentially is the truth. On the other hand, we may be permitted to suggest that, while man's stature can be traced back in a line of continuous progress to the most primitive of cellular forms, yet we cannot

---

[1] *The Renaissance of the Drama* (lxvi, Dec. 8, 1888, 76).
[2] *Dramatic Progress* (lvii, Jan. 26, 1895, 17).
[3] In addition to the authorities cited there, see Ernest Reynolds, *Early Victorian Drama* (1830–70) (Cambridge, 1936) and L. Waitzkin, *The Witch of Wych Street: A Study of the Theatrical Reforms of Madame Vestris* (Cambridge, U.S.A., 1933).

speak of man, as an independent and recognisable being, until a particular stage of development has been reached. No doubt in the theatre of the forties, alongside the relics of the old romantic melodrama and the still primitive but potentially progressive domestic dramas, one may discern fresh tendencies which presage the coming of other and more vital forms of dramatic art, but it is not until the seventies that these vital forms take definite shape and are consciously exploited.

Any examination, however cursory, of theatrical literature during the second half of the nineteenth century must make apparent the truly extraordinary alteration in attitude and accomplishment which came after the year 1870. Fundamentally that alteration is to be explained, not as the result of any one man's effort or as the consequence of any single change in social life, but as a necessary natural outgrowth dependent upon a series of movements which, though separate and diverse, at this time met and harmonised. As is usual in the sphere of the drama, the theatre led the way. The new plays could not have been had there not come, in previous years, a fresh orientation among those specifically concerned with the stage. Histrionic method suffered a complete mutation between these years. We start with the "classic" school of J. P. Kemble and Mrs Siddons; we end with the naturalistic ease of an Alexander and with the romantic vigour of an Irving. In 1800 the playhouses were lighted precisely as playhouses had been lit since the sixteenth century; in 1870 gas illumination, with all its accompanying flexibility in manipulation, was well-nigh universal. When Hazlitt watched Edmund Kean, the antique apron stage had not quite vanished and proscenium doors still obtruded themselves upon the attention of spectators; when Fechter came to London in the sixties he was experimenting with sectional stages and cycloramas. Most important of all is the fact that during this period the conception of the stage-manager, producer or director was born. In 1800, as in the preceding years, plays, like Topsy, "just growed"; the chief player, no doubt, took command of the rehearsals, but these rehearsals were comparatively few in number and from them little more seems to have been hoped for than acquainting the actors with their parts and in general terms settling their movements and business. It is only when we reach the mid-nineteenth century that we begin to encounter the directorial principle and, with it, the conception of a unified performance. To several men has been given the credit of initiating this conception; some say Robertson and Bancroft, some say Gilbert, some say Boucicault. The probability is that no single individual was responsible. This was not a thing invented by a peculiar genius with revolutionary views; it was the result of a general desire. Only when a director, or "stage-manager" according to contemporary theatrical parlance, could take control, was anything in the nature of a genuinely realistic production possible.

Compared with this active growth, the drama seemed for long to lag behind. Robertson had tried to discover a literary medium adequate to harmonise with these new stage ideals, but his steps were but halting and his vision more than half obscured. Sir Arthur Pinero and H. A. Jones carried on the search more surely and with a greater sense of set and deliberate purpose; but the final achievement of their aims came not until near the close of the century. This delayed development was due to a variety of causes. Primarily, perhaps, must be taken into account the fact that only in the last years were these various progressive movements in the theatre brought to fulfilment and harmony; basically most important was the attitude of the audience. A new audience was growing from the year 1840, but it took long before that audience reached self-expression and, consequently, before there could be a co-ordination of forces before and behind the curtain. A definite change in attitude is apparent with the coming of Queen Victoria. Towards the end of the year 1848 Charles Kean was appointed to supervise what soon came to be known as the "Windsor theatricals"—performances at court of successful plays taken from the London theatres. Three years later the young queen engaged a special box at the Princess's Theatre, "which she has retained annually ever since, and still more satisfactorily marked her approbation of the theatre by constant personal attendance".[1] The encouragement of these theatricals and the royal visits to privileged London playhouses soon convinced the aristocracy that what for years had been regarded as an almost entirely popular amusement might be tolerated by society. This influence, however, did not produce any sudden and immediately appreciable difference in the nature of the audience; that Charles Kean made appeal, in his early performances at the Princess's, to at least a certain section of cultured persons is clear, but it was not until the seventies and eighties that we find a definite turning of the managers from the type of fare suitable for the more popular audiences of 1830 to that fit for the more representative audiences which had taken their place.

This representative audience, while no doubt it was mainly responsible for the rapid development in dramatic style at the close of the century, would not itself have produced so great an effect had it not coalesced with other forces. Extremely important was the fresh opportunity offered to the dramatists of obtaining really adequate financial awards for their labours. Between 1830 and 1860 little could be made by a practising playwright unless he were prepared to sacrifice all his literary ambitions and devote himself to hack-work— turning out hurriedly written farces and melodramas, monthly, to order. The breakdown in the old stock company system, however, and the consequent development of long runs introduced fresh conditions. The substitution of royalties for outright purchases, combined with the protection afforded by the law of copyright, came to guarantee to the author of a successful play an income which compared favourably with the remuneration received by a popular novelist or essayist. Art in its higher reaches may be independent of sordid monetary conditions, yet even playwrights must live. The majority of authors seek for at least a share of jam and honey; and the development of a new drama in the last decades of

---

[1] J. W. Cole, *The Life and Theatrical Times of Charles Kean* (1859), ii, 13.

the century is by no means unconnected with the larger financial rewards offered to the dramatists.

Only by an adequate appreciation of all these tendencies can we seek to understand that truly extraordinary "Renascence of the English drama", as H. A. Jones has styled it—extraordinary because, in spite of the gradual approach which we, standing on our historical vantage ground, are able clearly to distinguish, of its apparent suddenness and of the changes immediately consequent upon its coming. So complex are the conditions which made for this renascence that such a summary as has been given above is a necessary basis for adequate appreciation, but no mere summary can provide a satisfactory picture of the social and theatrical circumstances which wrought the miracle. It will be necessary now to examine in greater detail the factors which conspired together to provide a platform, strongly and stoutly enough built to bear the stalwart band of dramatic reformers who established what we know as the modern drama.

2. *The Audience*

The period which we are now about to examine opens with the glittering splendours of the Great Exhibition. Like a fairy palace of comfortably solid proportions grew the crystal halls, and men could not tire of wandering through them. The Great Exhibition was the symbol of an age that was passing away and the premonition of an age that was to come. It stood representative of early Victorianism, secure, industrious, pacific; what made it possible was a force destined to shatter that security.[1]

This Great Exhibition was the self-expression of a metropolis which had multiplied its inhabitants mightily within a short span of years. In 1801 London had some 865,000 citizens; these had grown to one and a half millions by 1831, and the following twenty years witnessed a vast increase. It was these who were the originators and first supporters of

---

[1] R. H. Mottram, *Town Life*, in *Early Victorian England*, ed. by G. M. Young (1934), i, 212–22.

the Exhibition. With their help alone, however, the project could not have hoped to succeed; it required the attendance of many thousands from all parts of Britain, required too the visits of other thousands from France and Germany. In 1800 such visits would have been an impossibility, but by 1850 practical scientific development had provided means of transport undreamed of in the past. Before 1830 London had miserably inadequate methods of conveying its inhabitants from one part of the city to another; twenty years later suburbia was in full process of growth. The first railway (between Manchester and Liverpool) did not come until 1828; by 1843 the foundations at least of the present railroad system had been definitely laid.

The very means of conveyance which brought the Great Exhibition from a dream to realisation were the same which wrought a complete change in the world theatrical. Up to the middle of the nineteenth century the potential playgoing public was exceedingly small. Although London might be increasing annually, the fact that no suitable provision was made whereby the ordinary citizens might traverse its extending area automatically cut off many of these from possible attendance—save on rare and festive occasions—at the metropolitan theatres. When, however, the railway and the omnibus became common and familiar, at once the circumstances were altered. The whole of the suburban area, west, north and south, was brought into easy association with the theatrical district and quantitatively the number of likely ticket buyers was increased a hundredfold.

The conditions rendered it possible for great masses of the middle class, resident in the outlying quarters, to come to the playhouse if they wished; but other causes must be sought to explain how these middle-class people obtained the desire to enter the theatres. The stage in the early part of the century was largely a "popular" affair, and for the most part bourgeois opinion regarded its delights with cringing disapproval.[1] Typical audiences were composed mainly of

[1] See *A History of Early Nineteenth Century Drama* (1930), i, 7-22. This book is referred to subsequently as *E.N.D.*

lower-class citizens with a sprinkling of representatives from the gayer and more libertine section of the aristocracy. The staid middle class and the respectable, dignified nobility tended to look upon the stage as a thing not to be supported in an active manner. Some advance towards a changed orientation is to be discerned during the forties; for this a few individuals, such as Macready and Phelps, may be regarded as responsible. The great alteration, however, does not come until after the middle of the century, and perhaps no single individual did more to effect its realisation than Queen Victoria.

Victoria and the theatre do not commonly associate themselves in our minds, yet the queen's encouragement of the royal "theatricals" not only instituted something fresh and significant but, as contemporaries realised, something destined to yield a rich harvest in the future.[1] "But now", lilts J. R. Planché,[2]

> But now a fresh start's given the Drama to,
> By royal patronage. "The play's the thing",
> And goes to Court.

"If the patronage by Royalty," writes a commentator in 1853, "which appears to be increasing with every year, is a sign of the Drama's palmy days, then most assuredly may it be said to be 'looking up'."[3] Four years earlier than that a critic in *The Times*[4] guessed rightly at the effect which would result from this royal interest. "When the highest personage in the land", he deemed,

considers that an English dramatic performance is such an entertainment as to merit the construction of a stage in her own drawing room, with all the appurtenances of a regular theatre, the opinion that the native drama is unfashionable receives an

[1] On these royal theatricals see J. W. Cole, *op. cit.* i, 346–8 and 351; B. Webster, *The Series of Dramatic Entertainments performed by Royal Command at Windsor Castle, 1848–9* (1849); and J. K. Chapman *A Complete History of Theatrical Entertainments, Dramas, Masques, and Triumphs, at the English Court* (1849).
[2] *Mr Buckstone's Ascent of Mount Parnassus* (H. 1853).
[3] *The Dramatic Register for 1853* (Lacy, 1854), p. 33.
[4] Jan. 26, 1849.

authoritative rebuke. The plays that are acted at Windsor Castle are the same that may be seen at the Haymarket and Lyceum, the actors in the Rouben's Room are precisely the same individuals as those who appear on the public boards and it would be absurd to say that an entertainment which acquired a high rank at Windsor loses that rank when it comes to the metropolis.

That this critic was justified is amply proved by later events; he was even correct in what must then have seemed his fanciful guess that "a new stock of dramatists, worthy to compete with those of the Elizabethan era, may spring into evidence from the effect of the Windsor Theatricals". Nor was Victoria content to honour the stage in this way only. As has been indicated above, until the death of the Prince Consort in 1861 she pursued her interest in the stage and, through her visits to the Haymarket, the Princess's and the St James's, encouraged the managers and stimulated enthusiasm for the drama. As Henry Elliott put it in 1896,

Acting, as a profession, now has the direct sanction and approval of the fount of honour in these islands; and it owes that recognition to the gracious sympathy and appreciation of the present wielder of the sceptre.[1]

That a complete alteration was not effected is but natural, and naturally, too, complaints continued to be made regarding popular taste—such are perennial things and were as common in the days of *Hamlet* as in those of *Abie's Irish Rose*. In 1871 Thomas Purnell took a melancholy view:

The chief supporters of our theatres are country people... those of the nobility afflicted with *ennui*...busy professional men who come at fixed intervals with their families...men who go to the theatres from habit, just as they smoke tobacco, and a large number of green grocers and other shop keepers, who have received orders for displaying play-bills in their windows.... At one time the most intellectual and scholarly people habitually visited the playhouse,

but these, in his opinion, now kept away, since

[1] *The Stage under Victoria* (*The Theatre*, N.S. xxviii, Nov. 1896, 242–3). Further remarks on this subject will be found in J. Knight, *The History of the English Stage during the Reign of Victoria* (1901), A. Filon, *The English Stage: an Account of the Victorian Drama* (1897) and R. F. Sharp, *A Short History of the English Stage to 1908* (1909).

their field of intellectual recreation is widened, and the social
changes of our time provide them with other and more profitable
means of mental excitement.[1]

"Though theatres have multiplied of late," complained F. C.
Broughton seven years later, "it cannot be said that audiences
have vastly increased."[2] At a time when even pessimists
could no longer deny that many more persons than before
were attending performances regularly, the complaints, keyed
to a different pitch, were still to be heard. Some averred
that the new public was responsible for the success of mere-
tricious productions—*A Gaiety Girl*, *The Prisoner of Zenda*
and *The Sign of the Cross*;[3] others blamed their constant
seeking for amusement (as though that were not the object
of all playgoers).[4] "Within the last two or three years",
declares W. Winter in *The Theatre* for 1887,

although noble and beautiful works have been shown, and several
important advance steps have been taken—a complete avalanche
of trash has been cast upon our stage, and our people have accepted
it and they have, practically, approved it. Why? For the reason,
partly, that scarcely a voice among public censors has been raised
against this flagrant abuse of the theatre.... It was unfortunate
that the custom of viewing the stage as an "amusement" ever
came to prevail; for the stage is an institution far higher and finer
than any amusement, and it possesses at the present epoch an
influence upon society second only to that of the hearthstone and
the altar. But even viewing it as one of the amusements, no man
has a right to degrade its character or impair its usefulness....
There is more than common need of wholesome censure, as well of
the public taste as of the pernicious doctrine that it is the province
and policy of thinkers, writers and managers to follow the people
instead of leading them.[5]

    [1] *Dramatists of the Present Day by "Q"* (i.e. Thomas Purnell) (1871),
pp. 14–16. This essay was reprinted from *The Athenaeum*.
    [2] *Modern Audiences* (*The Theatre*, N.S. i, Aug. 1878, 36).
    [3] W. Davenport Adams, *What is the Theatrical Public?* (*The Theatre*,
N.S. xxix, April 1897, 198–200).
    [4] H. A. Jones, *The Renascence of the English Drama* (1895), p. 3. This
essay first appeared in *The Nineteenth Century* for 1883.
    [5] *The Theatre*, N.S. x, Sept. 1887, 159. This is quoted from *The New
York Tribune*, but *The Theatre*'s editor comments that these "pertinent
remarks...apply, unfortunately, to the English as well as the American
stage".

Those who looked to the "hearthstone and the altar" thus vented their dissatisfaction, and here joined hands with the reformers, for whom otherwise they had but little sympathy. "Half a dozen visits in the year", thought G. B. Shaw in 1896, serve all the purposes of those respectably literate citizens who are...anxious to see whatever is good in the theatre. Let me turn to the index of William Archer's *Theatrical World of 1895*, and try to pick out 52 new plays that would have justified such a citizen in going once a week to the theatre,

and the effort, he imagines, would be in vain.[1] Taste in appreciation of acting, too, was taxed:

> Perhaps the greatest difficulty that faces the British dramatist, at any rate one of the more important obstacles to his success, is to be found in the histrionic taste of the public. We by no means intend to insinuate that it is deficient or unsound, or that even at times it does not assert itself in an advantageous and a commendable manner; but we think our readers will be with us when we affirm that too often the judgment of an audience is uncertain and its favour capricious. Triumph and failure do not always depend upon the merit and shortcomings of author or actor.... The intellectual acumen and force that are brought to the judgment of an opera, a sonata, a picture, or a poem will surely be found sufficient in the encouragement of the highest aspirations of the Drama. In the meanwhile, however, the public should seek to stimulate its theatrical taste, define and improve it.[2]

Opposed to these more gloomy denunciations, and more valid because seizing on the essential qualities of change which differentiated the theatre of 1890 from that of 1850, come the optimistic views of those who recognised in the new audience a power and a force apt to introduce a great era of dramatic productivity. The general growth of an intellectual public was noted even in the seventies.[3] The subject

[1] *On Nothing in Particular and the Theatre in General* (*The Saturday Review*, lxxxi, March 14, 1896, 273).

[2] *Taste and the Drama* (*The Era*, xli, Jan. 26, 1879, 12). There is an interesting article on *The English Stage* in *The Quarterly Review*, clv, April 1883, 354–88, in which the writer, after quoting William Archer's dictum that "modern Englishmen cannot be got to take the drama seriously", compares the audiences of his own time with those of the Elizabethan age.

[3] *Our Stage: Its Present and its probable Future* (*The Theatre*, N.S. i, Aug. 1878, 1–7).

of regenerating the stage, wrote one man in 1879, "is now taken up as a stock text by editors and their leader-writers in the leading daily journals, whereas a very short time ago it would have been felt that a leader on such a topic in the *Daily News* or *Daily Telegraph*, to say nothing of *The Times*, was a matter for a nine days' wonder".[1] By the nineties the increase of interest taken in the drama had become incontrovertible. "The theatre", it was said in 1898, "is growing in importance as a social organ. Modern civilisation is rapidly multiplying the class to which the theatre is both school and church, and when the dramatic art is practised rightly...The national importance of the theatre will be as unquestioned as that of the army, the fleet, the Church, the law and the schools."[2] In spite of his shortcomings as a critic, H. A. Jones proved himself a clear-sighted observer when he looked on the spectators of his own time. The first thing, he imagined, that would strike a stranger visiting the London theatres would be the enormous popularity of the playhouse among all classes;[3] "the material prosperity of the English drama was never so great as at the present moment", he declared in 1891;[4] and he was eager in his defence of at least one section of the audience:

We have on our first nights, interspersed with perhaps a few ticklish but easily quieted elements of mischief, that serried pack of bright earnest intelligent faces in the first row of the pit, lovers of the drama for the drama's sake, whose self-appointed duty it is to give a loud and unmistakable verdict of approval or condemnation.[5]

Of one thing everyone was assured—that audiences were

[1] *Regenerating the Stage* (id. N.S. iii, Nov. 1879, 181–4). This article calls attention to the discussion on the theatre at the Art Section of the Social Science Congress, presided over by the Bishop of Manchester.
[2] *The Stage and its Critics* (*Blackwood's Edinburgh Magazine*, clxiii, June 1898, 871–4).
[3] *The Renascence of the English Drama* (1895), p. 154; essay first printed in *The English Illustrated Magazine*, Jan. and Feb. 1885, pp. 280 and 341.
[4] *Id.* p. 96; essay first printed in *The New Review*, July 1891, p. 86.
[5] *Id.* pp. 18–19; essay first printed in *The Nineteenth Century*, Sept. 1883, p. 452. These remarks, of course, are to be qualified by Jones's other strictures on theatrical taste in general.

more decorous and better-mannered than they had been in the past. Even in 1859 J. W. Cole could comment on the fact that

modern audiences are less easily worked up to strong demonstration than they were at the beginning of the present century.... Audiences now-a-days are more numerous than ever; but they sit, for the most part, in silent admiration.... The stalls, boxes, and even the pit, are too genteel to clap their hands; and the Olympian deities are awed into silence by their isolation, and the surrounding chill.[1]

The wild riots have disappeared;[2] and the disturbances which had been so common on first nights have given way to a new tolerance. In 1892, indeed, Alfred Berlyn was impelled to enquire whether contemporary audiences were not too patient.[3] Some writers might object that on these first nights the stall seats were now mostly filled with paper and that claques, organised by authors, managers and actors, were part of the ordinary theatre routine;[4] but such views were sternly rebutted by others.[5]

This new respectability in the playhouse was due partly to the fact that many of the potentially rowdy elements were being catered for in the music halls, but partly, at least, it was the result of a rather surprising alliance between church and stage. While an uncompromising Reverend John Robertson in Glasgow might still repeat the same arguments as had been employed by his predecessors, bitterly attacking Irving

---

[1] *Op. cit.* i, 92. It is true that lack of courtesy among spectators was noted in *The Theatre*, N.S. xiv, July 1889, 10–13, but no serious examples were there listed. The subject is also touched upon, *id.* N.S. iv, Aug. 1884, 91–2.

[2] Cf. those noted in *A History of Early Eighteenth-Century Drama* (Cambridge, 1937; referred to hereafter as *E.E.D.*), pp. 5–10, *A History of Late Eighteenth-Century Drama* (Cambridge, 1929; referred to hereafter as *L.E.D.*), p. 12, and *E.N.D.* i, 7–11. Some of the relatively rare disturbances chronicled during this period are listed by Wyndham Albery, *The Dramatic Works of James Albery* (1939) i, xcvii–cii.

[3] *The Theatre*, N.S. xix, Mar. 1892, 140–2.

[4] J. F. Nisbet, *The Composition of London Audiences* (*id.* N.S. xxx, Nov. 1897, 226–9).

[5] A. W. à Beckett, *"Organised Disturbance" Criticised* (*id.* N.S. xxix, Feb. 1897, 74–8).

for his supposed delinquencies,[1] that sort of thing was becoming rare. Since the days of the Church Fathers ecclesiastical opinion had been opposed to the playhouse, yet now,
as Alfred Halstead noted in 1897, even the Non-Conformists
were losing their old hatred of the stage.[2] The Reverend
H. C. Dimsdale, we learn, who was "spiritual pastor of the
Eton Mission, Hackney", in 1889 "produced a pantomime
called *Dick Whittington and his Cat* at his Mission Hall",[3]
and was not immediately blasted therefore either by heaven
or by his superiors. A dozen years earlier, the Reverend J.
Panton Ham, a Unitarian minister, in lecturing on the theatre,

denied that there was a very great deal to reform on our Stage;
that it was constantly watched by vigilant and honest critics, and
that there were many noble-minded managers who, like Macready,
were only too anxious to elevate the tone of the Drama. He called
on religious people to aid them in their work.[4]

A few months before this, the Bishop of Manchester delivered
addresses to audiences of actors and actresses from the stages
of Drury Lane and the Prince's, when he emphasised that
"he did not want to abolish the Theatre, but to purify it".[5]
"Socially", said the Reverend H. R. Haweis in a sermon
delivered at St James's, Marylebone, "we have reached a
critical time in the history of the Stage; a time when prelates
and play-actors shake hands."[6] The cue was taken by many
in the seventies. The Reverend C. C. Coe referred to "the
desire to give the player the social status which his calling,
if properly pursued, most justly demanded".[7] "Shall a man

[1] *Id.* N.S. xxv, Jan. 1895, 61–2. For the church-and-stage controversy
see J. Macdonald, *What is the Theatre?* (Edinburgh, 1851) and *The Theatre*
(1866); W. Keddie, *The Theatre: Its Pernicious Tendency* (Glasgow, 1853);
A. J. Baxter, *The Theatre a Religious Institution* (1865); R. B. Drummond,
The Theatre, its Bearings on Morals (Edinburgh, 1875). On the Bishop
of London's views see Frank Marshall, *The Stage and its Detractors* (*The
Theatre*, N.S. vi, Nov. 1885, 233–40).
[2] *Id.* N.S. xxx, Aug. 1897, 78–80; N.S. xxix, June 1897, 308–9.
[3] *The Church on the Stage* (*The Era*, li, Jan. 26, 1889, 13).
[4] *The Pulpit and the Stage* (*id.* xl, Oct. 21, 1877, 12). This was in
America; see note, p. 11 *infra*.
[5] *A Bishop on the Stage* (*id.* xxxix, Feb. 11, 1877, 7); *The Theatre*,
i, Feb. 1877, 21.
[6] *The Era*, xli, Oct. 19, 1879, 5.
[7] *The Theatre*, i, Feb. 1877, 34.

go to the Theatre?" enquired another, and gave the answer:
"Yes, if only as a reformer.... Go... as you ought to go
anywhere, to enjoy the good, encourage actors and Managers
in their strife for that.... Help the art to climb and re-establish
itself."[1] Men took pains to point out the essential morality
of the theatre now:

> Be it remembered this vital influence for good is not a thing of
> late existence; in all the struggles that the Stage has had with
> intolerance; in spite of the temptation that a certain number of
> people in every crowded city may offer to Managers to seek advan-
> tage by pandering to the vicious impulse of our nature... and
> even with the desire of the audiences of so-called minor Theatres
> to have their entertainment highly spiced, the English dramatist
> has for the most part kept the principle of his work sound....
> The stale contrivance of the penitence and confession of many
> a heavy villain at the end of Transpontine melodramas... might
> be cited as further evidence of the truly moral teaching with
> which the English Stage was instinct.[2]

The more liberal ideas thus naïvely expressed were destined
to win their way. Professor Blackie in Edinburgh added his
weight to the new movement[3] and various churchmen, sensing
the tendencies of the time, hastened to disassociate themselves
from former ecclesiastical condemnatory remarks. In 1878
the Church Congress, meeting at Sheffield, found that "the
discussion which aroused most interest" concerned the stage.
A few years later, at another Church Congress held at
Leicester, the Reverend H. C. Shuttleworth declared his
opinion that "of all the influences upon Society, the Drama"
had "ever been one of the most powerful. The dramatic
instinct", he thought, was "natural to mankind, and the
Stage will never cease to be an instrument of tremendous
power for good or evil. Church and Stage should go hand
in hand", he added, and concluded his comments by turning
upon the church and flaying it for its former attitude towards

---

[1] *The Era*, xxxiii, March 12, 1871, 10. This was part of a lecture
delivered in Baltimore, but the sentiments are akin to those encountered
in England.
[2] *The Stage as a Teacher of Morality* (*id.* xxxix, Jan. 14, 1877, 12).
[3] *The Theatre*, i, April 1877, 119.

the theatre.[1] From this changed orientation ultimately came
the Church and Stage Guild, organised "to promote religious
and social sympathy between the members of the Church
and Stage".[2]

No doubt this movement was largely responsible for the
imposition of a stricter and more formal "morality" in the
drama. A review in *The Theatre* of a play in which conjugal
infidelity was dealt with amusingly opined that this drama
could

> only be regarded as a direct hindrance to those who are just now
> striving by every means in their reach to win for the acted drama
> its recognition as a high moral influence, a social power, and an
> intellectual instrument, worthy of the strongest support which
> the culture of the nation can afford.[3]

On the same grounds, this journal displayed considerable
nervousness when it learned that the National Sunday League
was thinking of pleading for theatrical representations on the
sabbath; in the writer's opinion such a move would result
only in giving argumentative material to the enemy and in
estranging new friends.[4] The danger, may be, was a real
one; for after all, there was something in the remark of
a contemporary that "the young clergymen on the council"
of the Church and Stage Guild might "not realize that their
penchant for the conversion of young actresses" was "open,
to say the least of it, to misconception".[5]

The approval of the Church, whatever disadvantages and
misconceptions might arise, was of immense value to the
theatre; without it the audience could not have become truly
representative of the community. In the seventies the discussions in congresses and the sermons from the pulpit were
beginning to draw back to the auditorium certain sections
of the community which had refrained from attendance at
dramatic representations or attended seldom and in mental

---

[1] *The Era*, xliii, Oct. 10, 1880, 7.
[2] *The Church and Stage Guild* (*id.* xlii, Jan. 25, 1880, 4); *The Theatre*,
N.S. iii, Oct. 1878, 183–5.
[3] *The Theatre*, i, May 1877, 183–4.
[4] *Id.* N.S. i, Oct. 1878, 182–5.
[5] *Id.* N.S. iii, Dec. 1879, 247.

perturbation. A decade later all was assured. When in 1897
Henry Irving received his knighthood, gave a reading of
Becket in Canterbury Cathedral and unveiled a statue in
Paddington Green to the memory of Mrs Siddons—the first
statue to a player erected in London—he demonstrated in
himself the result of a new tolerance which had brought the
stage and those associated with it into an entirely fresh realm.[1]
The player was now received into society; he was recognised
as an artist worthy of distinguished remembrance; he was
even accepted within the walls of that church which, save
for temporary encouragement of religious plays in the Middle
Ages, had severely frowned on him and on his profession.

Gradually, the tone of the public attitude towards the
stage thus altered, and various elements, physical and spiritual,
in the theatre altered accordingly. Marie Wilton provided
a carpet for the stalls at the Prince of Wales's in 1865,[2] and
her action was symbolic. The old front rows of the severely
benched pit were becoming refined. The dress circle, referred
to in a letter of February 18, 1869,[3] rapidly assumed a new
importance. The theatre had become fashionable. A novel
significance now was attached to the dinner hour, which
had not worried the high-tea and supper partakers on whom
Sadler's Wells and the Adelphi had previously subsisted.
During these years the formal hour of dinner was being
advanced, and when eventually it reached seven o'clock it
had the effect of completely revolutionising playhouse pro-
grammes.[4] In earlier days popular audiences had demanded
their full money's worth. A performance which started at
6.30 might close about midnight and was expected to include
a farce, a tragedy or comedy, a pantomime and a few other
divertisements. The new patrons had chaster predilections;
coming to the theatre decorously at eight o'clock, they were

[1] *The Progress of the Player* (*The Theatre*, N.S. xxx, July 1897, 1–4);
cf. *id.* N.S. xxvi, July 1895, 1–9.
[2] Bradlee Watson, *Sheridan to Robertson* (1926). See also M. St C.
Byrne, *Stalls and Places in the Orchestra* (*The Times Literary Supplement*,
June 29, 1933).
[3] Frank Archer, *An Actor's Notebooks* (1912), p. 66.
[4] On the dinner hour see Mrs C. S. Peel, *Homes and Habits* (*Early
Victorian England, 1830–1865* (1934), i, 98).

content to depart homeward about eleven, and soon showed
themselves completely satisfied with the presentation of one
long play.[1] Charles Kean seems to have started the fashion
for one major play preceded by a curtain-raiser; even the
curtain-raiser was abandoned by the Bancrofts. Perhaps it
were not too much to say that the characteristic modern
dramatic performance was created by a change in society's
dinner hour. Created by this society, too, was the modern
matinée. Matinées would have been impossible in 1830; but
the presence within the new audience of numerous leisured
persons able to attend the theatres in the morning or the
afternoon had made such performances all the rage in 1880.
Inaugurated about 1869, they gradually increased in number
until a correspondent of 1889 could refer to "these days of
endless matinées".[2] The significance of this innovation must
be reserved for later discussion.[3]

The presence of more intelligent and sophisticated spectators in the playhouses made inevitably for the opening up
of dramatic realms forbidden by law or social taboo in the
past. Sydney Grundy in his reactionary age might see
seeds of disaster in this extension of theme. In 1896 he felt
sure the stage was "marching to its doom" because the
serious drama was in the hands of "a coterie of enthusiastic
eccentrics".[4] Now, looking back, we realise that the "enthusiastic eccentrics", both behind and before the curtain, were
preparing fresh soil for tillage. The office of the Licenser of
Plays, reflecting the tastes of the new audience, was slowly
becoming more liberal. True, the scrutiny of texts was still
severe. "Omit all oaths" is a common rubric in the manuscripts of plays preserved in the custody of the Lord Chamber-

---

[1] *The Theatre*, N.S. xxiii, Jan. 1894, 19; *The Era*, xxxiii, Oct. 23, 1870,
10. In 1871 T. Purnell (*op. cit.* p. 70) noted that "the late dinner-hour
of our day, combined with the increasing disposition of cultured people
to show no emotion, is inimical to farce".
[2] *The Theatre*, N.S. xiv, July 1889, 12. S. J. Adair Fitz-Gerald has an
interesting note on *The Matinée Question* (*id.* N.S. xviii, Oct. 1891, 159–60).
[3] *Infra*, pp. 59–60.
[4] *The Theatre*, N.S. xxvii, March 1896, 131. For Grundy's position see
also William Archer, *What does the Public want?* (*id.* N.S. v, June 1885,
269–75).

lain.[1] "However she persists in saying, there is something more between us than meets the naked eye" was cut; "Jael had but a nail for a weapon, Delilah her scissors" was cut; throughout the entirety of Browning's *Colombe's Birthday* (H. 1853) "Heaven" was substituted for "God"; in a version of *Hard Times* (Str. 1854) objection was taken to "Lord! I do give thee humble and hearty thanks for this my deliverance". The later attitude to these oaths is well displayed in a comment on *Our Wives* (Eastbourne, 1885):

Omit the frequent swearing, which, it should be understood, is no longer usual in these days in respectable drawing rooms, and in the company of ladies, and is calculated to give offence to any intelligent and respectable audience.

Not only oaths, of course, were regarded as reprehensible; topical references, too, were frequently lined out. "Proclamation—BEARBAITING! This Act is not licensed by the Lord Chamberlain" was duly censored in a pantomime, *Harlequin Hudibras* (D.L. 1852), and in a burlesque, *William Tell* (Str. 1857), the reader of plays found occasion to object to a piece of dialogue:

—Tell me of something that will make one sad.
—See Kean play Hamlet, that will do it, lad.
—Oh! dear! that remedy's much too severe:
    My nerves would never stand the shock, I fear.

When Sergeant Towner and Frank Beaumont submitted their drama, *Called to the Front* (Brit. 1885), they were informed that the villain of the piece must positively not be described as belonging to the Guards.

The whole question of the censorship was much discussed in these years,[2] praise or blame being awarded in accordance with the beliefs of the critical camp to which the particular writer belonged. Again, it is in the seventies that we first encounter the development of conscious likes and dislikes.

[1] The references to deletions ordered by the Lord Chamberlain are taken from an examination of the copies officially deposited at St James's Palace.
[2] On the censorship generally see G. M. G. *The Stage Censor* (1905) and W. Nicholson, *The Struggle for a Free Stage* (1906).

The censoring of some French plays called forth a protest in *The Athenaeum* in 1873,[1] and this perhaps occasioned the writing of a long article on the licensing laws in *The Era* for 1874.[2] Then came a growl from Sydney Grundy five years later,[3] which in turn led to a general series of complaints from the company of younger writers during the last decades of the century. This "theatrical anachronism" was attacked in *The Pall Mall Gazette* in 1880;[4] William Archer never ceased denouncing the iniquities of the censor's office;[5] and finally G. B. Shaw came forward with caustic pen to scourge and lacerate.[6] In spite of such attacks, however, there can be no doubt but that the censorship had grown in those years more tolerant and that it displayed a willingness to permit the public representation of dramas which would have shocked earlier society into convulsions.

The force of the new audience in the theatre is to be seen nowhere more clearly than in the widespread periodical discussions which, as has been noted above, occupied considerable space in the newspapers and journals of the time—especially clearly is this indicated in the broad lines of demarcation between two powerful groups of critics and essayists, the groups themselves being characteristic of a split among the spectators. The two schools of thought were described by W. A. Lewis Bettany in 1892 as "the Ancients and the Moderns";[7] the description is apt, for the one represented

---

[1] No. 2372, April 12, 1873, 482. Cf. *The Lord Chamberlain and the Drama* (*The Era*, xxxiv, Jan. 14, 1872, 12); in the same issue is a letter from the Licenser of Plays, W. B. Donne.

[2] *The Examiner of Stage Plays* (xxxvi, July 26, 1874, 9).

[3] *The Theatre*, N.S. ii, March 1879, 99–103. An article entitled *Theatrical Fenianism* in *The Saturday Review* (xli, Jan. 15, 1876, 76) also has a close bearing on this subject. Cf. "*A False Step*" *towards discrediting the Censorship* (*The Theatre*, N.S. i, Nov. 1878, 259–62) and *The Censorship on its Trial* (*id.* N.S. i, Dec. 1878, 332–5).

[4] xxxi, May 13, 1880, 11.

[5] *Mr Archer and the Censorship* (*The Era*, liv, March 21, 1892, 15); *The Pall Mall Gazette*, lx, March 23, 1895, 3. See also Arthur Goodrich, *The Dramatic Censorship* (*The Theatre*, N.S. xix, May 1892, 232–7) and Robert Buchanan, *The Ethics of Play-Licensing* (*id.* N.S. xxvii, May 1896, 254–7).

[6] *The Saturday Review*, lxxix, March 2, 1895, 280–2.

[7] *Criticism and the Renascent Drama* (*The Theatre*, N.S. xix, June 1892, 277–83).

the great mass of stolid, respectable, middle-class opinion
and the other reflected the tastes of the younger intellectuals
who, sensing the change in the theatre, had come to look
upon it as a place where high aspirations and daring thought
might find scope. "The present controversy between these
rival schools", Bettany informs us, "has been simmering
ever since 1880, and long before the production of 'A Doll's
House' in 1889 there had been signs of the coming clash.…
Nevertheless, it may be fairly said that up to the year 1889,
'the new criticism' had but a solitary champion—Mr William
Archer. Since then, however, several younger writers have
rallied to Mr Archer's support." Before 1892, "the dispute
had mainly consisted in an occasional difference of opinion
between the opposing leaders, caused by the production now
of Mr Pinero's 'Lords and Commons', now of Mr Grundy's
'Clito', and now of Mr Jones's 'The Noble Vagabond'. The
events of the past three years have tended to make the struggle
much more bitter and much more personal. Ibsen has been
thrown like an apple of discord…and over every important
new play the battle has been fiercely renewed, Mr Archer
ably championing the cause of modernity, and being stoutly
backed up by his adroit guerilla lieutenant 'Spectator', of
the *Star*."

The recognised leader of the Ancients was the redoubtable
Clement Scott. In him, thought a writer in *Blackwood's
Edinburgh Magazine*,[1] "our English theatre has found…
precisely the critic which it deserved". The immense personal
esteem in which he was held by the public at large was merely
the reflection of a tendency which produced a Henry Irving
and a Beerbohm Tree. "Other men", said Shaw in 1896,[2]

may have hurried from the theatre to the newspaper office to
prepare, red hot, a notice of the night's performance for the
morning's paper; but nobody did it before him with the knowledge
that the notice was awaited by a vast body of readers conscious
of his personality and anxious to hear his opinion, and that the

----

[1] clxvii, Jan. 1900, 98–108. For a penetrating study of Scott see W. L.
Courtney, *The Passing Hour* (n.d.), pp. 213–20.
[2] *The Saturday Review*, lxxxi, May 30, 1896, 548–9.

editor must respect it, and the sub-editor reserve space for it, as the most important feature of the paper. This strong position Mr Scott has made for himself. His opportunity has of course been made by circumstance—by the growth of mammoth newspapers like the *Daily Telegraph*, the multiplication of theatres, and the spread of interest in them.

The real secret of Clement Scott's popularity lay, as Shaw readily divined, in the superabundance of his sympathy and the impression of heartfelt integrity which he introduced into his writings. His critiques

are alive: their admiration is sincere and moving: their sentiment is vivid and genuine....The public believes in Mr Scott because he interprets the plays by feeling with the actor or author...and giving his feeling unrestrained expression in his notices.

There can be no question concerning Scott's ability, but he applied that ability to discredit the new drama. What appealed to his sentimental heart he praised; what aimed at appealing to his mind he was incapable of appreciating. In *Ghosts* he viewed, not a work calculated to penetrate deeply into a serious social problem, but a sociological pamphlet which introduced topics about which he was resolutely determined to keep grim silence in public. That his own defence was justified we may agree:

We who are entrusted with the difficult and delicate task of criticising our fellow men and women, write, we are proud to say, unbiassed, unfettered, at the dictates of our own impressions, and fortified by an experience that justifies us in speaking—[1]

but it cannot be denied that he did his best to kill the rising spirit of a renascent drama. In his youth he was among the revolutionaries who rallied around the teacup-and-saucer comedy; in his age he was a likable and vigorous reactionary.

Among his followers may be noted J. F. Nisbet, of *The Times*, less emotional than he, one who, although he welcomed Jones, Pinero and Grundy, took but a pessimistic view of the newer drama and constantly pleaded for old-time conventionality. To the same group belonged Alfred Watson,

---

[1] *The Theatre*, N.S. xvii, Feb. 1891, 86.

of *The Standard*, Wedmore, "most self-satisfied of critics", and Edward Morton, "most rollicking of dramatic Philistines".

The Moderns found their earliest and, in many respects, their most stalwart champion in William Archer. Despite a certain woodenness, Archer showed himself the farthest-seeing and the most broad-minded of the younger group. In method he was the direct opposite of Scott. Where the one judged by emotion, the other always judged by reason. Coldly analytical in his appreciations, he yet at times could summon a glow of mental vigour hardly less inspiring than Scott's most impassioned outbursts. The pair met, indeed, in an arena of dramatic fanaticism, for both were champions. That Archer was wrong in condemning entirely the conventional drama of the past seems now clear to most of us; but his service to the theatre in acclaiming Ibsen and in welcoming younger writers of the naturalistic school can in no way be minimised.[1]

Those who rallied to his standard, men who followed a new set of commandments, by which the critic

should praise Ibsen, Maeterlinck, and Zola...should slate melo-drama, "the well-made play", farce, and burlesque...should pooh-pooh Messrs Pinero and Jones...should regard Mr Irving with a wondering pity...should occasionally conceal his contempt for the actor...should support the Independent Theatre at least with praises...should condemn Clement Scott and all his *Tele-graph*-ese notes and criticism; and...should write his critiques on Impressionist principles,

were, although at first few in numbers, soon an influential group. A. B. Walkley, of *The Star* and *The Times*, became noted for his apt combination of scholarly exactitude and witty style. In *The Sunday Sun* and *The Gentleman's Magazine* young Justin McCarthy made himself a noted controversialist, while Addison Bright, of *The Lady's Pictorial*, won admiration by his acute judgment of acting and by his critical analysis

---

[1] Cf. Sydney Grundy, *Marching to our Doom* (*The Theatre*, N.S. xxvii, April 1896 196–200) and Oliver Bluff, *Critics? and Criticism* (*id.* N.S. xviii, Oct. 1891, 153–7).

of contemporary drama. Vigour characterised the writing of
E. F. Spence in *The Pall Mall Gazette*, scholarship that of
Joseph Knight in *The Athenaeum*, and chastened enthusiasm
that of the anonymous reviewers of *The Daily Graphic* and
Sporting Life.

Quite naturally, a few critical authors gave no formal
allegiance to either contrasted party, but for the most part
these men suffered from the spinelessness which Dante pilloried in the *Inferno*. Timidity, as was pointed out by a contemporary, prevented their joining the new school, while
conviction forbade their adopting the stereotyped formulae
of Scott. Among these, most notable were Davenport Adams
of *The Globe*, Malcolm Watson of *The Saturday Review*,
Pollock of *The St James's Gazette* and Jope Slade of *The
Echo*.[1]

As we survey this varied array of regular critics, we realise
with absolute clarity how far theatrical interest had progressed
by the end of the nineteenth century. Criticism now was
no longer a perfunctory thing, nor was it an affair which
appealed in the main only to the intellectuals; it had become
part of the public's interest, and the Parnassian controversies
were followed eagerly even by the common mortals on the
plains beneath. Not many save authors and actors had been
actively concerned with the charming delinquencies of Mr
Puff, but now the shortcomings of criticism were matters of
fundamental importance. Special articles on the functions
of the critic appear in the journals of the time;[2] the weaknesses
of the minor reviews are alternately attacked and defended;
the tendency towards greater kindliness of tone finds comment:

That theatrical criticism is stingless is a complaint now generally
heard. One has, indeed, only to compare the utterances of men

---

[1] Interesting individualists among the critics were W. S. Gilbert (*Fun*),
Frank Burnand (*Punch*) and Lewis Wingfield, "Whyte Tyghe" (*The
Globe*).

[2] In addition to those cited above, see S. J. A. Fitz-Gerald, *The True
Power of Criticism* (*The Theatre*, N.S. xxvii, Jan. 1896, 29–31), A.J.D.,
The Degeneracy of Dramatic Criticism (*id.* N.S. xv, May 1890, 253–6),
W. Davenport Adams, *Dramatic Criticism* (*id.* N.S. xvi, Aug. 1890, 55–9).

of judgment such as Leigh Hunt and Hazlitt, to say nothing of prejudiced and vituperative writers such as Theodore Hook, with those of the modern press, to see how far we have gone in the direction of "respective lenity". The idea that failure in ambitious effort is offence seems to have been dismissed.[1]

Dion Boucicault, in a letter to Charles Reade, attributed the "decline" of the drama, partly at least, to "the mischievious influence of the press".[2] The playwrights regularly uttered their "growls" against the critics of the time. One such[3] complained of the gradual disappearance of the old "first night" review, bringing to his aid tortuous arguments:

At a time when it was considered that a notice of a new play should appear in the morrow's paper as a piece of actual *news* which the reader had a right to expect, such notices were naturally written under great disadvantages, and, knowing this, the critics, as a rule, wielded their midnight pens with a certain air of kindly reservation. But recently theatrical matters have assumed a prominence altogether remarkable, and dramatic criticisms are looked for with eagerness, not only in the London papers, but in all the principal provincial ones, several of these latter receiving "criticisms" wired by telegraph "after the play"....I maintain that in most cases new plays, of any importance at all, should be seen a second time by the critic before he ventures to give any elaborate comment upon their merits, or upon the manner of their representation.

This question of first-night criticism attracted much attention during the period, and there was a great deal of somewhat acrimonious controversy devoted to it in the journals.[4] Other writers drew attention to the arduous labours of the ordinary dramatic reviewer, declaring that too many enter the theatre "already weary and *distrait*"—which is "altogether unfair, alike to managers, playwrights, and players".[5] The problem

---

[1] *The Athenaeum*, No. 3287, Oct. 25, 1890, 557–8.

[2] *The Theatre*, i, Sept. 1877, 141–2.

[3] H. J. Byron, *Growls from a Playwright* (*id.* N.S. i, Jan. 1880, 20–24).

[4] *"First Night" Criticisms* (*The Era*, xxxii, April 10, 1870, 9); *First Night Audiences* (*id.* xli, April 13, 1879, 14); *A Cry in the Wilderness* (*The Theatre*, N.S. xxi, May 1893, 255–9); Clement Scott, *The First Night Criticism* (*id.* N.S. xxiv, Sept. 1894, 100–5); *The Saturday Review*, lxxxix, Jan. 6, 1900, 13.

[5] *The Theatre*, N.S. xxvi, Dec. 1895, 340–3.

of whether a dramatist might justifiably discuss, as a critic, the productions of his fellow-dramatists was another frequent subject of discussion,[1] and the gentle art of puffing still called for attention.[2] Some said the critics were not cultured enough;[3] others declared with equal enthusiasm that their main fault was their inability to see through the eyes of ordinary uncultured spectators.[4]

These discussions are typical of the time. No age hitherto had shown itself so deeply interested in such problems. Schools of Criticism, Censorship, and, as we shall see, Dramatic Academies, National Theatres—these had become matters of general interest to thousands who previously would have dismissed them as unimportant or sinful. The theatre had become an institution of universal appeal.

3. *The Theatre*

In 1843 the stage had been freed from the monopoly which weighed heavily upon it since the days of Charles II;[5] but for some years it hardly grasped the full significance of its liberty. Samuel Phelps, it is true, was enabled by the new Act to put on his notable series of productions at Sadler's Wells from 1844 to 1862,[6] but the true start in a fresh direction was not taken until, on September 28, 1850, Charles Kean opened the Princess's with the first of his classic revivals.

During the decade 1843–53 there was practically no theatre-building in London, and for a time it looked as though this

---

[1] *The Critic-Dramatist: Old Type and New* (*The Theatre*, N.S. xxvi, Oct. 1895, 187–90); *Should Dramatic Critics write Plays?* (*id.* N.S. xxvi, Dec. 1895, 317–24); and see *The Saturday Review*, lxxx, Nov. 16, 1895, 650.

[2] *The Theatre*, iii, June 1878, 318–19.

[3] *Id.* N.S. xxii, July 1893, 3–8.

[4] Evelyn Ballantyne, *The Stalls, the Pit, and the Critic* (*id.* N.S. xvi, July 1890, 20–4); Charles Dickens, *The Public's Point of View* (*id.* N.S. xxiv, Nov. 1894, 220–6).

[5] See *E.N.D.* i, 22–3 and Ernest Reynolds, *Early Victorian Drama (1830–70)* (Cambridge, 1936), pp. 26–9.

[6] On his activities see John Coleman, *Memoirs of Samuel Phelps* (1886) and W. M. Phelps and John Forbes-Robertson, *The Life and Life-Work of Samuel Phelps* (1886).

Act, so long struggled for, was not to be of any practical assistance to the stage. Then suddenly there came an awakening. The new audiences which were arising both in the metropolis and in the provinces demanded new theatres—demanded, too, that many of the older theatres should be remodelled in accordance with the spirit of a later age. Between 1860 and 1870 came the rebuilt *Royalty*, *The Gaiety*, *The Charing Cross*, *The Globe*, *The Holborn*, *The Queen's* and *The Prince of Wales's*;[1] between 1870 and 1880 *The Court*, *The Opera Comique*, *The Vaudeville*, *The Criterion*, *The Philharmonic* and *The Imperial*; the following decade saw *The Comedy*, *The Savoy*, *The Avenue*, *The Novelty*, *Terry's*, *The Lyric*, *The Shaftesbury*, *The Prince's*, *The Empire* and *The Garrick*; while in the last ten years of the century were opened *The Duke of York's*, *Daly's*, *Her Majesty's* and *Wyndham's*. This brief list, which does not include any of the music halls or of the important suburban houses, amply testifies to the awakened and steadily increasing interest in the stage. The West End playhouses could now easily be reached, by means of omnibus or railroad, by an increasing population and those in the new suburban districts catered for such individuals as, because of lack of means or energy, preferred to take their pleasures nearer home.

"During the summer of 1851", noted J. W. Cole,[2] "there were nineteen theatres open in London, exclusive of the two Italian operas and the St James's, devoted entirely to French tragedy and comedy." The year 1851 was exceptional, for the great Exhibition had attracted thousands of country visitors and of foreigners to London; but even then there was less than a score of playhouses functioning in the metropolis. Barely half a century later, in 1899, London boasted sixty-one theatres—thirty-eight in the West End and twenty-three in the nearby suburban districts. Nor could these regular theatres by any means supply all the dramatic and semi-dramatic entertainment sought for by the public. Cer-

---

[1] Important reconstructions are noted here as well as the erection of entirely new theatres.
[2] *Op. cit.* ii, 10–11.

tainly in the fifties there were numerous houses which presented "dioramas, waxworks, pyrotechnics, astronomical and scientific experiments, Chinese villages, *poses plastiques* and aquatic performances",[1] but these were as nothing compared with the thirty-nine music halls which flourished at the end of the century. Quite apart from the fact that these music halls occasionally produced short plays, their influence on the general fortunes of the theatre and their significance as centres of entertainment was enormous. In some respects, the music hall was as characteristic a growth of Victorian England as the plays of Robertson, Pinero and Jones.[2]

Architecturally, the playhouse of this time reached a form after which men had been vaguely groping for two hundred years. That tendency which, beginning at the close of the seventeenth century, gradually cut away the old Restoration apron and its attendant stage-doors, now attained its culmination. The apron vanished entirely and the picture-frame stage, apt for realistic and spectacular experiments, was established. Percy Fitzgerald, commenting on the new Haymarket, drew attention to a "novel arrangement" introduced by Bancroft:

A rich and elaborate gold border, about two feet broad, after the pattern of a picture frame, is continued all round the proscenium, and carried even below the actor's feet—There can be no doubt the sense of illusion is increased, and for the reason just given; the actors seem cut off from the domain of prose; there is no borderland or platform in front; and, stranger still, the whole has the air of a picture projected on a surface.[3]

Here the picture-frame stage is not only recognised but consciousness of its function and significance is clearly expressed. With this picture-frame effect, far more could be achieved scenically than had ever been dreamed of before. True, the old conventional devices clung tenaciously to the boards of the stage and for long impeded the development of fresh theatrical ideals. Managers still made use of antiquated customs, and some of them showed not the slightest

---

[1] Ernest Reynolds, *op. cit.* p. 74.
[2] M. Willson Disher, *Winkles and Champagne* (1938).
[3] *The World behind the Scenes* (1881), pp. 20-1.

appreciation of what might be done with the instruments now at their command.

An interesting example of this is provided by the front curtain. Even as late as 1881 Percy Fitzgerald found himself compelled to call attention to the fact that the use of this curtain was but sparing. "What", he enquires sarcastically,

can be more absurd or ludicrous than to see a table and two chairs moving on the scene, of themselves apparently, but drawn on by a cord? or, more singular still, to see, on the prompter's whistle being heard, the table hurrying off at one side, the sofa and chairs at the other? After all, the invariable law that each scene can only be terminated by another taking its place, seems unmeaning. If a curtain fell for a moment or two while the change was made, it would be as logical as letting the "drop" fall at the end of each act.[1]

Although Charles Kean had employed "folding curtains of magnificent velvet"[2] to conceal scenic changes in his production of *Henry VIII*, the ancient methods of altering the sets persisted until the eighties.[3] Thus audiences might see a "canvas landscape" ascend "as though it were a vast window-blind, its wooden lath swinging below", and "the average representation of 'a bridge breaking down'" must have been but a clumsy picture when spectators could "distinctly see the 'broken' portion working smoothly on a hinge."[4]

The eighties, however, saw the new take the place of the old. Had Fitzgerald been penning his work in 1891 instead of in 1881 its comments would have been vastly different. Two things are here to be observed—first, the definite improvement in scenic discipline, and, second, the definite change in orientation, from conventionalism to naturalistic effect.

[1] *Op. cit.* p. 35. Already, however, the familiar modern iron curtain (or "asbestos") had been introduced at the Apollo.
[2] *The Illustrated London News*, June 2, 1855.
[3] *Between the Acts* (*The Saturday Review*, lxvi, Sept. 15, 1888, 321–2).
[4] Percy Fitzgerald, *op. cit.* p. 3; cf. Bradlee Watson, *op. cit.* p. 276 (with references from *The Theatrical Journal*, Feb. 6, 1859). It is interesting to note that Irving used the device of darkening the theatre in order to conceal scene-changes (Mrs Alec Tweedie, *Behind the Footlights* (1904), p. 223).

It was in this period that the modern producer or director—stage-manager, he was called then—was born. Up to the seventies things theatrical were often chaotic and confused. Some managers attempted to supervise and control, but there was in general no real endeavour to establish co-ordination and co-operative effort among the many workers back-stage. Murray of Edinburgh was considered peculiar because he "insisted upon every member of his company *acting* at rehearsal exactly as they intended to do at night".[1] The condition of the theatre "in 1865 was absolutely disheartening", declared a writer twenty years later,[2] and that in spite of the fact that we recognise now how much had already been done to prepare the way for a fresh conception. When *King John* was reclothed under the direction of Planché in 1828 a move was made towards the securing of unity in visual effect; only externals were influenced, it is true, but we may readily see how this innovation might lead to others. A further development came when, in the fifties, Charles Kean set forth his versions of Shakespeare. No doubt little was done towards controlling the styles of individual actors or towards building up mass effects by strict attention to detail, but unquestionably his productions were heavily stamped with the impress of a single mind. More significant still was the work of Bancroft at his little theatre in Tottenham Court Road. "Decency and order" were demanded there[3] and an ideal was set up for a unified realism in stage presentation.[4] Now a clear line of progress was set towards the concept of an art theatre, wherein many workers should contribute to secure a pre-designed effect. With the Bancrofts "the star system was revoked in favour of the individual merit system" and the stage-manager definitely had control of the rehearsals.

The Bancrofts used this method to produce a greater

[1] This was before 1850: J. C. Dibdin, *The Annals of the Edinburgh Stage* (Edinburgh, 1888), p. 423.
[2] *The Theatre*, N.S. vi, July 1885, 49.
[3] *Id.* p. 50.
[4] A. W. à Beckett, *Is Realism on the Stage overdone?* (*The Theatre*, N.S. xxviii, Sept. 1896, 132–6).

illusion of the real; Dion Boucicault adopted it chiefly in
order to obtain more "theatrical" and more thrilling effects.
He has been claimed as the inaugurator of the directorial
idea, but a clearer view discerns him as one among many
in whose minds the age had implanted this vision. Boucicault
paid minute attention to the working of stage tricks, to the
controlling of the lights and to the placement of his actors.
In these ways he proved the forerunner of Sir Augustus
Harris who was noted by A. W. à Beckett to have "worked
a reformation on the stage" both in the *mise-en-scène* and in
the direction of performers participating in the production.[1]
His Drury Lane spectacles attained their perfection from his
personal managerial care and ability.

Among the innovators, too, was W. S. Gilbert, who acknowledged a considerable debt to the activities of the Bancrofts
and of Robertson. In no uncertain terms the author of the
Savoy operas declared that Robertson

invented stage-management. It was an unknown art before his
time. Formerly, in a conversation scene, for instance, you simply
brought down two or three chairs from the flat and placed them
in a row in the middle of the stage, and the people sat down
and talked, and when the conversation was ended the chairs were
replaced. Robertson showed how to give life and variety and nature
to the scene by breaking it up with all sorts of little incidents and
delicate by-play.[2]

Similar "life and variety" Gilbert injected into his own productions by taking complete control. Edmond Rickett recalls
that

he was probably the most dreaded director in London—for he
invariably directed personally and autocratically the production
of his own plays and operas. Nor does this apply merely to the
spoken word. He planned the scenery, the lighting and ordered
not only the groupings of the chorus but practically every inflection

---

[1] *Green-Room Recollections* (1896), p. 35. Attention may be called to
a short article in *The Theatre*, N.S. xiii, May 1889, 260–1, where the new
functions of the producer are discussed; a clear distinction is drawn here
between the old "stage manager" and this novel official in the theatre.

[2] Sidney Dark and Rowland Grey, *W. S. Gilbert: his Life and Letters*
(1923), p. 59.

of the voice and every gesture of the actors. And there was no argument and no appeal from his decision.[1]

It is important to remember that all these varied approaches towards a fresh conception were being made from the middle of the century onwards, although at the same time the fact must fully be recognised that the final establishment of new principles in the English theatre, while it was largely the result of native endeavour, owed much to the visits of foreign artists. In 1880 Londoners were enabled to see the performances of a Rotterdam company which aroused much admiration on account of "the completeness of their performances" and because "considerations of general effect" were "not subordinated to the pretensions of a 'star' actor or actress"; the players' "extreme clearness, significance and decision" in gesture also won critical esteem.[2] The troupe paved a way for the visit of the Saxe-Meiningen company (opening at Drury Lane, May 30, 1881). All that had been admired in the work of the Rotterdam players was here found in even greater perfection. To the English theatre, as to theatres in many other lands, they immediately provided a model.[3] Under their director Chronegk they "taught a lesson in the management of stage crowds",[4] and lessons in many other things besides. Their magnificent co-operation, their attention to detail and their archaeological accuracy brought to the age precisely what it had been seeking.

Thus, out of varied needs and influences was the producer brought into being. Old-stagers, of course, might look back through rosy spectacles into the past and declare that not

[1] *Certain Recollections of W. S. Gilbert* (*The New York Times*, April 1, 1934).
[2] *The Saturday Review*, xlix, June 19, 1880, 790; Joseph Knight, *Theatrical Notes* (1893), viii; *The Theatre*, N.S. ii, July 1880, 28–35.
[3] For their influence on Russia, see C. Stanislavski, *My Life in Art* (1924), pp. 196–206, and on their activities in general, C. Weiser, *Zehn Jahre Meininger: Ein Beitrag zur Theatergeschichte* (*Archiv für Theatergeschichte*, i, 1904, 118–26).
[4] Philip Beck, *Realism* (*The Theatre*, N.S. vii, Sept. 1883, 127–31; Sir Theodore Martin, *The Meiningen Company and the London Stage* (*Blackwood's Edinburgh Magazine*, cxxx, Aug. 1881, 248–63); *Die Meininger* (*The Theatre*, N.S. iv, Aug. 1881, 102–5).

so much, after all, had been accomplished. In 1891 Lady Martin, writing of the production of Browning's *Strafford* in 1837, asserted that that play had been "mounted in all matters with great care. Modern critics", she said, "seem to have little knowledge of the infinite pains bestowed in all respects before their day upon the representation of historical and Shakespearian plays."[1] Such statements, however, cannot be accepted at their face value. Unquestionably, with our perspective in time, we can now see how, between the time when *Strafford* was produced and the end of the century, opinion had moved forward and created the ideal of a producer who, without subordinating all to one particular part, engaged himself to obtain order and harmony from the manifold efforts of all those taking part in a performance.

During the period the producer's main task was to secure an impression of reality on the stage. This tendency towards naturalism proved to be the most determined and the most persistent of its age; indeed, by it may these fifty years of theatrical endeavour best be tested and understood. To grasp fully its significance one must bear in mind the fact that the romantic movement of the early nineteenth century had contained within itself the seeds both of a creative idealism and of a creative realism—both of these being in direct opposition to the ideals of the eighteenth-century Augustans.

Typical form was what the Augustans aimed at; class characters, alike in tragedy and in comedy, formal and conventional settings, acting that depended mainly upon relatively fixed gestures—these were the things upon which the eighteenth-century theatre was based. The critics might stalwartly clamour for verisimilitude, but audiences as a whole accepted the playhouse as a place where the exact representation of life had no business. With the coming of romanticism men started to explore—on the one hand, the realms of unreal, imaginative wonder, and, on the other, the forms of life immediately around them. *The Lyrical Ballads* demonstrates both these tendencies—Wordsworth aiming at the close and detailed observation of life and at the use of familiar

---

[1] Sir Theodore Martin, *Helena Faucit (Lady Martin)* (1900), p. 244.

speech, Coleridge seeking escape in the fantastic dream world
of *The Ancient Mariner*. For a time, particularly in poetry,
idealism triumphed; but gradually, and especially in the
novel and in the drama, the gropings toward naturalistic
expression took greater and greater hold of the public.

As early as 1827 Boaden could declare that, in his opinion,
"the modern stage affects reality infinitely beyond the proper
objects of dramatic representation",[1] and deplore a tendency
which made audiences forget they were in a theatre, watching
persons who were, after all, merely actors making pretence.
From this time on, the movement toward the extreme of
naturalism was constant. "The almost universal craving for
Realism", thought an observer in 1883, "just now is one of
the most curious signs of the times."[2] The public, he felt
sure, would not then rest content with Vincent Crummles's
real pump and two washing-tubs; it would demand "entire
rows of real tubs, with real suds, real soap, real thumb blue,
real washing-powder, and real hot water for the mutual
drenching of two real irate females". It is not uninteresting
to observe that, in this period when the public was clamorous
in demanding these naturalistic effects, many of those most
intelligently interested in the theatre divined the dangers
inherent in the new style. "Extreme confidence in the practical worth of stage accessories naturally leads to carelessness
in dramatic construction" decided the critic of *The Graphic*
in 1869,[3] and in other articles, principally one on "The
Limits of Scenic Effect",[4] gave arguments to justify his
position. "While play-maker, play-actor, and play-goer admit
reluctantly that there is something wrong in the British
drama," he wrote,

they can point triumphantly to what has done the mischief—
the glories of British scenery. This, at least, flourishes; and has
almost reached perfection.... Set scenes, perfect structures that

[1] *Memoirs of Mrs Siddons* (1827), ii, 355; cf. pp. 292–3.
[2] Philip Beck, *Realism* (*The Theatre*, N.S. ii, Sept. 1883, 127–31).
Three years earlier Walter Gordon, in an article on *Realism* (*id.* N.S. ii,
Nov. 1880, 283–5) found the stage fully gripped by the prevailing fashion.
[3] i, 31, Dec. 11, 1869.
[4] i, 11, Dec. 4, 1869.

have to be "built", have taken the place of the old "flats"; side scenes have given way to regular enclosures; and drawing-rooms and boudoirs appear ready furnished with hangings, buhl, clocks, etc.; in short, as the bills are careful to inform us, "the furniture in Act IV by Messrs —— and ——, of Oxford Street".

"This mimicry," he opines,

once begun, is endless; it becomes gigantic and insupportable. Whole houses and streets have to be built up with infinite toil and cost; mountains have to be constructed, bridges thrown across.... Yet still we are not in the least beguiled; we may venture to say that the skilfully, effectively painted flat scene is far more welcome to the eye, has more illusion, and has certainly no points of weakness or make-shift, which the most careful eye can detect.... Once we descend into archaeological minuteness, the eye is disturbed, criticism is challenged, or we become pledged to a minuteness of detail which the play does not require, and which is an insufferable burden to those who get up the play.

Fundamentally the same attitude was adopted by Henry Labouchere, of *Truth*. "The new mechanical machinery", he thought,[1] "is far more unnatural than the old full and front sets." Imagination, in his opinion, was being thrust aside; the time was come "to relieve the stage from the thraldom of the stage carpenter" who long enough had had "his wicked way". Labouchere added to his argument regarding the unimaginative quality of realistic scenery another respecting its cost and confusing characteristics when applied to any kind of play other than the familiar "domestic drama". Writers of more romantic plays, he stated,

must reconsider their tactics. They are overlaying their plays with unnecessary scenery, and burdening the action with superfluous characters. The manager whose treasury is sufficiently taxed already by vexatiously costly productions and extravagant salaries, would...welcome any reform that tended towards theatrical economy.

And that reform must lie either in the re-introduction of frankly conventional settings or in simplification. As things stood,

[1] *Truth*, xviii, Nov. 12, 1885.

all nature, repose, and reality are lost. Lights are lowered and raised again so frequently that the spectators are as worried as passengers are in a railway train passing through innumerable tunnels on a bright summer day. Midnight death-scenes change into Buckinghamshire lanes, homesteads whirl into Thames Embankments, Egyptian sphinxes and Cleopatra needles become village-pumps, moonlit spinnies resolve themselves into flash drinking-houses in squalid London.[1]

Labouchere was even prepared to defend and demand the retention of ancient conventions. In reviewing a revival of *The Iron Chest* at the Lyceum in 1879,[2] he expressed regret at the disappearance of that green carpet which for generations had been the familiar accompaniment of the serious drama. This "floor-covering", he thought, was "as necessary to the proper consideration of tragedy as is the extinction of all gas when a ghost story is told in a country house". Some years later, a still more redoubtable warrior tilted his lance against the naturalistic enemy; in 1890 Henry Arthur Jones, despite his interest in the domestic problem-play, saw cause to deplore the loss of imaginative reality through the over great emphasis upon realistic trappings:

The uneducated playgoer goes to a theatre and sees a real lamp-post and a real London street. He goes to another theatre and hears a gentleman in antique dress soliloquising in blank verse. He recognises certain features of the lamp-post and certain features of the London street, but soliloquies in blank verse are palpable and egregious impossibilities. He thinks that the lamp-post and the London street are "real life" and that Hamlet is not.[3]

That these men had ample reason innumerable instances persuade us. Ellen Terry describes how Charles Reade introduced into *Rachel the Reaper* (Qns. 1874) "*real* pigs, *real* sheep, a *real* goat, and a *real* dog" with "*real* litter... strewn all over the stage".[4] A real steam-launch on real water drew spectators to Leonard Grover's *Lost in New York* (Olym. 1896), and the whirligig of fashion could bring a judgment

[1] *Truth*, xviii, Aug. 27, 1885.
[2] *Id.* vi, Oct. 2, 1879, 416.
[3] *The Renascence of the English Drama* (1895), p. 86. This article appeared originally in *The New York Dramatic Mirror*, April 19, 1890.
[4] Ellen Terry, *The Story of my Life* (1908).

that Sarcey was behind the times precisely because he did not believe in historical realism.[1]

For realism, of course, could be interpreted in terms both historical and contemporary. While on the one hand it led towards a closer approach in dialogue to ordinary conversational usage, in setting to a more faithful simulating of nature's three-dimensional forms and in acting to a more restrained and less conventional method of delivery, the same tendency effected a vast alteration in the production of earlier classics and of original plays written about past themes. When W. G. Wills's *Charles I* was presented at the Lyceum in 1872, "the Scenery and Appointments", we are informed, were "prepared with the intention of giving reality to a reproduction of the actual period during which the incidents are supposed to have taken place"—and this statement succinctly expresses the ideal which most managers kept strictly before them in their efforts.

Of these managers, the most representative is Charles Kean. Not only did his work come early in the period but his enunciation of aim was uncompromising and extreme. At a banquet given in his honour at the conclusion of the 1859 season he rose to acknowledge the toast. "I may safely assert", he said, "that in no single instance have I ever permitted historical truth to be sacrificed to theatrical effect."[2] That assertion, so strangely opposed to modern conceptions, gives us the clue for an understanding of his work and that of his companions. Kean was as proud of being an F.S.A. as of being a distinguished producer. His playbills soon extended themselves into miniature essays in which his own learning was set forth and ample indication given of the scholarly assistance which his enthusiasm had evoked. The historical plays of Shakespeare were his delight, but even those dramas, such as *A Midsummer Night's Dream* and *A Winter's Tale*, which were set in fantastic realms came to be treated in a similar manner. Kean's biographer, J. W. Cole,[3] recognised that *A Midsummer Night's Dream* did not

[1] *The Theatre*, N.S. xxi, Jan. 1895, 62.
[2] J. W. Cole, *op. cit.* ii, 382.   [3] *Op. cit.* ii, 197–8.

offer much "scope for that illustrative and historical accuracy, or for that classical research, so peculiarly identified with Mr Kean's system of management";

nevertheless, he availed himself of the few opportunities afforded by the subject, of carrying out his favourite plan. So little is known of Greek manners and architecture in the time of Theseus, twelve hundred years before the Christian era, and so probable is it that the buildings were of the rudest form, that any attempt to represent them on the stage would have failed in the intended object of profitable instruction. Holding himself, for these reasons, "unfettered with regard to chronology", Mr Kean presented ancient Athens to us, in the opening scene, at the culminating period of its magnificence, "as it would have appeared to one of its own inhabitants at a time when it had attained its greatest splendour in literature and art". His scholastic taste took advantage of the specified scene of action, to place before the eyes of the spectators, on the rising of the curtain, a restored view of the famous city, "standing in its pride and glory", which excited the spontaneous sympathy, and called up some of the earliest and deepest impressions of every educated mind. We saw, on the hill of the Acropolis, the far-famed Parthenon, the Erichtheum, and the statue of the tutelary goddess Minerva, or Athena; by its side the theatre of Bacchus; in advance, the temple of Jupiter Olympus, partially hiding the hall of the Museum; and on the right, the temple of Theseus. The view also included the summit of that memorable eminence, "from whence the words of sacred truth were first promulgated to the Athenian citizens by apostolic inspiration".[1]

We must not, of course, allow ourselves to be misled by these accounts into assuming that historical accuracy stood separate from all other considerations. No doubt Kean felt sincere in his declaration which he made to the guests at the banquet of 1859, but a clue to another object is to be found in one phrase of the above account. Even if, says Cole, Kean had been able to obtain reliable information concerning prehistoric Athens, he would probably have found "that the buildings were of the rudest form". The implication

---

[1] An excellent conception of Charles Kean's care and method is to be gained from an examination of the volumes (preserved in the Victoria and Albert Museum) wherein are bound the scene designs and property drawings for several of his productions.

is obvious; all this research and historical endeavour was designed, not simply to depict the past accurately, but to choose from the past that which made a goodly show. While Planché was honest enough in his encouraging of the historical costuming of Shakespeare's plays, while Phelps and Kean trotted forth their "records of antiquity" and their "authorities" for this or that production, the historical aim was generally confused with, and at times even lost in, the desire to present a richly coloured spectacle. Propriety, too, and the dictates of Victorian fashion might disturb severest accuracy. A Roman-clad Antony might stalwartly stand beside a very demure and much petticoated Cleopatra. Even Mrs Kean, for all her husband's devotion to archaeology, persisted in wearing her hair in her own individual manner—drawn straight down from her forehead "in curtains" and twisted curiously round her ears. As Hermione in *A Winter's Tale* she donned underskirt after underskirt in true contemporary style and posed by her pedestal a most un-Grecian statue.

Fundamentally, then, Kean's productions depended upon show; the antiquarian "correctness" was a sop to public taste and to his own vanity. The ideal of correctness, of course, was always insisted upon, until eventually (in 1907) a critic could condemn Tree's production of *Antony and Cleopatra* precisely because of the accurately designed Egyptian garments worn by Cleopatra's court—Cleopatra, this critic pointed out, was of a Greek dynasty and probably would have introduced Athenian fashions to the élite of Alexandria. Never for a moment, however, was the passion for spectacle lost. Kean's explanation of his aims in producing *A Midsummer Night's Dream* may sound like the combination of a sermon and a text-book, but once we proceed to practical matters of the stage we find ourselves in a different world. "The Scenery", we read, is

under the Direction of Mr GRIEVE, and Painted by Mr GRIEVE, Mr W. GORDON, Mr F. LLOYDS, Mr CUTHBERT, Mr DAYES, Mr MORRIS, and numerous Assistants. The Music under the Direction of Mr J. L. HATTON. The Dances and Action by Mr OSCAR BYRN. The Decorations and Appointments by Mr E. W.

BRADWELL. The Dresses by Mrs and Miss HOGGINS. The Machinery by Mr G. HODSON.

With these in charge, we are carried, first, to "A Terrace adjoining the Palace of Theseus overlooking the City of Athens". In the second scene comes the "Workshop of Quince the Carpenter", where, we are relieved to discover, all "the Furniture and Tools...are Copied from Discoveries at Herculaneum". Then, in Act 2, comes "A Wood near Athens (Moonlight)", which gives way to a "Moving Diorama, Exhibiting Another Part of the Wood" and "Titania's Shadow Dance". The third act is ejaculatingly labelled "THE WOOD!" and brings on a general "Dance of Fairies". In the fourth act we have "Titania's Bower", "Athens. Interior of Quince's House" and "The Wood (Sunrise)", while for the final scene is reserved, in largest capitals,

ATHENS

INTERIOR OF THE PALACE OF THESEUS

These are the indications on the playbill. J. W. Cole adds some further details:

the introduction to the haunt of the supernatural beings; the first appearance of *Oberon* and *Titania*, with their attendant trains; the noiseless footsteps of the dance on the moonlit greensward, with the shadowed reflection of every rapid and graceful movement; the wood peopled with its innumerable fairy legions, whose voices lull their queen to sleep upon a bank of flowers; the melodious music composed by Mendelssohn to the words of the author.... The perpetual change of scene and incident; the shifting diorama; the beams of the rising sun glittering on the leaves; the gradual dispersion of the mist, discovering the fairy guardians, light and brilliant as gossamer, grouped around the unconsciously sleeping mortals; the dazzling magnificence of the palace of Theseus at the close, thronged on every staircase, balustrade and corridor, with myriads of aerial beings—

indeed, "an endless succession of skilfully-blended, pictorial, mechanical, and musical effects".[1]

---

[1] *Op. cit.* ii, 199. On Kean's activities in this direction see H. M. Cundall, *Charles Kean, F.S.A. and Theatrical Scenery* (*The Art Journal*, 1903, pp. 199–206), Edward F. Strange, *The Scenery of Charles Kean's*

Thus went realism and spectacle hand in hand. Who would profess to say which was which in *The Merchant of Venice*, where

the gradual illumination of the lighthouse and various mansions, in almost every window, the moon slowly rising and throwing her silver light upon the deep blue waters of the Mediterranean, were managed with imposing reality?[1]

Or who could tell for which purpose were introduced many of the mechanical devices of these years? The gauze that simulated mist in *A Midsummer Night's Dream* served both, as did the panoramic and dioramic effects. It was instructive to go up the Thames by barge and see, passing by, the various edifices of Henry VIII's time, but this formed also a rich and thrilling show. Even Pepper's Ghost may be regarded as a device calculated to excite with wonder, to raise scientific curiosity and to make the supernatural more "naturalistic". To cause a ghost to move laboriously over a creaking stage-floor and cast dark shadows on the scenery is clearly conventional; Pepper's Ghost simply made disembodied creatures look more like disembodied creatures, while at the same time succeeding in providing a novel spectacle.[2]

Pepper's Ghost does not seem to have been much utilised in ordinary dramatic productions, but its counterpart appeared in Fechter's presentation of *Hamlet*, wherein the ghost delivered his long speech, standing in an archway, apparently in the full light of the moon. "As he began to scent the early

Plays and the Great Scene-Painters of his Day (*The Magazine of Art*, 1901–2, pp. 454–9 and 514–18), *The English Stage* (*The Quarterly Review*, clv, April 1883, 354–88). Further notes on *mise-en-scène* will be found in *Scenery and Scene-Painters* (*The Era Almanack*, 1871, pp. 35–40) and Georges Bourdon, *Les théâtres anglais* (*Revue de Paris*, 1900, pp. 859–94).

[1] J. W. Cole, *op. cit.* ii, 333.

[2] Percy Fitzgerald, *The World Behind the Scenes* (1881), pp. 65–6, gives an account of this device: "Just behind the footlights a portion of the stage was raised; an enormous sheet of plate-glass, such as would be used for a great shop-window, was placed on the stage, slightly inclined forwards. It was thus that a person below the stage, in the pit made under the footlights, was reflected, unseen himself, to the audience from the glass." Dion Boucicault, writing on *The Decline of the Drama* (*The North American Review*, cxxv, Sept. 1877, 239), notes that "ghosts are now secured by patent and produced by machinery by Professor Pepper".

morning air, he began to fade, without any motion on his part or any darkening of the stage and grew dimmer by degrees until he vanished altogether. This was about as spectral a bit of business as could be imagined. It was brought about as follows: The ghost stood behind a large concealed wheel which, when started, caught up, at each revolution, a fresh piece of some almost transparent stuff, artfully tinted to match the background, until the requisite thickness was obtained. The ghost apparently melted into thin air."[1]

The built-up sets which became commoner after 1870 served the same double purpose.[2] In 1875 the Bancrofts, impelled by the desire for realism and intent upon spectacular display, caused "elaborate capitals of enormous weight" to be "cast in plaster" for a production of *The Merchant of Venice*, even although part of the wall of the theatre had to be cut away to find room for them "to be moved by means of trucks, on and off the small stage".[3] It was about the same time that the box-set came definitely to supplant the conventional wings and back-cloths which had been handed down from the period of the Restoration, although it is to be noted that, even after its introduction, it long left much to be desired. A critic in 1879,[4] noticing the production of *Fernande* at the Court, draws attention to a "happy innovation which, it is to be hoped, will be widely copied. In this representation of an interior, the two sides of the room come completely down to the proscenium. There are not those gaps through which people in the private boxes and in some of the stalls can see prompters, scene-shifters, and actors waiting for their cues, to the great detriment of all stage illusion."[5] Stage illusion, interpreted as naturalistic illusion,

---

[1] *The New York Evening Post Magazine*, Dec. 20, 1919.
[2] An appeal for a more conventional attitude towards scenic backgrounds is made by Percy Fitzgerald, *Thoughts on Scenery* (*The Theatre*, N.S. i, Oct. 1878, 201–4). See *supra*, p. 36.
[3] Sir Squire and Lady Bancroft, *Recollections of Sixty Years* (1909), p. 205.
[4] *The Saturday Review*, xlviii, Sept. 27, 1879, 386–7.
[5] On the introduction of the box-set see also Percy Fitzgerald, *Theatrical Anecdotes* (1874), p. 71, and on the exactitude of interiors, A. W. Bean, *Artistic Stage Interiors* (*The Theatre*, N.S. xviii, July 1891, 16–20).

is now the final ideal. That ideal is served by the complete box-set for interiors, while for exteriors the cyclorama—described as a "semicircular" background "with a coved ceiling"—provided both spectacular effect and the simulation of a real sky.[1]

Throughout the period continual experimentation was being carried out in the devising of new scenic effects. When Planché introduced in *The Golden Branch* (Lyc. 1847) a

ACT II.—SCENE 1. A Room in Ballyraggett House, in 1st groove. SCENE 2. Father Dolan's (repeat of Scene 4, Act I.), full set. SCENE 3. The Barrack Room, in 1st groove. SCENE 4. Mrs. O'Kelly's Cabin, in 1st groove. SCENE 5. The Gate Tower, full set.

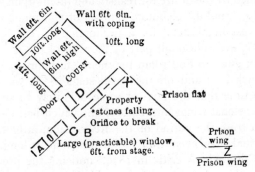

Fig. 1. *The Shaughraun*: scene-plot for Act II, scene 5, "The Gate Tower".

scene showing the "Spirit vaults beneath the Enchanter's Castle" and then made this "whole scene, together with the personages in it", vanish to reveal "The Brown Study of KING BROWN", he inaugurated the transformation so dear to later pantomimic tastes. Responsible for the carrying out of the device was William Beverley, "an ingenious machinist, as well as an admirable painter", according to the testimony of the author. New methods of scene change were being

---

[1] Percy Fitzgerald, *The World Behind the Scenes* (1881), p. 27. Fitzgerald, in *The Art of Acting* (1892), p. 162, notes that when the Paris Opera was being built "one M. Raymond submitted models of a kind of panoramic structure which filled the back of the stage in a semi-circular fashion, thus doing away with side scenes. The sky was formed by a hemisphere, so that the whole had the appearance of the apse of a cathedral."

substituted for the ancient use of grooves. Particularly interesting in this connection is the second act of Boucicault's *The Shaughraun* (D.L. 1875). The fifth scene of this act shows "The interior of a prison; large window, R., old fireplace, R.C., small window, C., door, L. Through window R. is seen exterior and courtyard." Robert, in prison, works to effect his escape while Conn assists him from without; part of the wall is broken when

The Scene moves—pivots on a point at the back. The prison moves off and shows the exterior of tower, with CONN clinging to the walls, and ROBERT creeping through the orifice. The walls of the yard appear to occupy three-fourths of stage.

How this was effected is shown in a scene-plot printed with the text of the play. It is explained that a man "inside boxed wall at A" moves that piece of scenery, which is pivoted at C;

when it gets square home at B a man at D pushes big boxed wall, the whole moves slowly, till smaller wall piece enters and disappears off at Z. The larger wall piece having pivoted on X will now be close to prison flat, the three walls of court will be drawn after it, and occupy the stage.

As an example of the way in which the stage of the seventies was breaking with earlier principles hardly anything better could have been found. Almost equally significant is the scene-plot for the last scene of the act, showing "The Ruins of St Bridget's Abbey". It will be noted in this that, while built-up scenery is freely employed, flat side-wings are still preserved. The set is midway between those of 1800 and those of 1900 and thus harmonises with the spirit and technique of the play for which it was designed. One may add that the five full-stage scenes in *The Shaughraun* are divided by others set in the familiar "grooves".

Boucicault, who was one of the greatest experimenters in this direction, was also an active experimenter in the manipulation of light effects—and these light effects proved possibly the most serviceable instrument in the realisation of those fresh aims which were animating the age. "All the great triumphs of modern stage effect", deemed Fitzgerald justly, date from the introduction of a strong light. When gas was introduced, it was found that a more gaudy display of colours could be effected; but it was the application of the lime-light that really threw open the realms of glittering fairyland to the scenic artist.[1]

In 1826 the whole theatre remained in an even glare of light, with no attempt made to concentrate the illuminant;[2] by 1849 the gas had been put "wholly under the control of the prompter",[3] the auditorium was darkened during the performance and endeavours were made, particularly by Charles Kean, to secure adequate direction and shading of the lights.

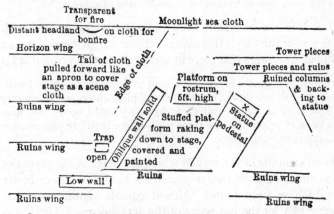

In case no special borders are painted, use cut woods in 1, 2, and 3.
Arched sky in 4 and 5.

Fig. 2. *The Shaughraun*: scene-plot for Act ii, scene ii, "Ruins of St Bridget's Abbey".

Limelight seems to have been tentatively employed by Macready, but it was Kean who first made it a definite and necessary part of theatre equipment; he was using it regularly in his productions of the fifties. Twenty years later came the invention of arclight, and the introduction of the incandescent mantle in 1890 brought further possibilities, possibilities immeasurably increased when electricity came to take the

[1] *The World behind the Scenes* (1881), p. 41.
[2] *The Theatrical Observer*, Sept. 15, 1826.
[3] *The Theatrical Journal*, Dec. 13, 1849.

place of gas illumination.[1] Independent research in spectacular devices was soon brought into association with the
stage. In New York Steele MacKaye opened his Spectatorium
in 1893;[2] in 1896 E. L. Bruce exhibited his "aerial grapho-
scope" at Kensington; and about the same time Professor
Herkomer was experimenting independently with projected
cloud effects.[3] In all of these show and illusion travelled
together.

Sometimes, of course, one prevailed, sometimes the other.
Often unadorned realism held such charms that but to see
reproduced upon the stage what anyone might see without
effort on the streets outside the theatre was very ecstasy and
bliss. A real cow could make the success of a play, not
because it was a strange cow or a prize cow or a sagacious
cow—simply because it, a cow of cows, was made to appear
in a faithfully imitated farmyard scene. A real lamp-post on
the stage was a wonder, and a real hansom cab the realisation
of a dream. Men began to pay attention now to things they
had never heeded before. Alfred Wigan, for example, observed that, if an interior set had a mirror placed facing the
audience, this mirror could reflect part of the auditorium,
which, according to the new creed, was as absurd as any
absurdity tantalisingly demonstrated by Euclid. Accordingly,
he introduced a mirror which, instead of a silvered surface,
was covered with a piece of wallpaper similar to that on the
rest of the scenery; in other words, the mirror was made to
simulate a reflection of the invisible fourth wall.[4]

Peculiarly enough—and yet not peculiarly when one considers aright the philosophic principles at work—this very
same tendency towards naturalism which incidentally en-

---

[1] E. Ack, *Machinerie électrique du théâtre de Drury Lane à Londres*
(*Genie civil*, xxxiv, Jan. 28, 1899, 204-5) and W. W. Davies, *Electric
Light in the Theatre* (*Notes and Queries*, viii, 8, 1895, 288-9).

[2] Percy MacKaye, *Epoch: The Life of Steele MacKaye* (New York,
1927), ii, 345-8.

[3] An early use of the magic lantern for the projection of a scene is
recorded in connection with *The Flying Dutchman* by E. Fitzball, *Thirty-
Five Years of a Dramatic Author's Life* (1859), ii, 13-14.

[4] Godfrey Turner, *Show and its Value* (*The Theatre*, N.S. iii, May 1884,
234).

couraged the elaborately spectacular productions of Shakespeare's plays was responsible for experimentation in the
highly conventional manner of Elizabethan staging. Charles
Kean applied the realistic method for the purpose of making
Lear look like an ancient British monarch and Hamlet seem
a genuine melancholy Dane; others, employing an identical
method, demanded that Shakespeare's stage be reproduced
in all exactitude and his characters be costumed as they might
have appeared in the original productions. Thus was the
historical-real sponsored and guided by William Poel. Found-
ing an Elizabethan Reading Society, that innovator first produced the early *Hamlet* at St George's Hall in April 1887
and followed that by performances of a series of Elizabethan
plays. Webster's *The Duchess of Malfi* appeared at the Opera
Comique in October 1892, Marlowe's *Doctor Faustus* at St
George's Hall in July 1896, *Arden of Feversham* at the same
place in July 1897, Beaumont and Fletcher's *The Coxcomb*
at the Inner Temple Hall in February 1898, Middleton and
Rowley's *The Spanish Gipsy* at St George's Hall in April
1898, Ford's *The Broken Heart* in June of that year, and
Ben Jonson's *The Sad Shepherd* in July—a truly remarkable
series of experiments.[1] Such experiments could not have
been conducted before this time, for during these years only
had there come the desire and the knowledge; hitherto there
had been but slight understanding of the true features exhibited by an Elizabethan playhouse. At the beginning of
the century Edmund Malone had groped blindly towards
the truth, but not till De Witt's famous sketch of The Swan
was published (in 1888) could men obtain any adequate conception of what a playhouse of 1600 looked like. Once this
conception had been gained, the ideal might be realised of
reconstructing that playhouse and of performing Shakespeare's
dramas in their original manner. In 1893 a bare "Elizabethan"
stage of this kind was used for a production of *Twelfth Night*
and in 1896 for a production of *The Two Gentlemen of Verona*.

In these ways an age of invention and materialism affected

[1] *William Poel and his Stage Productions* (privately printed for the
William Poel Portrait Committee, 1933).

the theatre, and amid the conflicting manifestations of a single aim we must tread in our path towards an understanding of the nineteenth-century playhouse. On the one hand there is the unadorned Elizabethan stage companioned by the rather drab and barren middle-class interior, reproduced with pains-taking exactness; on the other there is that scenic splendour by which both poet and actor "were subordinated to the antiquary" while "the costumier helped still further to de-bauch the public taste".[1]

4. *Actors, Managers and Authors*

The audience changed; the theatre changed; and with them the actor, too, altered his methods and, chameleon-like, assumed the colouring of his age. In spite of all Garrick's efforts, the chief histrionic tendency at the beginning of the century was that which may be described as "classical". J. P. Kemble and Mrs Siddons were the leaders of a school which recognised acting as a conventional art and strove to exhibit skill rather than simulate real life.[2] For them and for their audiences plays and dramatic characters existed mainly for the opportunities they provided to the performer. Typical is the scene at Mrs Siddons's farewell in 1812 as narrated by Cole. The play was *Macbeth* and, we are informed, "her friends insisted on having" it "terminated when she made her final exit, in the sleeping scene".[3] The tragedy and its persons mattered little; the artistry of the actress alone had significance. That continual "playing for points", so characteristic of these theatres, tells the same tale, for in the "point", made or lost, the character depicted had perforce to be forgotten.

[1] *The Drama in England* (*The Quarterly Review*, cxxxii, Jan. 1872, 1–26).
[2] By far the finest account of the various styles of acting in the early nineteenth century appears in Bradlee Watson, *Sheridan to Robertson* (Cambridge, U.S.A. 1926). See also C. F. Armstrong, *A Century of Great Actors: 1750–1850* (1912), H. B. Baker, *Our Old Actors* (1881), H. Simpson and C. Brown, *A Century of Famous Actresses, 1750–1850* (1913). Information regarding the Kembles will be found in Percy Fitzgerald, *The Kembles* (2 vols. 1871), J. Boaden, *Memoirs of the Life of John Philip Kemble* (2 vols. 1825) and J. Boaden, *Memoirs of the Life of Mrs Siddons* (2 vols. 1827).
[3] *Op. cit.* i, 33.

Opposed to this highly intellectualised "classic" model, Edmund Kean established, in the second decade of the century, a highly romantic method, and for years his passionate and perfervid style, suited to the mood of an age which produced a Byron and a Shelley, continued to flourish.[1] Flamboyant in the hands of Kean himself, of G. F. Cooke,[2] of G. V. Brooke, it reflected now the satanic idealism of the one poet and now the rapturous ecstasies of the other. In the sphere of comedy a like absence of restraint proved popular. Burlesque methods were by no means confined to extravaganza; they coloured vividly the interpretation of both farce and comedy. Here, too, the "idealism" inherent in the romantic mould found clear (if somewhat strange and perverse) expression.

Romanticism, however, as has been seen, contained within itself the seeds of realism and it is consequently not surprising to find, in the period when domestic melodrama flourished and Lytton essayed his first experiments in the comedy of manners, the arising of more naturalistic styles. Macready[3] and Samuel Phelps[4] were more colloquial than Kean; Kean's son, Charles, brought a "gentlemanly" air to melodrama and Alfred Wigan strained towards reality. In comedy Madame Vestris[5] and Charles Mathews[6] set new standards which provided a foundation for what was to come; the low comedian who had been so popular in the days of Charles Lamb gave place to performers of a more refined, more "genteel" and more versatile sort.

Thus was the way being paved for the theatre of the sixties and seventies. On April 15, 1865, Squire Bancroft made his debut in London under the management of Marie Wilton,

[1] The best account of his work is H. M. Hillebrand, *Edmund Kean* (New York, 1933).
[2] William Dunlap, *Memoirs of George Fred. Cooke* (2 vols. 1813).
[3] See *Macready's Reminiscences*, ed. Sir Frederick Pollock (2 vols. 1875) and W. Archer, *W. C. Macready* (1890).
[4] John Coleman, *Memoirs of Samuel Phelps* (1886), W. M. Phelps and J. Forbes-Robertson, *The Life and Life-work of Samuel Phelps* (1886).
[5] L. Waitzkin, *The Witch of Wych Street. A Study of the Reforms of Madame Vestris* (Cambridge, U.S.A. 1933).
[6] *Memoirs of Charles Mathews, Comedian* (4 vols. 1838–9).

who was later to become his wife, and with their conjunction a new era of comedy acting began.[1] This was recognised by contemporaries. "The new school of acting", writes one critic in the year 1888,[2]

dates from the early days of the Bancrofts at the Prince of Wales's Theatre, and was the result of a most praiseworthy stand against the absurd artificialities and conventionalities then in vogue on the stage....How delighted fashionable audiences were with a system which replaced the grossest caricature of themselves, their manners and customs, with the closest and most faithful reproduction was at once proved by the rapid bounds by which the theatre at which that system first saw the light progressed in public esteem. The managers of the other houses, bewildered by the success which attended this new competition for public favour, at first attempted to explain it away, but ended by copying much of their rivals' method; and the new school thus spread from the stage of the Prince of Wales's to the other theatres of London. Still as the popularity of the Prince of Wales's flourished unabated, so also flourished and increased the new school of actors. That its efforts are uniformly successful from an artistic point of view can hardly be averred by any who desire to see on the stage any more lively display of the passions or humours of life than they can witness for nothing in their own houses....The dread of over-accentuating any display of the feelings has led to a diluted method of playing what should be strong scenes, and a half-hearted handling of strong characters, which have so long prevailed throughout the London Theatres that it is now impossible to expect a full-bodied performance, instinct with life and passion, save from a few players of the old regime.

This critic divined an essential truth. There can be no doubt but that the Bancrofts succeeded in banishing many follies and absurdities which had encrusted themselves upon the stage. Typical is Sir Squire Bancroft's account of the preparations for *Caste* (P.W. 1867).[3] Fred Younge was given the role of D'Alroy and Bancroft took that of Hawtree. The former was "amazed" when the latter "asked if he would mind being the fair man";

[1] Marie and Squire Bancroft, *The Bancrofts* (1909) and *Mr and Mrs Bancroft on and off the Stage* (1889).
[2] *The Saturday Review*, lxvi, Dec. 22, 1888, 741–2.
[3] *Mr and Mrs Bancroft on and off the Stage* (1889), p. 110.

he said how on earth could he do such a thing! He was the sentimental hero, and of course was intended to be dark; while, as what he described as the comic dandy or fop, I was equally compelled to be fair, and wear long flaxen whiskers.

Such things the Bancrofts put to shame, and in doing so inevitably they lost much of the old ranting vigour of the old-timers. Actors now, coming into society, were afraid to express their passions freely. Edmund Kean may have been lionised by lords and ladies in his day, but at a fashionable dinner-table he was rather an eccentric oddity than a genuinely honoured guest; his son, Charles Kean, was master of theatrical ceremonies to Queen Victoria and mingled freely with society. By the end of the century men did not gasp with indignant amazement when an actor was formally knighted by the crown—not for his contributions to charity, but because of his eminence on the stage. The contemporary change in histrionic method, observed the same critic in *The Saturday Review*,[1] was "founded essentially on the manners of the politer classes of society...as a protest against the exaggeration of which the old school of actors was continually guilty", and these politer classes could now be studied at first hand.[2] In place of "the stilted and declamatory style of an earlier generation" there was substituted a "suppressed emotion" and a "reserved force" which, when carried to excess, resulted in underacting. True, the most prominent member of the profession during those years, Sir Henry

[1] lxvi, Sept. 1, 1888, 266.
[2] Numerous books are concerned with the activities of actors during this period; among these may be mentioned Frank Archer, *An Actor's Notebooks* (1912); J. H. Barnes, *Forty Years on the Stage* (1914); A. H. Calvert, *Sixty-eight Years on the Stage* (1911); Mrs Patrick Campbell, *My Life and Some Letters* (1922); J. Coleman, *Players and Playwrights I have Known* (2 vols. 1888); C. and E. Compton, *Memoirs of Henry Compton* (1879); Dutton Cook, *Hours with the Players* (2 vols. 1881), *Nights at the Play* (2 vols. 1883) and *On the Stage* (2 vols. 1883); W. A. Donaldson, *Recollections of an Actor* (1865); A. Ellerslie, *The Diary of an Actress* (1885); D. Frohman, *Memories of a Manager* (1911); J. K. Jerome, *On the Stage—and Off* (1885); J. W. Marston, *Our Recent Actors* (2 vols. 1888); T. E. Pemberton, *The Kendals* (1900); A. J. Smythe, *The Life of William Terriss* (1898); J. L. Toole, *Reminiscences of J. L. Toole* (2 vols. 1889); C. M. Younge, *A Memoir of Charles Mayne Younge* (2 vols. 1891); A. E. W. Mason, *Sir George Alexander and the St James' Theatre* (1935).

Irving, did not accept the restraint and persisted in his own particular style of romantic interpretation; but Irving's method was a kind of *tour de force* and is not strictly typical of the dominant forces of the age.[1]

Unquestionably the English actors of this generation were considerably aided in their efforts by foreign example. On November 3, 1860, Fechter first performed in England and his influence may readily be traced on others. Although we might not now recognise his style as realistic, it contributed something to the new school. The Rotterdam and Saxe-Meiningen companies, even although—or perhaps precisely because—they included no star players, later made their influence felt. Nor must one forget the successive visits of Augustin Daly's actors from 1884 until, in 1893, Daly's Theatre was formally opened in London. The original visit, with the opening of Toole's Theatre on July 19, 1884, marks an historic occasion. From the time when, about the year 1700, Tony Aston sailed across the Atlantic, many English players had toured to America or had settled down there. For long, however, the passage was an arduous and difficult one. Even when Charles Kean crossed the ocean in 1833 the voyage lasted forty days. This, remarks his biographer, "was before the broad Atlantic had been spanned by steamers as with a bridge, reducing to hours what had formerly occupied days", so that the three thousand mile journey took about as long as "it took our ancestors a few generations back to rumble in a lumbering *diligence* from Edinburgh to London".[2]

[1] On Irving see E. Gordon Craig, *Henry Irving* (1930); W. Archer, *Henry Irving, Actor and Manager* (1883); A. Brereton, *The Life of Henry Irving* (1908) and *The Lyceum and Henry Irving* (1903); W. Calvert, *Sir Henry Irving and Miss Ellen Terry* (1897); H. A. Clapp, *Reminiscences of a Dramatic Critic. With an Essay on the Art of Henry Irving* (1902); P. Fitzgerald, *Henry Irving* (1893) and *Sir Henry Irving* (1906); C. Hiatt, *Henry Irving* (1899); F. Marshall, *Henry Irving, Actor and Manager* (1883); Clement Scott, *From The Bells to King Arthur* (1896). W. Archer and R. W. Lowe have a (now rare) satire, *The Fashionable Tragedian* (Edinburgh, 1877). On Ellen Terry see Clement Scott, *Ellen Terry* (N.Y., revised edition, 1900); Ellen Terry, *The Story of My Life* (1908) and *Memoirs* (1933); C. Hiatt, *Ellen Terry and her Impersonations* (1898); T. E. Pemberton, *Ellen Terry and her Sisters* (1902). On Tree see Max Beerbohm, *Herbert Beerbohm Tree* (1921).

[2] J. W. Cole, *op. cit.* i, 203.

Up to this time, hardly anyone thought of a reciprocal movement of actors to England, but, with the greater facilities for
travel and with the rapid growth of the American stage, at last
the time was reached when Daly could dare to bring over an
entire American company—incidentally meeting with critical
acclaim for his excellent stage management and for the performances of Ada Rehan and John Drew.[1]

With the introduction of new histrionic ideals and with
the closer co-operation between stage and society, when it
became no shame for persons "of gentle birth and education"
to tread the boards,[2] many things which before had been
passed over in indifference aroused public interest. In 1877
a "Dramatic Reform Association" is formally promulgated,
its aim being to introduce a "higher standard of taste".[3]
The question of child performers—hitherto undiscussed—
becomes "a serious one", not lightly to be dismissed.[4] The
schoolboards begin to take an interest in boys "who attended
school in the morning, and in the afternoon and evening
personified a Colorado Beetle and a French soldier" for
a salary of 9s. weekly.[5] The actors come to take themselves
more seriously, and in 1891 is held the first meeting of the
Actors' Association, "an event", says *The Era*, "which may
well be regarded with joy and triumph by the whole of the
theatrical profession".[6]

By far the most sweeping change in conditions, however,
effected by this new movement in the theatre was the complete dissolution of the stock company and the establishment
of the long run. In the good old days a perfectly normal
system was universally recognised. London had a number
of theatres, in each of which was established a stock company

---

[1] J. F. Daly, *The Life of Augustin Daly* (New York, 1917). It is to be
observed that from the very first Daly broke away from the traditional
"lines of business" (*op. cit.* p. 90).

[2] *The Saturday Review*, lxvi, Dec. 15, 1888, 710.

[3] *The Theatre*, ii, Dec. 1877, 298–9.

[4] *The Era*, xl, Feb. 17, 1878, 12; *id.* xlix, May 21, 1887, 13.

[5] *The School Board and the Theatres* (*id.* xl, Feb. 10, 1878, 7); cf.
The Theatre, N.S. xxv, March 1895, 140–3.

[6] *The Era*, liv, March 3, 1892, 13; cf. *id.* Dec. 3, 1892, 11; *id.* lv,
July 22, 1893, 13; *The Athenaeum*, No. 3327, Aug. 1, 1891, p. 172.

or at least a company engaged for the season. When any deficiencies had to be made up, the managers looked for fresh talent among the scores of other stock companies which could be found either stationed in the larger provincial cities or else working the various circuits of smaller towns. It was recognised that, in ordinary circumstances, any young man or woman who intended to follow the profession had to put in a few years of training at these provincial schools; only rarely could a genius or a child of good fortune make his debut in London and be accepted into the Drury Lane or Covent Garden companies. Even when the days of stardom dawned and a Kean or a Macready went to glitter for a space in Birmingham or in Edinburgh, the troupe with which he played was the ordinary stock troupe of the town. Thus the "good stock company was a kind of histrionic nursery, the young actors and actresses of which were literally in a dramatic school", gaining excellent experience both by reason of the constant variation in the repertoire and by their occasional conjunction with visiting stars.[1]

Then arose the new public in London and the resultant long run. Actors became social personalities and were sought after by admiring audiences; the audiences had increased and found easy means of reaching the theatres; foreign visitors, because of accelerated Channel crossings, more frequently appeared in the auditoriums—for these and a dozen other reasons the long run became inevitable in London.[2] Starting tentatively in the abnormal days of the Great Exhibition of 1851, the movement rapidly gained in impetus as the years advanced. Charles Kean created a record with the hundred nights of his *Henry VIII* (P'cess, 1855), beat that record by fifty with *A Midsummer Night's Dream* (P'cess, 1856) and was easily outdistanced in a few years by Sothern's production of Taylor's *Our American Cousin* (H. 1861), and by Robertson's *Caste* (P.W. 1867). Instead of a constant change of bill, necessitating the maintenance of a salaried group of performers chosen for their recognised skill in portraying

[1] *The Stock Company Question* (*The Era*, lii, Dec. 14, 1889, 13).
[2] *The Theatre*, iii, Feb. 1878, 76.

type parts, the theatres subsisted on plays which ran for
hundreds of nights, plays which were becoming increasingly
naturalistic and hence demanded an interpretation of characters, not according to type parts but according to indi-
vidualities. Naturally, the managers found that their most
profitable plan was to get their play, study the *dramatis
personae*, and engaged such performers as might best suit
the requirements of the script.

This system established in London, the managers soon
discovered a new additional source of income. The provincial
cities were, like the metropolis, rapidly increasing and there
too a vast audience was arising. Speedier methods of com-
munication brought to them news of London's latest successes
and inevitably was born a desire to see these successes reproduced. As a result, the metropolitan managers gathered a first,
a second and even a third touring company and sent these
out over the country.[1] Of necessity, because of this competition, the provincial stock companies disappeared and the
old Theatres Royal, instead of being managed by men qualified
in repertory work, passed into the hands of directors interested
in nothing but profitable "bookings". Since these provincial
theatres could now be hired or contracted for on a sharing
basis, still another development occurred, for London managers
came to find it convenient to produce a play first in the provinces and then bring it, polished after the "try-out", to the
metropolis.[2]

---

[1] Considerable doubt exists concerning the origin of this practice.
Ernest Reynolds, in *Early Victorian Drama (1830–70)* (Cambridge, 1936),
pp. 67–8, declares that the earliest professional company touring with
a single play was that of *Caste* in 1867. This tour was anticipated by the
distinguished amateurs who, inspired by Dickens, took Lytton's *Not so
bad as we seem* to the provinces in 1851. In 1892 it was noted (by Walter
Baynham, in *The Glasgow Stage* (1892), p. 209) that "Mr Boucicault has
been considered the first to introduce the present system of travelling
companies, although the Haymarket company had...appeared with almost
the full corps in 1849....The present system of bringing down a play
with a complete cast was then but in perspective. The members of
travelling corps eight and twenty years ago (i.e. in 1864) had to depend
upon aid from those of the stock resident company."

[2] On this subject and on the growth of the suburban theatres see Robert
Buchanan, *An Interesting Experiment* (*The Theatre*, N.S. xxviii, July 1896,
9–11), Henry Elliott, *The Suburban Theatre* (*id.* N.S. xxix, April 1897,
202–5) and John Hollingshead, *The Theatrical Radius* (*id.* N.S. xxx, Dec.
1897, 302–6).

The establishment of the long run produced many changes in the theatrical world. One result was that the young actor found himself without an adequate opportunity for training; another was that, instead of being able to see a fairly extensive collection of old and new plays presented in repertoire, audiences now were regaled either with long-run successes or occasional and elaborate revivals; from this generated decreasing opportunities for the young author and the inception of the commercial manager. These may occupy our attention for a moment.

An apprentice actor might obtain a part in a touring company but, if he were successful in gaining this role, he might "easily go round the provinces for eighteen months perseveringly playing the same part", without having any chance of acquiring versatility. So serious was this that in 1898 Beerbohm Tree declared that "nothing in these days is more destructive of true theatrical art than the long run".[1] This was the first problem that the stage had to settle. The second concerned the disappearance of the old repertory. "What is wanted in London", declared a writer in *The Pall Mall Gazette*,[2]

is a theatre where it would be possible from time to time to play single performances of some of the plays that were once applauded as masterpieces and that now lie untroubled on the shelves by all save a few persistent students.... Such a work could, of course, only be done by private enterprise, by private enthusiasm. The revival of an old comedy at a regular theatre would not do, because it could not appeal to a public who would support it for a run.... The old tragedies, the old comedies, are not very expensive pieces to mount, and the chance of interpreting them now and then might be of no small advantage to young actors and to young actresses. The number of persons in London who would go sometimes to see a Restoration comedy or an Elizabethan tragedy is not in all probability very large, but also, in all probability, is larger than many would imagine.

[1] *The Pall Mall Gazette*, lxvi, June 16, 1898, 3. There is an important article on this subject, *The Provinces as a Dramatic School*, in *The Saturday Review*, lxvi, Oct. 13, 1888, 433–4. See also *id.* Nov. 3, 1888, 522–3 and *The Era*, xl, April 14, 1878, 7.
[2] lvi, Sept. 19, 1893, 4–5.

If the public, or a part of it, were deprived of their old favourites, so that Jonson and others who had long held the stage were now theatrically forgotten, the playwrights had equally valid grounds for complaint. The long-run system had conduced to the establishment in London of two types of manager—the star actor, like Irving or Tree, who controlled the fortunes of a company, and the purely business man who, choosing what he considered to be a likely play, proceeded to finance its production. "The ease with which a man may become a manager without adequate equipment in money or knowledge of his business"[1] was a common theme of complaint. Against the actor-manager was preferred the accusation that he either subsisted on a series of revivals which cost him no royalties or else selected new plays which contained one fat part for himself.[2] That this objection was not without justification is easily demonstrated by a glance at the productions of Charles Kean at the Princess's and of Henry Irving at the Lyceum. So far as the commercial manager was concerned, the complaint most commonly expressed was that, in his want of knowledge and in his purely financial aims, he persisted in leaning upon the plays written by a limited number of already tried and recognised authors. His objection to the perusal of outsiders' manuscripts, his delay in returning these, his fondness for conventionality, his dread of novel ventures, and his profound belief in the value of a successful name on his playbill were all duly pilloried.[3] A letter written by W. Allingham to *The Athenaeum* demonstrates some of the difficulties and dangers associated with this attitude of the managers. "Your dramatic critic", he writes,

[1] *The Athenaeum*, No. 2394, Sept. 13, 1873, 347–8.
[2] *Dramatic Revivals* (*The Era*, xxxviii, July 9, 1876, 10). See on this subject *Dramatic Authors vs. Actor-Managers* (*The Saturday Review*, lxx, Aug. 9, 1890, 168–9) and Sydney Grundy, *The Dearth of Originality* (*The Theatre*, N.S. i, Nov. 1878, 274–7). Further discussions of this problem will be found in *The Fortnightly Review*, liii, April 1890, 499–516, June 1890, 922–36, liv, July 1890, 1–19, and in *The Nineteenth Century*, xxvii, June 1890, 1040–58.
[3] *The Theatre*, iii, no. 57, Feb. 27, 1878, pp. 74, 75; *The Era*, xxxix, Jan. 14, 1877, 4; *id.* xli, Sept. 22, 1878, 6; *The Pall Mall Gazette*, xxxi, May 14, 1880, 12; *The Athenaeum*, No. 3613, Jan. 23, 1897, 114.

having mentioned my play "Ashby Manor" in connexion with
"The Lord Harry" at the Princess's Theatre, I am emboldened
to send you a brief statement which seems to me to raise a not
unimportant question. In 1883 I sent my play in print to Mr
Wilson Barrett, and had, at his request, an interview with that
gentleman, and a second one in 1884. He said he was "much
struck" with "Ashby Manor", but it was not suitable for his
company, and in any case would require "a great deal of pulling
about". He made no proposal but asked if I had anything else
to show him. Since then I have heard nothing. Mr Barrett has
now produced "The Lord Harry", not only the germ of which
is unquestionably in "Ashby Manor", though there has been
extensive "pulling about" and much addition of sensational
incident and scenery, unconnected with any plot—but also the
personages in each are essentially identical.

The question, of some importance to the English drama, is
this, How shall a writer outside theatrical circles bring a play
under the eyes of managers without the risk that, should it contain
anything of value for stage purposes, this will be appropriated
without the smallest acknowledgement?[1]

One dramatic author in 1870 gave it as his belief that a play
"from an unknown writer, although as brilliant as Sheridan
or profound as Shakespeare" would stand little chance of
being "accepted by a Manager for representation".[2] The
existence of a "Dramatic Ring", due to "the cowardice of
English managers" and "none the less effectual although not
organised", was generally admitted.[3] "The cry that English
authorship is dead", declared Grundy, "ought to be, rather,
that English dramatic authorship has been murdered.... The
pressing requirement of the theatre is a manager who has the
courage to avail himself of the wealth of dramatic genius which
lies outside the Ring."

As a slight attempt to find a solution for these conditions
came the matinée. The matinée system, whereby an author
could hire a theatre for an afternoon or morning and present
his untried play, served a useful purpose in mitigating the

---

[1] *The Athenaeum*, No. 3045, March 6, 1886, 338.
[2] *The Era*, xxxii, Jan. 23, 1870, 6.
[3] Sydney Grundy, *The Dramatic Ring* (*The Theatre*, N.S. iii, Dec.
1879, 273–7); H. A. Jones, *op. cit.* 163 (article first printed in *The English
Illustrated Magazine*, Jan.–Feb. 1885); *The Era*, xxxix, Jan. 14, 1877, 4.

force of the established ring. No doubt the system brought with it many disadvantages, making "every third person one meets" consider himself a born dramatist, insistent "on putting his efforts before the public",[1] but the virtues of the device are apparent. It is true that the matinée soon ceased to present merely new plays and became an occasion for the addition of two weekly performances of popular productions, but throughout the greater part of this period it preserved its other functions.

The independent matinée, however, was not enough. Those with vision realised that to meet the needs of the time co-operative action was essential; the matinée idea might be used, but in a resolute and determined manner. Hence the growth of an element entirely new to the theatre—the stage society. Typical is the organisation known as The Dramatic Students, founded in 1886. Of it *The Saturday Review* has this to say:

> The Dramatic Students are a society of young professional actors, who, finding that the long runs now common in successful plays give them scant occasion to gain variety of skill in their art, have determined to bring out, in single morning performances, the less known masterpieces of English dramatic literature. They eschew such plays as are included in the ordinary repertory.... We follow their efforts with great interest, for we believe that these form the nucleus of a very wholesome revival of interest in the best theatrical writing....By-and-bye this seed will, we do not doubt, bear fruit, and the public will insist on seeing more of these interesting pieces, and on seeing them repeated. It is a sheer absurdity that our seventeenth century dramatic literature should be without dispute one of the richest ornaments of our language and yet that none of it, except three or four plays of Shakespeare's, should ever be seen, even for a moment on the stage.[2]

William Poel's activities[3] had a similar object and there were other ventures of the kind during the period. Akin to these was the Independent Theatre Society. Started by a few audacious and vigorous enthusiasts in 1891, it eventually

[1] *The Theatre*, N.S. xiv, July 1889, 12.
[2] lxi, Jan. 23, 1886, 116.   [3] *Supra*, p. 48.

passed on its mantle to The Stage Society eight years later.
Perhaps it did not do all it set out to accomplish. In reviewing
one of the plays presented under its auspices, the critic of
The Theatre, at any rate, opined that it was sufficient to say
"Independent Theatre play" in order "to indicate that its
construction is amateurish and its theme unpleasant".[1] But,
whatever its shortcomings, it undoubtedly achieved a great
deal. "The Independent Theatre", wrote G. B. Shaw in
1895,

is an excellent institution, simply because it is independent. The
disparagers ask what it is independent of.... It is, of course,
independent of commercial success.... If Mr Grein had not taken
the dramatic critics of London and put them in a row before
"Ghosts" and "The Wild Duck", with a certain small but
inquisitive and influential body of enthusiasts behind them, we
should be far less advanced today than we are. The real history
of the drama for the last ten years is not the history of the prosperous enterprises of Mr Hare, Mr Irving, and the established
West-end theatres, but of the forlorn hopes led by Mr Vernon,
Mr Charrington, Mr Grein, Messrs Henly and Stevenson, Miss
Achurch, Miss Robins and Miss Lea, Miss Farr and the rest of
the Impossibilists.[2]

One danger of the Independent Theatre was that it might
become a highbrow society, extolling commercial failure as
an artistic virtue. "No author", notes Shaw, "whose play
strikes, or is aimed at, the commercially successful pitch will
give it to Mr Grein", and consequently he pleads for the
presentation of one marketable play each year. Thus, in his
opinion, the London managers might be persuaded to

help and cherish the Independent Theatre as a sort of laboratory
in which they can have experiments tried on the public from time
to time without the cost and responsibility incurred by, for example,
Mr Beerbohm Tree in the experiments he made at the Haymarket
with "Beau Austin" and "An Enemy of the People".

Another danger, commented on boldly by Antoine,[3] lay in

[1] *The Theatre*, N.S. xxv, Feb. 1895, 107.
[2] *The Saturday Review*, lxxix, Jan. 26, 1895, 126; cf. an article in
The Athenaeum, No. 3557, Dec. 28, 1895, 912.
[3] See *The Pall Mall Gazette*, lxv, Sept. 28, 1897, 7.

the fact that this association directed its attention to the production of foreign plays rather than to the cultivation of native talent; but that, no doubt, was natural when Ibsen had swum into the horizon of the younger writers but was still looked on as a cloudy and rather ominous symbol by the over-respectable audiences in the commercial theatres.

Most important of all these movements were those which aimed at the establishment either of permanent endowed theatres or of dramatic schools. In the year 1875, the annual birthday exercises at Stratford were marked by "the inauguration of a Shakespearian scheme on a far grander scale than any which has preceded it". "It is contemplated", we are informed, "to build a Shakespeare Theatre in Shakespeare's native town, and it is considered feasible that a School, or University of Dramatic Art, can be established there, with its libraries, class-rooms, houses for instructors, scholarships for students, and special chairs for Professors."[1] This concept by many was combined with another—that of setting up in London a dramatic academy which might serve as a training school for young players and be to the theatre what the Royal Academy was to the world of art. In recording the Stratford proposals, *The Era* seized the opportunity to plead this cause:

We would, at the outset, implore the prime movers in the scheme to decide definitely, and once for all, if the Shakespeare Memorial is intended as a tribute to mere sentiment, or is destined to have some sound and practical outcome.... There is but one place in England which should be the headquarters of dramatic art—in London. Only in one place can a Shakespeare Theatre be erected—in London.... For years and years we have talked of the institution of an Academy of [Dramatic] Art. Over and over again in these columns it has been urged that either Government aid or generous private enterprise would establish a dramatic mutual society like the Comedie Francaise of Molière in Paris, or an art school like the Parisian Conservatoire. Here at last is the foundation of one or other such scheme.... Where... can Shakespeare's plays be better acted than in London, where we have the very pick of the Dramatic Profession?[2]

[1] *The Era*, xxxvii, May 2, 1875, 13. See also W. A. Chevalier, *A Tribute to the Shakespeare Memorial at Stratford-on-Avon. Outlines of a Scheme for Reforming the Stage* (1875).   [2] *Id.* 13.

The prominence given to this subject in the newspapers of the time may not be overlooked. Dramatic academies of a sort had, of course, existed in earlier years, but they were trivial or private institutions. The Restoration "Nursery"[1] was one such; another, later, was the Musical and Dramatic Academy started by Glover and his wife at 21 *a* Soho Square in 1848.[2] This new movement pointed to something on a larger, more ambitious scale, and, moreover, called into being a controversy which, not yet dead, indicated by its acrimony and persistence the widespread general interest in the subject. A serious attempt to start such a Dramatic College was made in 1876,[3] but objections were brought forward to its institution as "false in principle and useless in practice". "The radical mistake", it was thought, "was made in erecting such a building without the prospect of an endowment, and in believing that the housing of a few old pensioners of indifferent fame was the outcome of the theatrical revolution in this country."[4] A year later the chairman of the governors, Lord William Lennox, commented on the same subject. "The first stone of the Royal Dramatic College", he stated,

was laid by the late Prince Consort. It was opened by his Royal Highness the Prince of Wales, and, therefore, we would suppose that, under such distinguished auspices, the Royal Dramatic College would not have had to do—what it does today—appeal to the public for funds to carry it on.[5]

The performances given by the students of the College met with some approval, but apparently it soon ceased to function for lack of support; at any rate a new plea was being made in 1879 for "an academy of acting",[6] followed again by a

[1] *A History of Restoration Drama* (1928), pp. 280–1.
[2] *The Theatrical Journal* Feb. 24, 1848.
[3] Already on Jan. 12, 1859, a meeting had been called at the Adelphi Theatre for the purpose of discussing the establishment of a Royal Dramatic College; Charles Kean, Benjamin Webster, Charles Dickens and W. M. Thackeray were made trustees of this venture. See H. Dodd, *Royal Dramatic College: Correspondence respecting proposed gift of land* (1859).
[4] *The Era*, xxxviii, July 30, 1876, 10; cf. also *id.* July 23, 1876, 10.
[5] *Id.* xxix, Feb. 25, 1877, 12.
[6] *The Theatre*, N.S. iii, Sept. 1879, 61–4.

proposal to establish a Royal Academy of Dramatic Art. This met with the unqualified approval of W. E. Henley.[1] For it he envisaged many useful functions:

> It might sit as a jury on unpublished plays and unknown playwrights....In time it might build a theatre...and the National Theatre would be the issue...it would create, organise, and control a complete system of instruction.

and, he thought, if the instructors "did but half their duty, they would make technical incapacity far rarer on the English stage than it is". In 1882 the question was still being debated. Hamilton Aidé then launched a fresh plea, arguing the case rather more fully than his predecessors had done:

> It is rather singular that, of all the arts, the one which is perhaps the most popular, judging by the crowds that flock nightly to an increasing number of theatres, is the only one for which, up to the present time, no school or organised system of education upon any considerable scale has been provided. There was a time when the want of such definite routine of instruction was supplied by means no longer at our command—the constant variety of practice in country theatres, and the stream of tradition unbroken for several generations, simultaneously training and exercising the capacities of actors, and maintaining a standard whereby their efforts might be gauged. But the stream of tradition is dry, and country theatres have no longer stock companies. The system of long runs in London, and of importing the pieces which have enjoyed them into the provinces, is disastrous to the true interests of the Drama. That the performances must suffer after a time, and that the best artists in the world must unconsciously exaggerate or flag, after the weary iteration of months, is self-evident. What the audience is less likely to remember is, how this condition of things on the stage necessarily affects the beginners in the profession....It is with the view of raising the standard of education on the stage, and, by offering some obstacles to indolent incompetency, of clearing the ground for the more active and industrious, that an association has lately been formed in the hope of creating a School of Dramatic Art. Other schemes of a like character have in past years been projected; but, for some cause or another, they have all of them collapsed before they reached maturity....

---

[1] *A Corporation of Actors* (*The Theatre*, N.S. ii, Nov. 1880, 274–9).

The present association, however, is formed under exceptional conditions.[1]

The committee of this new venture included Lytton, Tennyson, Mathew Arnold, Henry Morley and Wilkie Collins. Tentatively an academy was opened in October 1882, but was forced to close in 1885. *The Quarterly Review* in 1883 had a long article dealing with the disappearance of the old stock companies,[2] and five years later *The Saturday Review* was still commenting on the imperative need of a dramatic school in London.[3] "The supplanting of the stock companies by casts engaged for the run of the piece in town and by touring companies in the country" was here again noted as having effected a revolution. "The provinces, theatrically considered," it was found, "have in fact so completely surrendered their importance and independence to the preponderating influence of the metropolis, and have for so many years been content to take their dramatic supply at secondhand from that fountain-head, that it is useless to expect the origination of any important change except in town." The method, as this writer saw it, was to arouse the self-seeking London managers to some kind of disinterested effort.[4]

About this time, several articles were published, complaining of the want of proper theatrical instruction and proposing a revival of ancient traditions. In 1890, however, B. W. Findon, in a general survey of the whole subject, decided that nothing could be done towards a resuscitation of the old provincial stock companies. That solution, he believed, was hopeless. Although he fully realised that something positive had to be done, he feared, on the other hand, that "a State-aided school would quickly become fossilized, and produce nothing but dramatic dummies". Hence followed an interesting suggestion that "the future School of

---

[1] *A Dramatic School (The Theatre*, N.S. v, Feb. 1882, 73–6). See also, *A Dramatic School of Art (Truth*, xi, June 1, 1882, 756), *A Subventioned Theatre (id.* iii, March 21, 1878, 361) and *A Dramatic Academy (id.* vii, Jan. 22, 1880, 109).
[2] clv, April 1883, 354–88.
[3] lxvi, Nov. 17, 1888, 581–2.
[4] Cf. *id.* lxvi, Nov. 24, 1888, 615.

Dramatic Art is the amateur dramatic club". With this idea in mind, Findon proposed "the formation of a Grand Central Club"—the British Drama League of to-day—"to which all amateur clubs" should "have the right to be affiliated on payment of an annual subscription". The whole movement, he thought, should be initiated and controlled by professionals, for it

> must, above all things, have the active support of the theatrical manager. It must be clearly and distinctly understood that he will regard it as his recruiting ground, and that it shall be to the stage what our great military schools are to the army.[1]

So the various efforts proceeded. In 1895 S. J. Adair Fitzgerald was pleading once more for a Royal Academy of Dramatic Art[2]—"a sort of dramatic Athenaeum and Museum combined, containing a theatre, lecture rooms, galleries, and a library". And when we leave this half-century, in 1900, a writer in *The Era* is still proclaiming that

> it would be the grandest thing of all if the committee which is to be formed by, or for, the Actor's Association could permanently establish an academy of acting—the "Royal Academy of the Drama" would follow after.[3]

That but little success attended the efforts of the several sponsors counts as nothing compared with the vast amount of public interest involved and with the fact that eventually out of all this discussion grew the present Royal Academy of Dramatic Art. Similarly, the failure to establish a National Theatre should not blind our eyes to the immense publicity which the idea of a permanent home for the classic drama received between 1870 and 1900. A scheme for such a national theatre had been promulgated as early as 1848, but once more the seventies witnessed the first determined effort in that direction, Tom Taylor arguing in favour[4] and Thomas Purnell

---

[1] *The Amateur Club as a Stepping-Stone to the Stage* (*The Theatre*, N.S. xvi, Aug. 1890, 63–7).

[2] *Id.* N.S. xxv, June 1895, 344–6.

[3] lxiii, April 14, 1900, 11.

[4] See the series of letters contributed by him to *The Echo* on June 7, 1871, and subsequent dates.

against.[1] The controversy proceeded apace. H. J. Byron, George Godwin and others took various sides in *The Theatre* during the years 1878 and 1879.[2] On October 8, 1879, Mrs Pfeiffer restimulated interest in the subject by a letter contributed to *The Times*, and an offer of £100 towards its accomplishment was announced towards the end of that month.[3] Ten years later, in *A Plea for an Endowed Theatre*, William Archer went over again the same old arguments,[4] receiving the critical and enthusiastic support of *The Saturday Review*.[5] William Poel discussed *The Functions of a National Theatre* in 1893;[6] Sir Edward Russell put forward another plan in 1897;[7] and Sir Henry Irving, in an address delivered in 1894, discussed the desirability of having subsidised municipal theatres.[8] As we reach the end of the period, we find that the seemingly interminable discussion results in a prospectus issued for a National Theatre Company, Limited.[9]

The space devoted to these projects is justified in that nothing could present a clearer picture of the atmosphere amid which authors and actors worked and of the definite needs of the time. If, however, the authors complained and felt that only subsidised theatres could provide alleviation for the abuses of the time, it is to be noted that their fortunes, during the last two decades of the century, had markedly

[1] *Op. cit.* pp. 13–17. A plea for a national theatre was separately put forward by Henry Neville in *The Stage: Its Past and Present in Relation to Fine Art*, an address delivered in 1871 and published in 1875.
[2] *A Subsidised Theatre for London* (*The Theatre*, N.S. i, Aug. 1878, 7–11), H. J. Byron, *The Other Side of the Question* (*id.* Sept. 1878, 109–12), George Godwin, *The National Theatre Question* (*id.* Dec. 1878, 346–52), Henry Peat, *Objections to State Aid* (*id.* N.S. ii, Feb. 1879, 28–31), *A National Theatre* (*id.* April 1879, 147–50), *A National Theatre* (*Truth*, v, Feb. 6, 1879, 160).
[3] *The Era*, xli, Oct. 26, 1879, 5. For other contemporary comments see *The Era*, xxxiii, July 23, 1871, 12; xxxvii, Jan. 10, 1875, 11; xli, Nov. 2, 1879, 12; xli, Oct. 12, 1879, 12; *The Quarterly Review*, cxxxii, No. 263, Jan. 1872, 1–26.
[4] *The Fortnightly Review*, xlv, May 1889, 610–26.
[5] lxvii, May 11, 1889, 567.
[6] *The Theatre*, xxii, Sept. 1893, 164–6.
[7] *Id.* xxx, July 1897, 10–14.
[8] *The Pall Mall Gazette*, lix, Sept. 27, 1894, 8.
[9] *Id.* lxxi, July 21, 1900.

improved. In the seventies Dion Boucicault could still complain of low income from playwriting and of French competition. As an example he narrates how some thirty years before he had been offered £100 for a new drama and how, on his protesting, the manager had replied: "I can go to Paris and select a first-class comedy; having seen it performed, I feel certain of its effect. To get this comedy translated will cost me £25. Why should I give £300 or £500 for your comedy, of the success of which I cannot feel so assured?"[1] There was no wonder that Boucicault bitterly pilloried this type of man who, "in most instances, received his education in a bar room, possibly on the far side of the counter". About the same time, Frank Marshall[2] declared that "the difficulties which beset the path of a dramatist nowadays who would give us original plays of real literary merit are almost insuperable". Among his reasons for making this statement he adduces the popularity of French adaptations, the small fame and profits accruing from dramatic composition and the fact that plays could not be printed without the loss of acting rights.

Yet even then, in the seventies, a revolution had occurred which was destined to transform the entire profession of playwriting. In 1847, or thereabouts, Boucicault had been offered £100 for an original play.[3] This was a fairly normal recompense. Charles Reade and Tom Taylor received a total of £150 for *Masks and Faces* (H. 1852) and £100 for *Two Loves and a Life* (Adel. 1854).[4] The latter's *Our American Cousin* (H. 1861), which netted the management over £20,000, brought the author only £150.[5] A few privileged writers might expect a trifle more; Charles Kean paid G. W. Lovell £400 for *The Wife's Secret* (H. 1848), gave Douglas Jerrold

---

[1] *The Theatre*, i, Sept. 1877, 141–2; cf. *The Era*, xxxix, June 3, 1877, 12 and *id.* xli, April 13, 1879, 7–8.

[2] *The Drama of the Day in its Relation to Literature* (*The Theatre*, N.S. i, Aug. 1878, 23–6).

[3] No mention is made in this reference to benefits. The change in stage economics is to be seen in the attack made, during the seventies, on the benefit system (*The Athenaeum*, No. 2394, Sept. 13, 1873, 347–8).

[4] Malcolm Elwin, *Charles Reade* (1931), pp. 85 and 101.

[5] *The Theatre*, N.S. iii, Dec. 1879, 265.

£300 each for *A Heart of Gold* (P'cess, 1854) and *St Cupid* (P'cess, 1853), and even went so far as to offer Knowles £1000 for a new play;[1] but the ordinary author could not look for more than a maximum of about £50 per act. For this reason many of them were willing to hire themselves out as stock-dramatists at annual salaries; for a time Morton and Boucicault wrote exclusively for the Princess's,[2] MacDermott for the Grecian, Hazlewood for the Britannia, à Beckett for the St James's, W. Brough for the Lyceum and Faucit for the Victoria.[3] All this was before a startling revolution casually introduced by Boucicault. In the year 1860, when he took his *Colleen Bawn* (Adel. 1860) to Webster, he made a novel proposal; instead of asking for a lump sum, he suggested sharing terms—and found himself eventually the richer by £10,000.[4] At first the full significance of this was not recognised. Some of the astuter authors—such as Burnand who, by making similar arrangements, cleared £2000 for his *Ixion* (Roy. 1863) and as much for *Black-eyed Susan* (Roy. 1866) —eagerly followed Boucicault's example, but the practice did not become universal until the eighties. Even in 1879 F. C. Burnand found it necessary to remind his fellows that every playwright ought to demand 10% of the gross receipts of the production;[5] it is known that James Albery received a flat sum of only £3 a performance for *Two Roses* (Vaud. 1870) and of £2 a performance for *Tweedie's Rights* (Vaud. 1871).[6] The general adoption of the new plan brought considerable changes; instead of a bevy of hack authors there came into being the privileged members of the "Dramatic Ring". "It is easier to make a fortune than to earn a livelihood by

[1] J. W. Cole, *op. cit.* i, 343 and 323.
[2] Townsend Walsh, *The Career of Dion Boucicault* (New York, 1915), p. 42; J. W. Cole, *op. cit.* ii, 133.
[3] Errol Sherson, *London's Lost Theatres of the Nineteenth Century* (1925), p. 97.
[4] Arthur à Beckett, *The Earnings of Playwrights and Players* (*The Theatre*, N.S. xxvi, Oct. 1895, 209–13). In 1874 Boucicault asked Augustin Daly for a 12% royalty (to be divided between himself and Bret Harte) for a play (J. F. Daly, *op. cit.* p. 173).
[5] *Authors and Managers* (*The Theatre*, N.S. ii, Feb. 1879, 14–17).
[6] *The Dramatic Works of James Albery*, ed. by W. Albery (1939), i, xxviii.

writing plays" had become a just judgment by the year
1896.[1]

The possibility of making their fortunes had the result of
attracting to the theatre many men who in previous years
would have devoted themselves entirely to the novel. G. B.
Shaw, despite his vivid theatricality, almost certainly would
have joined Thackeray and Dickens had he flourished in
1840.[2] For a time, it is true, one other thing served to hold
back these authors from the stage. The Copyright Act of
1833 had brought the work of the dramatists alongside the
work of other literary artists, but some doubts and difficulties
remained.[3] One was of a practical kind, for stage copyright
was based on actual performance of the play. To comply
with the law, authors and managers turned to the provinces,
where many "copyright performances" were presented, or
else made use of the newly developing matinee for a similar
purpose. Many of these productions seem to have been
little more than perfunctory readings, and consequently induced complaints.[4] More serious was the problem of American
copyrights. The United States had now become a great
theatrical centre, and much additional income, it was seen,
might accrue from the successful performance of new dramas
there. But no law prevented a manager in New York from
taking the printed text of such a drama and presenting it
without payment of a single cent. Of this a moving testimony
remains in Lacy's edition of *Maud's Peril* (Adel. 1867); this

[1] Leopold Wagner, *Playwriting: Past and Present* (*The Theatre*, N.S.
xxviii, Aug. 1896, 66–8). It should be noted that, in addition to London
royalties, additional sums could now be made from "country royalties".
Morton, it is said, drew over £500 a year from this source, the money
being collected by the Dramatic Authors' Society (A. W. à Beckett, *Green-
Room Recollections* (1896), p. 254).

[2] This movement of literary men to the theatre, because of increased
returns, is emphasised by Mrs Alec Tweedie, *Behind the Footlights*
(1904), pp. 95–7.

[3] *Dramatic Copyright* (*The Era*, xlvi, Aug. 30, 1884, 7–8); *Dramatic
Copyright* (*The Athenaeum*, Nov. 21, 1874). The conditions of 1873
are fully outlined in J. Coryton's *Stage Right. A Compendium of the Law
relating to Dramatic Authors* (1873). See also *A Handy-book on the Law
of the Drama and Music* (1864) and B. W. Weller, *Stage Copyright at
Home and Abroad* (1912).

[4] Mrs Alec Tweedie, *Behind the Footlights* (1904), pp. 95–7.

is dedicated by Watts Phillips, "with feelings of deep disgust, to the Thief of Thieves, who, by means of shorthand, or other petty larceny devices, caused a mutilated copy of the work to be circulated in America, to the detriment of the Author". Hoping that such "petty larceny devices" would not be successful, the English dramatist frequently found that it was to his advantage to keep his play unpublished, and the careful guarding of manuscript became almost an echo of a similar treasuring of precious prompt-books in the days of Elizabeth. By the eighties, however, this state of affairs had attracted sufficient attention to call for immediate action. An international copyright agreement was signed in 1887;[1] this covered most of the European countries. Much more important was the American copyright bill which came at the beginning of the last decade of the century.[2] Quite apart from the additional incomes it now offered to successful dramatists, it established an entirely new set of conditions. Already in its first comment on the agreement, *The Era* hinted at its possible influence:

There is...one ray of hope for English authors in the act. It has been often suggested that they should more frequently publish their plays for reading purposes. As is well known, this is done to a great extent in France, and the French dramatists reap no inconsiderable rewards from this source. On this side of the Channel, Mr W. S. Gilbert is, we believe, almost the only modern author who has published his works; but we understand that the experiment has not been unprofitable to him. If the English authors, indeed, would take the trouble—as the French dramatists do—to prepare their plays for the press in a readable form, and not present them in the "acting edition" shape, with its irritating stage directions, and with the names of the speakers at the side of the page, we believe that the best works of such authors as Mr H. A. Jones and Mr Pinero would be perused by no small section of the British public....We are never likely to have a native drama of much literary merit without the practice of publication to emphasise conscientious finish and rebuke slovenly writing.[3]

[1] *The Era*, i, Dec. 10, 1887, 9.
[2] See *A Petition to the Senate...for the Amendment of the Copyright Law...from the Dramatists, Theatrical Managers and other Members of the Dramatic Profession* (New York, 1891).
[3] *The Era*, liii, Jan. 10, 1891, 15. H. A. Jones's comments on this Act in the preface to *Saints and Sinners* (Vaud. 1884) are well known.

The hope expressed by the editor of *The Era* was carried to realisation. From the year when this Act was passed a complete change came to the printed drama. Samuel French still continues to issue his "acting plays", but the more ambitious authors turn now to address their works to a reading public. Stage directions are completely revolutionised; instead of the old L.C. and P.S. and R.C., intelligible only to those versed in theatrical abbreviations and designed for the guidance of acting groups, there are introduced ever lengthier and lengthier descriptions of the set, of the characters, of the movements until the descriptive material has sometimes come to assume equal importance with the dialogue. Dramatically, of course, these new stage directions have little interest for us; carried to excess, they have led some authors seriously astray; but they serve to demonstrate the fresh appeal which was being made by the modern drama.

In every way now men of literary genius could be attracted to the theatre; they were tempted by the possibility of great material rewards and they knew that their work, if worthy, would no longer be forced to remain in guarded manuscript or, at best, be issued in cheap series of stage texts, but were likely to appear in dignified form apt to appeal to the ordinary reading public.

CHAPTER II

CONTEMPORARY DRAMATIC CONDITIONS

THE stage was thus set in the seventies for the dramatic renascence. The audience had increased and become more representative of all classes in the nation; the theatre had found a new ideal which, if ridiculous when carried to excess, had vitality and inspiration in it; the dramatic.author suddenly discovered that he had walked into a realm, spiritually and materially different from that inhabited by the melodramatists and extravaganza writers who, fifty years before, had been compelled to turn out hundreds upon hundreds of plays if they were to hope that the howling wolf might be directed from their doors.

That this revival may be traced back evenly in the evolution of the English stage is obvious; equally obvious is the fact that it was not confined to England. Indeed, such progressive strides had been taken during the nineteenth century by the French, Russian and Scandinavian theatres that there has been a tendency among some writers on this subject to explain the awakening of dramatic interest in London by reference to outside influences. Such an interpretation of events is unquestionably false, yet it is impossible to pass to another extreme and attempt to deny those influences. The truth lies between the two positions. The English stage was independently moving towards this "renascence", but, when conditions were favourable, various European developments certainly stimulated and strengthened the movement of youth in London.

Even the most cursory glance at the fortunes of the European stage during the nineteenth century makes clear the fact that the revolutions already described had their counterparts abroad and also that generally these revolutions reached fulfilment at a considerably earlier period than they did in London. Work of a genuinely modern character does not proceed from the pens of English dramatists till the eighties and nineties; indeed, one might go further and say that plays of this sort are hardly to be found before the year 1895. Yet by 1868 Henri Becque, a man responsible for developing a strong and vital naturalism in the playhouse, had produced *Le prodigue*, and by 1882, with *Les corbeaux*, had reached his full maturity.[1] Partly through the influence of Becque's naturalism, the Théâtre Libre was established by Antoine in 1887, and with the stimulus provided by this organisation came into being a group of notable dramatists—François de Curel, Villiers de l'Isle Adam, Georges Ancey, Léon Hennique, Jean Jullien, Georges de Porto-Riche, Pierre Wolff, Georges Courteline and Eugène Brieux. To compare the work that these men were doing in the eighties and nineties with the contemporary repertoire of London playhouses brings an immediate realisation of the relatively fettered expression exhibited by the English stage. Realism may seem to us now an outworn ideal; in following its paths the dramatists of this time may appear to be following idols false because uninspired with any imaginative glow; but undoubtedly we are forced to admit that the playwrights in Paris were more successful than their English confrères in attaining what they sought. These French dramatists wanted a realistic approach and

[1] On the "advance" movement in Europe during this time see Anna Irene Miller, *The Independent Theatre in Europe: 1887 to the Present* (1931) and S. M. Waxman, *Antoine and the Théâtre Libre* (1926). There are many studies of the major dramatists; of these may be mentioned Storm Jameson, *Modern Drama in Europe* (1920), L. Lewisohn, *The Modern Drama* (1915), A. Henderson, *European Dramatists* (1914), E. E. Hale, *Dramatists of Today* (1911), J. G. Huneker, *Iconoclasts: A Book of Dramatists* (1905), Ashley Dukes, *Modern Dramatists* (1912) and G. Brandes, *Creative Spirits of the XX Century* (1903). A useful survey is Barrett H. Clark's *A Study of the Modern Drama* (1925). On the French theatre of the time see Brander Matthews, *French Dramatists of the Nineteenth Century* (New York, 1924), F. W. Chandler, *The Contemporary Drama of France* (1920), N. C. Arvin, *Eugene Scribe and the French Theatre, 1815–1860* (1924), H. A. Smith, *Main Currents of Modern French Drama* (1925), J. A. Hart, *Sardou and the Sardou Play* (1913) and Barrett H. Clark, *Contemporary French Dramatists* (1915).

they found it; most of the English dramatists obviously wished to build their plays out of the common stuff of life, but only too frequently they permitted the old conventionalism to distract them and thwart them in their aims. That occasionally these old conventions, because they were born of an essentially popular theatre, gave a kind of melodramatic vigour to the English plays is certainly true; nevertheless, such vigour proved often but a poor compensation for the loss of unity and harmony attendant upon this confusion of spirit.

Germany displayed a similar energy and forcefulness. There, far off in the days when London was subsisting on extravaganza and melodramatic excitement, Friedrich Hebbel was writing in a strain definitely "modern" because of its intensity and technical brilliance, while Otto Ludwig with *Der Erbförster* (1849) explored the possibilities of the naturalistic method in a manner hitherto untried.[1] By the year 1889 the Freie Bühne had been founded in Berlin; during that year came the production of Hauptmann's *Vor Sonnenaufgang*. *Die Weber*, a play far in advance of anything the London theatres had then to offer, was written three years later, in 1892. Hermann Sudermann's dramatic debut occurred contemporaneously, his *Die Ehre* being presented in 1889 and *Die Heimat* in 1893; the year 1889 saw the appearance of Frank Wedekind's *Die junge Welt*, and two years later *Frühlings Erwachen* was given to the public. While this movement was thus progressing in Berlin, Vienna remained by no means inactive. By 1887 Hermann Bahr had started to experiment with his ironic social comedy; Anton Schnitzler in 1893 first displayed his peculiarly brilliant and mordant genius; in 1891 Hugo von Hofmannsthal presented the earliest of a series of plays in which to dramaturgic skill was united a literary grace unique in its individuality.

During the time when France and Germany were thus awakening to a new spirit in the theatre, other countries,

---

[1] Georg Witkowski, *The German Drama of the Nineteenth Century* (1909), C. von Klenze, *From Goethe to Hauptmann* (1926) and M. Martersteig, *Das deutsche Theater im neunzehnten Jahrhundert* (Leipzig, 1924).

even the most remote, experienced a similar renascence. To have said in a London greenroom of the eighties that any drama of worth might be discovered in the land of the almighty Tsar would, no doubt, have aroused a burst of jeering merriment; yet Russia was at that time building up a stage whereon were displayed a fine sense of character delineation, an appreciation of subtle dramatic values and an enthusiasm far surpassing anything yet accomplished in England.[1] Leo Tolstoi's *The Nihilist* was written as early as 1863, some years before Tom Robertson's initial efforts in social comedy; *The Power of Darkness*, which, whatever we may think of its dramatic quality, displays a vigour and an intransigent spirit unrecognisable in any English plays of the time, appeared in 1886. Two years before that, in 1884, Anton Chekhov completed *On the High Road*, while the year 1889 brought *The Swan Song* and 1896 *The Sea-Gull*.[2] Not until the twentieth century was this Russian drama appreciated in the rest of Europe, yet its worth and its vision could have caused no surprise in the minds of those able to compare such a play as A. S. Griboiedov's *The Misfortune of Being Clever*, written in 1823, with any work of a similar kind contemporaneously presented in the London theatres.

The most extraordinary and significant development, however, came from a land even more distant from men's minds than Russia. Henrik Ibsen was born at Skien, Norway, in 1828.[3] His first play, *Catiline*, was written when he was twenty-two years of age and ushered in a series of historical romances. From *The Warrior's Barrow* of 1854 to *Emperor and Galilean* his dramas were historical or legendary in subject-matter and idealistically lyrical in mood. Then came *Pillars*

[1] Leo Wiener, *The Contemporary Drama of Russia* (1924), Oliver M. Sayler, *The Russian Theater* (1922), Alexander Bakshy, *The Path of the Modern Russian Stage* (1916). *The Russian Theatre* (1930) by René Fülöp-Miller and Joseph Gregor presents a well-illustrated survey with special attention to the Soviet playhouse.

[2] Anton Chekhov, *Literary and Theatrical Reminiscences*, translated by S. S. Koteliansky (1923) and C. Stanislavski, *My Life in Art* (1924).

[3] H. Koht, *The Life of Ibsen* (1931), E. Gosse, *Henrik Ibsen* (1908), H. Rose, *Henrik Ibsen* (1913), O. Heller, *Henrik Ibsen, Plays and Problems* (1912), M. J. Moses, *Henrik Ibsen: the Man and his Plays* (1908), and H. J. Weigand, *Modern Ibsen: A Reconsideration* (1925).

of Society in 1877, followed by *A Doll's House* (1879), *Ghosts* (1881), *An Enemy of the People* (1882), and *The Wild Duck* (1884). In *The Wild Duck* a new mood entered; the barer realism shaded into symbolism, with a definite progression from *Rosmersholm* (1886), through *The Lady from the Sea* (1888), *Hedda Gabler* (1890), *The Master Builder* (1892), *Little Eyolf* (1894) and *John Gabriel Borkman* (1894), to *When We Dead Awaken* (1899). It is truly extraordinary to think that Ibsen's work was completed ere Shaw's had barely begun—completed when the English stage was still struggling to secure its freedom. Nor was Ibsen alone in the Scandinavian countries. Björnstjerne Björnson was born only four years later than he, and, after a kindred series of experiments in historical drama, also turned, with *The Newly-married Couple* (1865), to realistic treatment of ordinary life. *A Gauntlet*, perhaps his best play, was produced in 1883.[1] Then, strangest and in some respects strongest figure of all, came August Strindberg, whose *The Father* (1887), *Comrades* (1888) and *Miss Julie* (1888) provide a stark penetration into life and a piercing psychological analysis unique in their uncompromising vigour.[2]

Although many of the more revolutionary plays did not come to English authors' notice until the twentieth century, there is no need of trying to demonstrate that this widespread European movement did not contribute largely to London's dramatic renascence; all we may do is to emphasise, first, that the London theatres assumed a fresh vitality quite independently of the continental movement, secondly, that this fresh vitality is to be easily traced back to the melodramatic theatre of the forties, and thirdly, that even when we reach the last years of the century we can see the popular interest in the stage often battling against instead of alongside the newer continental ideals. When the half-century opened, we are in the midst of a free filching from the French—a filching, moreover, which, with a monotonous regularity, selected only

---

[1] W. M. Payne, *Björnstjerne Björnson* (1903).
[2] V. J. McGill, *August Strindberg, the Bedeviled Viking* (1930) and L. Lind-af-Hageby, *August Strindberg, the Spirit of Revolt* (1913).

the lesser, the least thoughtful and technically the most conservative of plays. "At this moment", remarks Percy Fitzgerald as late as 1881,

it may be said that the English stage is virtually subsisting on the
French. What a contrast this to the old days of exuberant native
production, when Dibdin, dying so lately as 1841, was stated to
be the author of 200 pieces, and Mr Planché of over 100!—[1]

forgetting the wholesale borrowing from Paris in these good
old times. The complaints continued down to the end of the
century; in 1897 Edward Morton lamented that

the theatrical entertainment offered by the capital of the greatest
empire of the world includes one play, and only one, by an English
dramatist of repute.[2]

The rest were merely "versions" of Gallic dramas.

This was the usual kind of adaptation; only in the last
decade of the century did there arise any real appreciation
either of new technical methods or of the fresh ideals exemplified in the plays of Ibsen and his companions. To William
Archer belongs the credit of preaching Ibsen's worth and of
introducing him to the English public[3]—a task in which he
received considerable aid from J. T. Grein and G. B. Shaw.
This task was an uphill one. Even such a "modern" as
Max Beerbohm could not find sympathy for "Mr Shaw's
desire to Ibsenise the English stage from footlights to flies",[4]
although he recognised the eminence of the Norwegian dramatist.[5] In 1893 Joseph Knight declared that his influence was
"not as yet far-reaching",[6] even among the more progressive
writers. The plays, in English dress, started to come before
the public in the eighties, but it was not until the next decade
that the fame of the author became promulgated. *Quicksands;*

[1] *Op. cit.* p. 289.
[2] *The French Invasion (The Theatre,* N.S. xxx, July 1897, 27–9); see
also *French Authors and English Adapters (id.* N.S. i, Dec. 1878, 329–32).
[3] On Ibsen in England see Robert Huber, *Ibsens Bedeutung für das
englische Drama* (Marburg, 1914), G. B. Shaw, *The Quintessence of
Ibsenism* (1913) and Miriam A. Franc, *Ibsen in England* (1919).
[4] *The Saturday Review,* lxxxv, April 9, 1898, 482.
[5] *Id.* lxxxviii, July 1899, 102.
[6] *Theatrical Notes* (1893), xv.

or, *The Pillars of Society* appeared at the Gaiety as early as 1880, but *Rosmersholm* had to wait until 1891[1] for production. When they eventually arrived they were met by a blast of sometimes good-natured but more frequently embittered abuse. Burlesques like *Rosmer of Rosmersholm* (1891) and *Jerry-Builder Solness* (St G. 1893) made fun of their novel features, while critics and correspondents reviled their ideas in the press. An open letter addressed to William Archer in 1897 described Ibsen as

a dramatist who, apart from the non-construction of his alleged plays, deliberately selects his subjects from the most sordid, abject, even the most revolting corners of human life, relieving the crushing effect of their hideous monotony only by a mechanical joyless mirth like the crackling of thorns.[2]

"Go out from the moral leper house", trumpeted Clement Scott,

and hospital and society dissecting room, reeking with the smell of dissolution, and tell us something of the cleanliness that is next to Godliness; something of the trials and struggles of the just, the sorely-tried, the tempted, and the pure.[3]

"Candidly," wrote another critic of an "Ibsenite" play,

this continued harping upon nauseous topics is becoming something more than tiresome, and it is high time an emphatic protest were made against the growing custom of turning the theatre into a social lazar-house.[4]

Ibsen, then, was introduced with much difficulty to the stage, and many heartburning controversies had to be indulged in before he became accepted by all as a master undoubted and supreme. Throughout this period his influence was less than that of many another continental author—such as Scribe —who, less daring, tried pathos made familiar by the tread of unadventuresome feet.

Among the influences on the drama of this time must be

---

[1] *Rosmersholm* (Vaud. 1891) and *Beata* (Glo. 1892).
[2] *The Theatre*, N.S. xxx, July 1897, 7.
[3] *The Modern Society Play* (*The Theatre*, N.S. xxv, Jan. 1895, 6–10).
[4] *Id.* p. 46.

reckoned that of contemporary fiction, both native and foreign. Scott and Dickens had already provided founts of inspiration for the melodramatists of the preceding half-century, and still their works continued to be used for plot material. It is instructive to note that no less than eight versions of *Ivanhoe* are recorded between 1850 and 1900,[1] and five of *The Heart of Midlothian*.[2] New novels by Dickens were eagerly seized upon and old ones were redramatised. There were at least eight versions of *Bleak House*;[3] from *David Copperfield* Andrew Halliday took *Little Emily* (Olym. 1869) and E. H. Brooke *Little Em'ly's Trials* (S.W. 1871), while anonymous plays called *Little Emily* were licensed for Croydon in 1870 and the Albion in 1877. Other early novelists, too, had their writings seized upon. There were, for example, four versions of *Jane Eyre* and a burlesque.[4] But naturally it was the contemporary writers of fiction who most appealed. Thus, when Ouida brought out *Moths*, there was a general rush to bring its excitements to the stage. Five adaptations were written in 1882, three during the seasons 1883 and 1884, while two burlesques were soon on the boards.[5] These few examples may serve to stand for many hundreds. To record here the various adaptations from fiction made during these fifty years would indeed be a lengthy task.

In passing, however, we must note one thing. The con-

[1] Anonymous (Ast. 1859), L.C. licensed for Queen's 1859, Queen's 1863 and Garrick 1872, R. Cowie (Dundee, 1875), J. Sturgis (R.E.O.H. 1891), E. Stevens (Grand, Glasgow, 1896), R. Edgar (Amphi. L'pool, 1871); a burlesque by H. J. Byron appeared at the Strand in 1862.

[2] D. Boucicault (Ast. 1863), J. Bennett (Lyc. Edinburgh, 1894), L.C. licensed for Albion 1877, Standard 1862 and Pavilion 1863.

[3] Anonymous (M'bone, 1853), Elphinstone and Neale (C.L. 1853), anonymous (Str. 1854), P. Burnett (P.W. L'pool, 1875), G. Lander (Pav. 1876), Eliza Thorne (Alex. Sheffield, 1876), L.C. licensed for Globe 1876 and Grand, Walsall, 1892.

[4] L.C. licensed for Surrey 1867 and Coventry 1877, T. H. Paul (Adel. Oldham, 1879), W. G. Wills (Glo. 1882); J. Willing's *Poor Relations; or, Jane Eyre*, appeared at the Park in 1879.

[5] H. Hamilton (Glo. 1882), John Chute (Croydon, 1882), anonymous (S.W. 1882), L.C. licensed for Greenwich and Torquay 1882; W. F. Lyon (Peterborough, 1883), M. A. Seaton (L'pool, 1883), Mervyn Dallas (Str. 1884). The first burlesque was D. W. Edgar's *Moth's Quitoes; or, Ouida's Moths* (Middlesbrough, 1882), the second F. H. Herbert's *Moths à la Mode* (P'cess, Edinburgh, 1883).

temporary fiction was developing a style different from that of the early nineteenth century. Love of incident and grotesque characterisation had appealed in the past; now a deeper psychological note and a franker treatment of intimate domestic life became the fashion. How much the imitation of this on the stage contributed to the development of the characteristic problem-play may readily be realised.

CHAPTER III

BOUCICAULT AND TAYLOR:
PLAYS OF THE FIFTIES

1. *Domestic and Historical Drama*

To survey in detail the dramatic fare between 1850 and 1860 would be, largely, to cover ground so similar to that already traversed between 1840 and 1850 that it would seem common and familiar. For this section of the theatrical highway, accordingly, we may walk without taking intimate stock of the road surface or of the surrounding landscape. That both were slightly different from what immediately preceded them is true, but the difference is but slight. Farce, extravaganza, melodrama and comic opera flourish now as they flourished in the earlier years.

From J. R. Planché's *The Camp at the Olympic* (Olym. 1853) we may obtain a good bird's-eye view of prevailing conditions. This skit, written for Alfred Wigan when he took over the Olympic Theatre, imagines the manager and his wife totally at a loss to know what they should present to the public. Suddenly Fancy, attired in a jester's costume, pounces up through a trap. By means of her magic the scene becomes "*the Camp of the Combined British Dramatic Forces*". Tragedy enters first and is soon joined by Comedy. The former, we learn, is now superannuated and the latter's spirit has grown dull—

> Wit! oh, my dear, don't mention such a thing!
> Wit on the stage what wit away would fling?
> There are so few who know it when they hear it,
> And half of those don't like so much as fear it.

Dramatic taste is both low and fickle:

> O mercy! Tell me, pray.
> What horse will win the Derby, sir? You may,

I'm sure, as easily as I tell you
What the dear British public will come to!
Just what they like—whatever that may be—
Not much to hear, and something strange to see.

Popular are Burlesque—"a vice of kings! a king of shreds
and patches!"—English Opera "with a foreign band", Ballet,
Melodrama, Pantomime, Hippo-Drame and Spectacle. "Immortal Shakespeare!" cries the last ironically, echoing a
remark made by Tragedy,

Immortal Shakespeare! come, the less you say
The better on that head. There's not a play
Of his for many a year the town has taken,
If I've not buttered preciously his bacon.

The playlet ends on a characteristic note. "I am completely
bothered," confesses Wigan, "that's a fact, And, like some
actors, don't know how to act!"

TRAGEDY.	But screw your courage to the sticking place!
MR WIGAN.	I have—and stuck quite fast—that's just my case.
MRS WIGAN.	I'll tell you what to do.
MR WIGAN.	I wish you would.
MRS WIGAN.	In each of them there's something that is good.
	Without committing ourselves here to fix 'em,
	Let's take the best and mix 'em.
MR WIGAN.	Mix 'em!
MRS WIGAN.	Mix 'em.
MR WIGAN.	Like pickles? or like physic? what a notion!
	D'ye think the town will swallow such a potion?
	Why, Tragedy's a black dose of itself!
MRS WIGAN.	Who talks of taking *all*, you silly elf?
	I mean an extract of each spirit—Tragic,
	Comic, Satiric, Operatic, Magic,
	Romantic, Pantomimic, Choreographic,
	Spectacular, Hip-
MR WIGAN.	Spare that tongue seraphic
	Such vain exertion—for they would but call
	Your mixture melo-drama, after all.
MRS WIGAN.	With all my heart, I say, I don't care what
	It's called.

This satiric picture is by no means untrue to the spirit of

the time. Mixed forms were what the public desired. In
1868 Dion Boucicault told Mrs Bancroft that although the
audience might pretend it wanted pure comedy, it really
sought for other things. "What they want", he opined,
"is *domestic drama*, treated with broad comic character."
"A sentimental, pathetic play, comically rendered", was their
desire.[1] These words are as valid for 1858 as they were for
ten years later. The public wanted nothing pure except its
heroines.

In spite of this, we do recognise that the tread of the
dramatists is unquestionably firmer, and that the movement
towards surer and franker delineation of life begins to wring
a changed form out of the antique melodrama. In this period
perhaps the most original and influential of dramatists was
Dion Boucicault, who had already associated himself with
the new spirit in comedy by the writing of *London Assurance*
(C.G. 1841).[2] *London Assurance* and its companion plays of
the forties marked, however, only a beginning, and Boucicault
first definitely found his footing when he produced *The
Corsican Brothers* at the Princess's in 1852. From this time
on, his most characteristic pieces were plays wherein were
mingled elements taken from all worlds—of sentimentalism
much, a flash or two of broad wit and above all a series of
exciting incidents recalling the familiar technique of early
melodrama. Boucicault's importance as a dramatist rests on
two things—his uncanny sense of theatrical values and his
keenly observant eye. No man knew better than he just what
would appeal on the stage. The construction of his plays, if
we make allowance for their frankly melodramatic framework,
is excellent; and of countless theatrical devices he was the

---

[1] *Mr and Mrs Bancroft on and off the Stage* (1889), p. 118.
[2] See T. Walsh, *The Career of Dion Boucicault* (New York, 1915)
and article on *Mr Boucicault and Mr Barnum* (*The Saturday Review*,
lxi, May 1886, 607–8). On the drama of this period generally see J. W.
Cunliffe, *Modern English Playwrights: A Short History of the English
Drama from 1825* (1927), A. E. Morgan, *Tendencies of Modern English
Drama* (1924), P. M. A. Filon, *The English Stage* (1897), Mario Borsa,
The English Stage of To-day (1908), Ernst L. Stahl, *Das englische Theater
im 19. Jahrhundert* (Munich, 1914) and C. F. Armstrong, *Shakespeare to
Shaw* (1913).

eager inventor. From revolving towers to sham locomotives
he sounded the whole range of scenic sensationalism. Yet his
plays do not derive their interest entirely from this exciting
incident. Crude as many of his effects may seem to us, he
had an acute eye for oddity in real life, and many of his best
scenes rely, not on scenic splendour, but on the depiction,
through laughter or tears, of domestic interiors. It was this—
the cultivation of naturalistically conceived scenes allied to
melodramatic excitement—which gave him his contemporary
importance. *The Streets of London* (P'cess, 1864) may appear
merely amusing to modern audiences, but, since realism in art
is no fundamental or static method, it appealed in its own day
as a truthful picture of social events. The atmosphere of the
later Irish dramas may seem absurd, but they were to Victorian spectators what the plays of Sean O'Casey are to
audiences of to-day.

That in 1882 Boucicault was a "dramatist of yesterday"
as William Archer styled him[1] is unquestionably true, but
our concern is with the development of dramatic art during
this whole period and, in our endeavour to assess Boucicault's
value right, it is our business to place ourselves imaginatively
in his own time and thus judge him in relation to contemporary moods and desires. It is also true that he was a skilful
adaptor, taking much from sources diverse in their scope;[2]
but no one can deny that he gave theatrical quality to what
he borrowed, that he surpassed every other playwright of the
time in sensing the wishes of the public and that to his alien
material he added much that came from his own observation
of life.

Boucicault's career, of course, carries us well beyond the
fifties, just as its beginnings carry us to the other side of this
half-century, but we shall not be far wrong in saying that the
decade 1850–60 exhibited his most characteristic and influential work. With his sure appreciation of public taste he
divined that romantic supernaturalism was what the audiences

---

[1] *English Dramatists of Today* (1882), pp. 38–48.
[2] Cf. Thomas Purnell, *op. cit.* pp. 58–68; A. H. Thorndike, *English
Comedy* (New York, 1929), pp. 519–20.

most desired in the early fifties; and the result was *The Corsican Brothers* (P'cess, 1852). This drama immediately received "the stamp of current fashion", so that it led the van in a sweeping rush of dramatisations of the same theme. For a time, says Cole,[1] "the subject became a perfect mania". His success naturally induced Boucicault to exploit for a time further romantic possibilities of adventurous and supernatural action. In *The Vampire* (P'cess, 1852), *Geneviève; or, The Reign of Terror* (Adel. 1853) and *Louis XI* (P'cess, 1855) he freely exploited a flamboyant dramatic style which corresponded to the romantically melodramatic acting method rendered fashionable by Charles Kean. The last-mentioned play, an adaptation from the French of Casimir de la Vigne, gained a run of sixty-two nights and that largely because of the complete harmony between the spirit of the drama and its histrionic interpretation. Audiences were in raptures. "The enthusiastic feeling of the house on the first night", declares Cole,[2]

reminded us of the excitement we had witnessed during the best days of his father's *Othello*. Even when the play was over, and the principal character lay dead before the audience, they trembled lest he should start up again, and work fresh mischief with the revivified influence of a ghoul or a vampire....The success of "Louis the Eleventh" established a decisive period in Mr C. Kean's career as an actor.

No doubt can remain that this combination was thoroughly representative of at any rate one mood of the time; Kean's romantic impersonations were as typical as was Boucicault's flamboyant, yet decisively refined, melodramatic method.

By the close of the fifties, however, Boucicault was sensing the necessity of a change, if not in theme at least in outward semblance. Out of these historical or pseudo-historical romances grew the plays which, after all, form his most characteristic contribution to the theatre of his day. With *The Octoroon; or, Life in Louisiana* (New York, 1859; Adel. 1861) and *The Colleen Bawn; or, The Brides of Garryowen* (New York, 1860; Adel. 1860) a definite approach was made

[1] *Op. cit.* ii, 32.   [2] *Id.* pp. 124-5.

towards reproducing the conditions of real life; in that life
Boucicault discovered new material to exploit, new appeals
which he might make to the public. Cleverly, however, he
chose spheres of interest where he might freely introduce
a flavour of romance, a dash of patriotic sentiment, a certain
semblance of the real allied to a richness of spectacle. *The
Colleen Bawn*, with its musical accompaniments, is thus
obviously related to the older melodrama. In the printed
text and in the original play-bills the scenic show is fully
advertised; that was part of the appeal. At the same time this
melodramatic basis and this pleasing spectacle are subtly
related to actual existence; instead of wizards' caverns and
vampires' dens *The Colleen Bawn* introduces us to the familiar
made rosy and imaginative. Those prospective playgoers who
read the original list of scenes would have appreciated this
to the full:

Act I

LAKE OF KILLARNEY (MOONLIGHT)
The Signal Light!
Gap of Dunloe
Cottage on Muckross Head
The Irish Fireside—The Cruiskeen Lawn—The Oath!

Act II

Torc Cregan
COTTAGE OF THE COLLEEN BAWN
"The Pretty Girl Milking Her Cow"
Mac Gillicuddy's Reeks
The O'Donoghue's Stables
The Water Cave

Act III

THE HUT   CASTLE CHUTE
THE CASTLE GARDENS
Illuminated Hall and Garden in Castle Chute

From romantic moonlight on the fair Lake of Killarney
through the splendour of the castle gardens to the lonely

cottage; from the thrilling signal light through the oath to
the pretty girl milking her cow—Boucicault sounds the gamut
of a particular style. The plot fully accords with the scenery;
it is full of exciting incidents and of dramatic suspense.
Hardress Cregan has secretly married Eily O'Connor, but
finds himself faced with ruin unless he marries Anne Chute.
The dilemma for him is a terrible one; and the confusion in
which the characters are placed is rendered greater by the
fact that Anne, loving Kyrle Daly, is led to believe that he,
not Cregan, is Eily's husband. Cregan has a faithful devoted
servant in Danny Mann; to relieve his master he attempts
to slay Eily, but she is saved by Myles-na-Coppalean, the
stock, pathetically dog-like lover. It is all very exciting and
not for one moment is the attention of the audience permitted
to flag. But if it is exciting, it is also very appealing in its
apparent realism. The Irish dialect employed has a kind of
double effect—it gives a pleasing air of wild romantic remote-
ness to the action and at the same time creates the illusion
that all these events are definitely related to life.

A similar combination of elements appears in *The Octoroon*.
No one could fail to be impressed by the author's rich vitality
and dramatic inventiveness. The love of George Peyton for
Zoe, the octoroon; the poverty threatening Mrs Peyton; the
villainies of McClosky; the apparent disasters and the ultimate
triumph of good—all these keep the plot moving swiftly.
And again theatrical use is made of the life known to the
audience. To us this use of material things may seem more
than a trifle absurd and forced; but the sense of novelty
which would accompany their original introduction must have
amply compensated for any dim feeling of dissatisfaction.
Take the camera episode. McClosky is the brutal villain of
the regular melodramatic tradition, and in Act II he murders
Paul, thinking that no eye has seen his crime. Unfortunately
for him, however, a camera belonging to Scudder has been
standing facing him all the time, and, as he is muttering
"What a find! this infernal letter would have saved all", the
stage direction declares that "*he remains nearly motionless
under the focus of camera*". The result of this becomes apparent

in the last scene. McClosky is accusing the Indian Wahnotee of killing Paul, while Scudder endeavours to plead for him:

Scudder. I appeal against your usurped authority; this Lynch law is a wild and lawless proceeding. Here's a pictur' for a civilized community to afford; yonder, a poor ignorant savage, and round him a circle of hearts, white with revenge and hate, thirsting for his blood; you call yourselves judges—you ain't—you're a jury of executioners. It is such scenes as these that bring disgrace upon our Western life.

M'Closky. Evidence! Evidence! give us evidence, we've had talk enough; now for proof.

Omnes. Yes, yes! Proof, proof.

Scudder. Where am I to get it? the proof is here, in my heart!

Pete (who has been looking about the camera). Top sar! top a bit! Oh, laws-a-mussey, see dis, here's pictur I found sticking in that yar telescope machine, sar! look sar!

Scudder. A photographic plate. (Pete *holds lantern up*) What's this, eh? two forms! the child—'tis he! dead—and above him— Ah, ah! Jacob McClosky—'twas you murdered that boy!

M'Closky. Me?

Scudder. You! You slew him with that tomahawk, and as you stood over his body with the letter in your hand, you thought that no witness saw the deed, that no eye was on you, but there was, Jacob McClosky, there was—the eye of the Eternal was on you— the blessed sun in heaven, that looking down struck upon this plate the image of the deed. Here you are, in the attitude of your crime!

Thus is the villain foiled. The means may be ridiculous and we may permit ourselves to smile superiorly, but Boucicault is sure of his business and recognises that the utilisation of this new invention (about which both the audience and he know little) will be exciting and thrilling. Things like these thrilled contemporary audiences on both sides of the Atlantic: Boucicault was able to write to a friend that "the sensation produced in New York" by this drama was "intense", the houses being "crammed to suffocation".[1]

The same skill is shown throughout the entirety of Bouci-cault's dramatic career. *Arrah-na-Pogue; or, The Wicklow*

---

[1] Letter to G. W. Riggs, formerly in the possession of the late Father Riggs of New Haven. It may be noted here that the source of this play was a story written by Hezekiah L. Hosmer, editor of *The Toledo Daily Blade.*

Wedding (Dublin, Nov. 1864; P'cess, March 1865) presents, in an Irish setting, a kindred mixture of diverse elements. Against a background of nationalist sentiment and revolutionary ardour Beamish MacCoul stages a robbery, for which the honest Shaun is arrested. Love, of course, has to play its part here and its path has to be duly crossed; Fanny Power, who adores and is adored by Beamish, comes to believe that Arrah is his mistress. Complications and complexities ensue, with frantic efforts made by O'Grady to save poor Shaun. At last Beamish, having given himself up, is about to be condemned, when a kind-hearted and liberal-souled Secretary decides to save him. *Arrah-na-Pogue* is no less thrilling than *The Octoroon*, and its hair-raising excitements are cleverly interspersed with a variety of comic business. Perhaps Boucicault's importance may best be gauged when we regard him as one of the masters—for such in a way he is—of George Bernard Shaw. Amid Boucicault's realms of sensation and laughter and propaganda the young Shaw wandered, and the result is to be viewed, not only in the melodramatic *Devil's Disciple*, but in *Arms and the Man, Caesar and Cleopatra, The Man of Destiny* as well. Nor is this indebtedness one merely of a general sort. "Technically", says Shaw in his preface to *Three Plays for Puritans*,

I do not find myself able to proceed otherwise than as former playwrights have done. True, my plays have the latest mechanical improvements; the action is not carried on by impossible soliloquys and asides; and my people get on and off the stage without requiring four doors to a room which in real life would have only one. But my stories are the old stories; my characters are the familiar harlequin and columbine, clown and pantaloon (note the harlequin's leap in the third act of Caesar and Cleopatra); my stage tricks and suspenses and thrills and jests are the ones in vogue when I was a boy, by which time my grandfather was tired of them.

How true this statement is may be realised by glancing at two scenes from *Arrah-na-Pogue* and *The Devil's Disciple* respectively. The former presents a court-martial scene. There is a severe Major and a kindly Colonel O'Grady; the prisoner is Shaun, who has allowed himself to be arrested in the stead of another:

MAJOR. Your name?

SHAUN. Is it my name, sir? Ah, you're jokin'! Sure there's his honour beside ye can answer for me, long life to him!

MAJOR. Will you give the Court your name, fellow?

SHAUN. Well, I'm not ashamed of it.

O'GRADY. Come, Shaun, my man.

SHAUN. There, didn't I tell ye! he knows me well enough.

MAJOR. Shaun (*writing*)...What is your other name?

SHAUN. My mother's name?

MAJOR. Your other name.

SHAUN. My other name? D'ye think I've taken anybody else's name? Did ye ever know me, boys, only as Shaun?...

O'GRADY. He is called Shaun the Post.

SHAUN. In regard of me carrying the letter-bag by the car, yer honour.

MAJOR. Now prisoner, are you guilty or not guilty?

SHAUN. Sure, Major, I thought that was what we'd all come here to find out.

Contrast this with the court-martial scene in Shaw's play. There is here too a severe Major (Swindon) and a good-humoured General (Burgoyne); the prisoner (Richard) has allowed himself to be arrested in the place of Anthony Anderson:

SWINDON. Your name, sir?

RICHARD. Come: you don't mean to say that you've brought me here without knowing who I am?

SWINDON. As a matter of form, sir, give me your name.

RICHARD. As a matter of form, then, my name is Anthony Anderson, Presbyterian minister in this town....

BURGOYNE. Any political views Mr Anderson?

RICHARD. I understand that that is just what we are here to find out.

The same situation; the same fundamental types; even in part the same expressions.

Throughout his dramatic career Boucicault displayed a rich theatrical exuberance and a keen appreciation of stage values. As Joseph Knight observed of *The Shaughraun* (New

York, 1874; D.L. Sept. 1875), he found the ordinary conditions of life in England "prosaic and commonplace" and
consequently turned to the richer material discoverable amidst
the romantically rebel Irish folk;[1] good fun abounds in all his
dramas; and in all is the effective utilisation of exciting esca-
pades, often with distinctively novel circumstances connected
therewith. In *The Shaughraun* there was "a revolving tower"
which showed, "from the inside first, and then from the
outside, the escape of the hero";[2] in *The Poor of New York*
(New York, 1857) occurred a scene showing two adjoining
rooms[3] and a most exciting conflagration:

> *Stage dark. The exterior of the tenement house, No.* 19½ *Cross
> Street, Five Points—the shutters of all the windows are closed.
> A light is seen through the round holes in the shutters of the upper
> windows—presently a flame rises—it is extinguished—then revives.
> The light is seen to descend as the bearer of it passes down the staircase,
> the door opens cautiously—*BLOODGOOD, *disguised, appears—he
> looks round—closes the door again—locks it.*
>
> BLOOD. (*aloud*). In a few hours, this accursed house will be
> in ruins. The receipt is concealed there—and it will be consumed
> in the flames. (*The glow of fire is seen to spread from room to room*)
> Now Badger—do your worst—I am safe! (*Exit*) *The house is
> gradually enveloped in fire, a cry outside is heard "Fi-er!" "Fi-er!";
> it is taken up by other voices more distant. The tocsin sounds—other
> churches take up the alarm—bells of Engines are heard. Enter a
> crowd of persons. Enter* BADGER, *without coat or hat—he tries
> the door—finds it fast; seizes a bar of iron and dashes in the ground
> floor window, the interior is seen in flames. Enter* DAN.
>
> DAN (*seeing* BADGER *climbing into the window*). Stop! Stop!
>
> BADGER *leaps in and disappears. Shouts from the mob;* DAN *leaps
> in—another shout.* DAN *leaps out again black and burned, staggers
> forward and seems overcome by the heat and smoke. The shutters
> of the garret fall and discover* BADGER *in the upper floor. Another
> cry from the crowd, a loud crash is heard,* BADGER *disappears as
> if falling with the inside of the building. The shutters of the windows
> fall away, and the inside of the house is seen, gutted by the fire; a
> cry of horror is uttered by the mob.* BADGER *drags himself from the
> ruins, and falls across the sill of the lower window.* DAN *and two of
> the mob run to help him forward but recoil before the heat; at length*

---

[1] *Theatrical Notes* (1893), pp. 56–9.
[2] See *supra*, p. 44.   [3] Act v, Scene 2.

they succeed in rescuing his body—which lies C. LIVINGSTONE, PAUL *and* PUFFY *rush on.* DAN *kneels over* BADGER *and extinguishes the fire which clings to parts of his clothes.*

That is the entirety of the scene, and a very thrilling one it must have been, brought the nearer to the spectators as it was by the fact that here Boucicault was treating of the great financial crash of 1837, still a vivid reality in men's memories. His merit ever consisted in this ability to give thrilling form to material which seemed to be the material of life and yet was always material of the theatre. Sometimes he achieved his end by visual means; sometimes, as in *The O'Dowd* (Adel. Oct. 1880), by skilful arrangement of the incidents. In this last-mentioned play Mike O'Dowd is first shown in London, embarrassed by a debt of £20,000. His friends rally round him, but even their efforts fail to stave off disaster. Emigrating to America, he at length succeeds in amassing wealth and returns to Europe. The play ends with a thrilling scene in which he saves a ship by guiding her through a channel of which only he and his father are aware. Inventiveness was always Boucicault's greatest gift and if the inventions were not always his own he proved felicitous in adapting the ideas of others. A semi-realistic "problem-play", for example, he transforms and makes interesting by devising a special framework. *Dot* (New York, 1859; Adel. April, 1862), based on *The Cricket on the Hearth*, is introduced by Oberon and Titania, conceived as wretched, poverty-stricken wanderers, forgotten by the modern world; their place is taken by Home, and this provides an opportunity for emphasising that poetry must now be sought in the quiet domestic interior.

Boucicault's knowledge of the stage and its possibilities was completer than that possessed by any of his contemporaries, and unlike so many of these he had a keen eye for whatsoever in real life might provide him with opportunities for the building up of melodramatic incident. The invention of the camera, a great financial failure, the problem of the octoroon, the conflict between Yankee and Virginian or between Irish and English—all were vigorously seized on and easily assimilated. His plays may lack literary finish; but at least they present in a bold way that theatrical effective- ness and that theatrical interest which are the primal demands we must make of a dramatist. Readily may we ridicule much of his work, but, when we seriously consider his accomplish- ment in terms of contemporary stage practice, it is hard indeed to deny him praise and esteem.

But few writers in this time vied with him in this com- bination of diverse interests. Most of the melodramas fol- lowed the time-worn lines laid down by the authors of the forties. *The Writing on the Wall* (H. Aug. 1852), by Thomas and J. M. Morton,[1] may be taken as representative of a thousand others. In this play the serious plot deals with Richard Oliver, who has murdered Walter Elton and who endeavours to cast the blame on the dead man's brother, Everhard Elton. This Everhard hovers round the side-wings in the disguise of Tobias the Blind Man. Not content with the slaying of one Elton and the traducing of another, Oliver proceeds darkly with his attempt to encompass the total destruction of the Elton family. With the horrid chuckle of the melodramatic villain, he purchases Elton Hall—only to discover there that the murdered man had scrawled upon a wall, in his own blood, the name of his slayer. Alongside of this story runs one of more comic import, introducing Lotty Smithers, famous in circus-land as Carlotta Smitherini, Gammon and Walker, two bucolic farmers, and Fergusson Trotter, a philanthropist who tries to start a model farm. Everything here is planned according to ancient formula. Oliver, in the first act, is asked why he hates the Eltons, and his reply is characteristic:

My hatred is at least honest, because open. I hate the Eltons because—but my hatred owns responsibility to no man: I hate them—because I hate them.

Which is a very correct sentiment in the mouth of a stage villain. The revealing of the murderer's identity is planned in similar wise:

[1] See C. Scott, *John Maddison Morton* (*London Society*, xlix, 1886).

Oliver. We've still clear time enough, and we'll make the most of it.

Smithers. What are you going to do?

Oliver (seizing crow-bar). To grind to dust, those damned and damning words—the Writing on the Wall!

Smithers. You dare not—sure—

Oliver. Dare not?—look here! (*advances to door, a loud crash is heard within followed by piercing shriek, twice or thrice repeated; falls back*) What's that? (*desperately*) Ah, the legend! Spite of all the legends of Hell, I'll enter! (*he batters the door, which at last falls forward with a heavy crash;* MARGARET *is discovered within, in white robe and dishevelled hair;* OLIVER *staggers back to front of stage;* SMITHERS *falls on his knees; the noise brings on* SIR PHILIP, LADY ELTON *and* JOSEPH, R.; GUESTS *and* SERVANTS, L.).

Margaret. Richard Oliver! (*she utters the name with peculiar solemnity, and they all start in recognition of the legend*) Are you come to claim your bride? Enter then: my father's spirit is here, to join our hands.

Sir Philip. (R.C.) Sister!

Lady Elton. (R.) Margaret, beloved child, come from that dreadful chamber.

Margaret (waves them back). Not till I discharge my father's will. In this room of horror, I took refuge from worse horror. Here, where my father's spirit flew to heaven, I invoked his aid to save me: at that moment, a huge oaken screen broke through the mouldering floor, and by the beams of light that streamed in radiant floods upon the wall, he sent his answer—look! (*points*) 'tis there!—"RICHARD OLIVER MY MURDERER!"

If another example of the kind be desired, it may be found in J. E. Carpenter's *Love and Honour, or Soldiers at Home—Heroes Abroad* (Surrey, Nov. 1855), wherein Captain Melville, the villain, forges a will to defraud his younger brother and aims at seducing Jessie Gray the miller's daughter. Strange how persistently the motif utilised by Thomas Southerne in *The Fatal Marriage* (D.L. 1694) and carried on through Schiller's *Die Raüber* continued to make its appeal. This particular evil brother is shot at by George St Clair, who is consequently court-martialled. The escape of St Clair is engineered by Jessie and, some evidence coming to light, Melville is dismissed. Finally, at the close of the drama, we find ourselves in Sebastopol, where St Clair is a colonel and

Melville a spy. The latter is shot and, dying, recognises in St Clair his much-injured brother. Typical, not only of this play but of many akin to it, is the close of the first act. The scene is a cottage exterior and Melville is addressing Briefwrit:

Melville. Cease your ill-timed and assumed mannerism. See! there is a light in the cottage—she has not retired to rest. I will try what persuasion can do first. 'Tis I—Melville!

(*He taps at the window—St Clair is seen at an upper window of the inn.*)

Jessie (At the window). Why do you seek me at this untimely hour?

Melville. Dearest Jessie, this moment is one of life or death to me. For your sake I have applied for my discharge from my regiment—I am about to put your love to the test: consent to fly with a friend I can trust; to-morrow I will join you, and, all necessary forms over, we can return, and claim your father's forgiveness.

Jessie. Do I dream! no! The soldier spoke the truth, and you are a villain. Leave me, sir: this secret flight were unnecessary, if your intentions are honourable. Your impetuosity reveals the baseness of your purpose. Leave me, I say again, or I will alarm the neighbours!

Melville. I expected such an answer from you, and am prepared. Resistance is vain;—you must comply with my desires.

Jessie. Father! Father! Where are you? Save your daughter.

Melville. Nay! before he can return, you will be far from hence. You are mine, and thus I gain you.

(*He jumps in at the window, and carries her out through the door, passing her to Briefwrit.*)

St Clair (At the upper window of the Inn). Hold, Captain! Unless your companion releases the girl, I fire—

Melville. Distraction! you dare not! (*Gets in front of them.*) Now, then, fire, if you dare—I am your superior officer.

St Clair. Stand aside.

Melville. Forward!

(*St Clair fires—the Captain falls—St Clair jumps from the window, and rescues Jessie—Stephen Gray rushes in—others enter from the house and at the back, form picture, and the drop descends.*)

This passage, strained and ridiculous, is no extreme example of the common melodramatic style of the period. To obtain an idea of the true depth to which the popular dramatists could descend we must turn to such plays as C. H. Hazlewood's *Waiting for the Verdict; or, Falsely Accused* (C.L. Jan. 1859). Compared with this, *Love and Honour* seems a masterpiece.

Out of these plays, however, something was germinating—something that promised a richer and a more plentiful harvest for the future. Boucicault's main tendencies were towards the sensational and the comic, but others were endeavouring to give more of vital content to the serious matter which formed a main part in the melodramatic mélange. Thus Charles Selby, one trained in the realm of the minor drama, penned *The Marble Heart; or, The Sculptor's Dream* (Adel. May 1854), calling it "A Romance of Real Life" and definitely making an experiment along novel lines.[1] This, although it springs from the melodramatic, is not an ordinary melodrama; rather might it be styled an essay in genuine tragic material. The first act opens in Athens and shows us the sculptor Phidias rejected, in favour of wealth, by the marble hearts of his time. The next scene carries us to the modern world and there we are confronted by a series of persons who are the counterparts or descendants of the ancient denizens of Athens—Ferdinand Volage (Diogenes), Raphael Duchatlet (Phidias), Mons. Veaudoré (Gorgias), Mlle Marco (Lais) and Marie (the Slave Thea). At the conclusion of the play the sculptor goes mad and dies. If only for the experimentation in the treatment *The Marble Heart* would be a notable drama for the year 1854.

Of all the dramatists who endeavoured to develop this popular drama into more profitable paths, perhaps Tom Taylor is the most interesting. That he borrowed many of his plots is unquestioned,[2] but, like Boucicault, he was a man

[1] It must be confessed that this play is adapted from *Les filles de marbre* of Barrière and Thiboust. Its French derivation ought not, however, to cause us to overlook the importance of this play's production in the fifties. The way in which the new movement in the French theatre might influence the English is to be seen in such a play as *The Barrister* (Surrey, March 1853), adapted trom Emile Augier, with its interesting treatment of domestic friction.

[2] T. Purnell, *op. cit.* pp. 94-126. See J. Sheehan, *Tom Taylor* (*Dublin University Magazine*, xc, 1877, pp. 142-158) and T. Hughes, *In Memoriam Tom Taylor* (*Macmillan's Magazine*, xlii, 1880, pp. 298-301).

who understood his theatre perfectly and always transformed
what he utilised. Taylor's dramatic work, which extends in
time from the forties to the seventies, is perplexing in its
variety, but he is sufficiently a man of his time to recognise
the desirability of mingling freely his humour and his pathos.
In many of his plays he indicated a distinct leaning towards
the historic theme; indeed, part of his merit consisted in
reviving the costume play, which had been so popular during
the Scott period, and in dealing with that in a bolder and
more realistic technique. In *Plot and Passion* (Olym. Oct.
1853) he turns to the Napoleonic régime for his subject-
matter, introducing the intrigues of Fouché, the loves of de
Neuville and Madame de Fontanges, the belated honesty of
the villain's accomplice, Desmarets. The Monmouth rebellion
forms the subject-matter for *A Sheep in Wolf's Clothing*
(Olym. Feb. 1857) which narrates how Anne Carew conceals
her husband, Jasper, from the authorities. To facilitate this
she permits Colonel Percy Kirke to make love to her and is
nearly involved in disaster through the impertinent busybody,
Keziah Mapletoft. At the conclusion Lord Churchill arrives
ex machina, cashiers Kirke and allows Jasper to escape. For
The Fool's Revenge (S.W. Oct. 1859) he takes Victor Hugo's
Le roi s'amuse as his basis,[1] and in writing *The Hidden Hand*
(Olym. Nov. 1864) he turns to *L'aïeule* of Dennery and
Edmond. The date of the action here is 1685, and the
characters are drawn so as to show the hatred of the Welsh
towards the English. A sentimental conclusion mars a play
otherwise rendered thrillingly exciting by its passion, intrigue
and poison. This period of the late seventeenth century
clearly fascinated Taylor, and once more he deals with it
melodramatically in *Lady Clancarty: or, Wedded and Wooed.
A Tale of the Assassination Plot 1696* (Olym. March 1874).

Besides these plays, Taylor wrote a few other historical
dramas of a more ambitious kind. Based on Charlotte Birch-
Pfeiffer's *Elizabeth von England, 'Twixt Axe and Crown;
or, The Lady Elizabeth* (Queen's, Jan. 1870) attempts a higher

[1] See an article by T.T., *Mr Phelps and The Fool's Revenge* (*The Theatre*,
N.S. i, Dec. 1878, 338–44).

flight with its blank verse dialogue and indicates a desire to give to the theatre something more of literary grace. That his effort was a worthy one may readily be allowed; but that he failed to reach true success in these more ambitious plays cannot be denied.

All these dramas, the literary and the melodramatic, must, however, cede place to the few historical plays which Taylor wrote in association with Charles Reade. Taylor himself was inclined towards the sentimental, and perhaps that sentimentality had to be tempered by the greater robustness and even brutality of Reade's talent.[1] *Two Loves and a Life* (Adel. March 1854) was one of the earliest of their collaborative efforts; in turning to it we recognise a greater firmness in the handling and a surer delineation of character than are to be found in Taylor's unaided efforts. Here we are introduced to Sir Gervase Rokewood and Father Radcliffe, who are organising the men at Morecombe Bay in support of Prince Charlie. Ruth Ravenscar, really the daughter of Radcliffe, saves the Duke of Cumberland and his men from disaster, while Anne, Rokewood's beloved, is forced by her father Musgrave to betray the conspirators. Rokewood is arrested, but is eventually saved by Ruth, who pleads to the Duke of Cumberland for his life. Comedy scenes introducing John Daw, the schoolmaster, and Potts, the barber, give the necessary relief to a well-planned, if melodramatic and occasionally sentimental, plot. Interesting, too, is *The King's Rival; or, The Court and the Stage* (St J. Oct. 1854), another collaborative venture. Here Charles II is the hero, and Miss Stewart the heroine. The former, ever captivated by a pretty face, becomes enamoured of the latter who, for her part, loves and is loved by the Duke of Richmond. The attentions of the Merry Monarch are proving somewhat of an embarrassment for the fair Stewart when kind-hearted Nell Gwynne steps in to set everything to rights. Perhaps Charles II, like Shakespeare, forms a kind of sociological thermometer. In the mid-eighteenth century a Georgian damsel wished she were

[1] See Malcolm Elwin, *Charles Reade* (1931) and E. G. Sutcliffe, *The Stage in Reade's Novels* (*Studies in Philology*, xxvii, Oct. 1930, 654–88).

back in good King Somebody's days.[1] About 1820 a Charles II drama endeavoured to demonstrate that affairs of the heart at Whitehall were of the purest and most honourable; a little flirtation, perhaps, but positive evil, never. Fifty years later come Taylor and Reade, interpreting the period sentimentally it is true, but honestly prepared to admit that Charles did have his mistresses and that there might be danger for a young girl in his court. Fifty years later came *And So To Bed*, which provided for the nineteen-twenties what *The King's Rival* and *Rochester* did for the mid-nineteenth century. Finally we reach G. B. Shaw's philosophic and political treatment of the good old days when the Merry Monarch reigned—a reflection of the interests of 1939.

Not all Taylor's dramas were of the historical kind. A link between these and his plays on domestic themes may be found in *Retribution* (Olym. May 1856), based on Charles de Bernard's novel, *La loi du talion*. Here Oscar de Beaupré is shown as having seduced the wife of Rodolphe. The latter, in the guise of Count Priuli, seeks revenge by attempting to seduce Madame de Beaupré, who is loved by Victor de Mornac, his brother. This play ends tragically with the deaths of both Victor and Oscar. There is here a slight flavour of the romantic drama, but the theme is one of more immediate contemporary interest and has a distinct "domestic" tone in spite of its romantic proclivities. Based on another French novel, *Le Gendre* (by the same author), *Still Waters Run Deep* (Olym. May 1855) introduces us to what was perhaps Taylor's greatest contribution to the theatre of his time. The plot of this play deals mainly with Mildmay, a man who has been married but a year and who has adopted an attitude of *laissez faire* while his wife's aunt, Mrs Sternhold, domineers over his household. His wife herself indulges in a flirtation with the rascally Captain Hawksley, a gentleman of fortune who had previously had an affair with Mrs Sternhold. Coming to learn of his attempt to seduce her niece, Mrs Sternhold tries to hinder him, but is silenced when he threatens to publish a number of her letters, addressed to him. Disaster

[1] See *E.E.D.* p. 160 and *E.N.D.* i, 16–17.

threatens, but is prevented by Mildmay's sudden change of front. Taking command of the situation, he succeeds in extracting the letters from Hawksley and in getting that disturber of the peace (or piece) sentenced for a forgery committed by him four years previously. In this play the most important thing is not the plot or the technique; it is the frankness with which the affairs of sex are discussed. In *The King's Rival* Charles, it is admitted, had mistresses; in *Still Waters Run Deep* is the equally important admission that illicit love was a fact of life. The scene wherein Mrs Sternhold confronts Hawksley may be lacking in vigour and intellectual honesty if we view it from our position in the twentieth century, but for its own age it marks a very deliberate break with convention. The way is being prepared for the dramas of the last decade of the century; the scope of the domestic play is being extended to include subjects and characters which before were taboo.

This greater intimacy and this application of the dramatist to contemporary material is marked clearly in what, after all, is Taylor's most interesting play, *The Ticket-of-Leave Man* (Olym. May 1863). Starting with an interesting crowd scene set in a restaurant (an innovation in itself), we are immediately introduced to the London underworld. The provincial Bob Brierly is taken in by Dalton (The Tiger) and is sent to prison. Released thence, he marries the little orphan, May Edwards, whom he had befriended, and secures honourable employment. Discovered by his former associates, he is threatened by them until he pretends to join them in their schemes. Actually, however, he works against them and aids the police in securing their capture. *The Ticket-of-Leave Man* is one of the first melodramas to deal with the criminal life of London, to take as a hero a man who had suffered imprisonment for association with these criminals, to introduce a detective (Hawkshaw) on the stage, and to break away from the familiar domestic interior sets in an attempt (as in the restaurant scene) to treat of the teeming world of contemporary social life. Marred by hopeless coincidences though it may be, this play definitely marks a stage in the development of

the nineteenth-century stage. It springs from the old melodrama; it borrows from the adaptations of Dickens' novels
which had been and still were so popular; but, in spite of these
things, it has a quality of its own which must induce us to
rate Taylor as one of the more noteworthy dramatic authors
of the century.

Perhaps it may not be unprofitable to glance at one or
two other plays which, either by reason of their intrinsic
merits or by reason of their authorship, deserve some particular attention. Of the historical plays, W. R. Markwell's
Louis XI (D.L. Feb. 1853) merits mention. Melodramatic
it is with its hero, Nemours, and its heroine, Marie de Comine,
and melodramatically bombastic is its dialogue. On the other
hand, Markwell, like Taylor, is here aiming at something
beyond what the minor writers of the forties indulged in;
his *Louis XI* indicated, albeit but crudely, how that minor
theatre was to become amalgamated with the literary. While
displaying a full consciousness of what the public wanted,
and while manifestly prepared to satisfy that want, Markwell
has a decidedly ambitious aim here and succeeds in striking
a note higher and more significant. Thrills there are, but the
thrills are subordinated to the building up of a serious
atmosphere and the delineation of character. C. S. Cheltnam's
Edendale (Charing Cross, June 1869) might be taken as repre-
senting the further development of this new note. Choosing
the American Civil War as a background, the author con-
centrates his attention on the loves of a Northerner, Fairholt,
and a Southerner, Ada Vandeleur. Whereas Markwell had
not learned how adequately to modulate his instrument,
Cheltnam shows a power of moving from the easy flippant
conversation of the early familiar scenes to the torment of
passion in which his persons are later involved. Still more
inclining towards the literary are the plays of Westland
Marston, who was regarded by Thomas Purnell in 1871 as
"with the possible exception of Lord Lytton, the sole living
representative of the legitimate drama".[1] This author's *Patri-*

---

[1] *Op. cit.* pp. 31–44. See R. H. Horne, *A New Spirit of the Age* (World's
Classics edition, pp. 358–78).

cian's Daughter, originally produced in 1842, is his best-known play, but he continued his theatrical career over two clear decades. The quality of living character he gives to his persons is probably his most noteworthy virtue. Thus in *A Hard Struggle* (Lyc. Feb. 1858) he contrives to make real a poor and improbable story by the vitality with which he delineates the noble lover, Reuben Holt, the passionate young doctor, Fergus Graham, and the distressed girl, Lilian Trevor. In Marston's plays clearly another step is being taken towards that union of popular and literary elements out of which the new drama was to grow.

More sentimentally inclined is J. Palgrave Simpson, an author whose work covers three decades. *Second Love* (H. July 1856) is fairly typical of his style. The serious here outweighs the comic. Knowing that she has been left a large sum of money, Colonel Dangerfield makes passionate advances to the blind girl Elinor. This Elinor has a devoted lover in the person of Ralph Thornhill, who is prepared to make any sacrifice to secure her happiness. Just when the villain seems about to win the day, Elinor is luckily cured of her affliction, literally sees Dangerfield's duplicity and the wedding bells ring out on her marriage to Ralph. Of similar tone is *Daddy Hardacre* (Olym. March 1857), featuring Daddy Hardacre himself (a miser), Esther (his lovable daughter) and Mary (the honest maid). To Hardacre comes his brother-in-law's son, Charles, with a letter stating that the writer, being on the brink of ruin, proposes to blow his brains out. Noble Esther hears of this, steals her father's money and sends it to London by Adolphus Jobling, her comic suitor. Of course Charles and Esther fall in love; and of course Charles's father is saved in the nick of time—the conventions of the Simpsonian drama could not have permitted anything else. All of the characters in these plays are stock types; of this a note to the list of dramatis personae in *Alone* (Court, Oct. 1873), in which Simpson collaborated with Herman C. Merivale, is characteristic. Of Stratton Strawless in this play Simpson observes that "the part does not belong to the line of the 'Old Man' but of the 'Eccentric Comedian'". His figures thus have a marked sameness, and this sameness intrudes into the plots as well. In *Alone* it is Colonel Challice, not the heroine, who is blind. Cruelly, this gentleman has thrown off his daughter years before, but she returns and reads *Lear* to him so prettily that he relents and takes her once more to his heart. *Shadows of the Past* (Brighton, Nov. 1867) shows Simpson approaching the problem drama, and *Broken Ties* (Olym. June 1872) reveals to perfection his strong sentimental leanings. In the latter, the happiness of the hero, Warner, is nearly destroyed by the fact that his wife is pursuing a career of her own. Disaster almost threatens when suddenly the wife decides that home, after all, is best—and throws herself sobbingly into her husband's arms.

2. *Comedy-Dramas and Farces*

Nearly all of the authors mentioned above aimed at the introduction of laughter as well as tears into their plays; the peculiar atmosphere of Boucicault's dramas, as we have seen, arises precisely from the skilful juxtaposition of these two elements. Sometimes, too, the use of historical material was designed, not to illustrate past events but to provide colour for a farcical situation; W. J. Sorrell's *A Border Marriage* (Adel. Nov. 1856) and Douglas Jerrold's *St Cupid; or, Dorothy's Fortune* (P'cess, Jan. 1853) may be mentioned as examples. On the whole, however, the historical plays were mainly tragic in theme or sensationally adventuresome, and in the domestic dramas comedy was subordinated to serious purpose. Now it is necessary to turn for a moment to that field of play-writing wherein the comic elements preponderated.

Tom Taylor was responsible for one of the most popular of all such pieces—*Our American Cousin* (New York, Oct. 1858; H. Nov. 1861), a comedy long remembered for the Dundreary of Sothern.[1] Structureless and indulgent of much farcical business, this play is nowise to be condemned. True, it seems that the spirit in which its performance was conceived

---

[1] See G. A. H. Sala, *Breakfast in Bed* (1863), pp. 7–32.

deviated markedly from that in which it was written. "From a comedy of a heavy type—in fact, a domestic drama," Arthur à Beckett declares, "it became a roaring farce."[1] The set of eccentric types, however, are well conceived—kind-hearted Asa Trenchard, foppish Lord Dundreary, "interesting" Georgina, gay Florence Trenchard, villainous Coyle—and equally well conceived is the series of ridiculous situations in which these characters are involved. With this comedy Taylor set a new fashion and stimulated many imitators.

As in the realm of melodrama, so in this of comedy-farce we may trace, if but vaguely, the signs of things to come. Thus *Victims* (H. July 1857), where Mrs Merryweather, who thinks herself persecuted, is flattered and fluttered by the attentions of the poetaster Fitzherbert and where the husband proves himself the magnanimous hero, presents a faint suspicion of the atmosphere which later produced *How He Lied to Her Husband*. One could not suggest, naturally, that Taylor is a neglected genius in whose works lies buried a comic talent equal to that of Shaw; but potentially *Victims* contains the material out of which the Shavian comedy was wrought. The same spirit animates *To Oblige Benson* (Olym. March 1854).[2] Here Mrs Benson is engaged in a flirtation with Meredith. A friend, Mrs Southdown, anxious to awaken Mrs Benson's mind to an appreciation of the dangers in her path, suggests to the husband that he make pretence at jealousy. This course the good man adopts, but only too rapidly passes from feigned to real passion. In vain Mrs Southdown, who imagines he is overacting just a little, endeavours to restrain him. The conception and the dialogue here have both a certain ease and style. Then there is the famous *Masks and Faces* (H. Nov. 1852) written in collaboration with Charles Reade. The treatment of Peg Woffington, if somewhat sentimental, has a decided lightness and delicacy and the character of Triplet is well managed. Taylor's worth may be gauged by the fact that *Masks and Faces* still gives pleasure in revival.

In connection with Taylor's *Victims* and *To Oblige Benson*

---

[1] *Green-Room Recollections* (1896), pp. 16–17.
[2] Adapted from *Un service à Blachard* by Vande.

it may be worthy of remark that the theme of married boredom was one which attracted much attention during this time. The theme itself may owe its popularity to French example (as in Augier), but so frequently is it exploited that we must believe it somehow in accordance with popular predilections. Sometimes the playwright will deal with it seriously, more often he will give it a humorous turn, as in Ben Webster's *A Novel Expedient* (H. June 1852) or George Henry Lewes' *A Cozy Couple* (Lyc. April 1854). In the former it is the wife who is dissatisfied; taking advice, she pretends to make love to Harry Damon who, playing up to her, succeeds in nearly scaring her out of her wits. The husband, Mr Dormouse, in the latter is the person bored and weary. When an old friend, Tom Russelton, appears and tells him of his adventures, he nearly breaks his chains and is prevented from doing so only by the fact that the wandering Tom, sensing the felicity of a domestic fireside, agrees to stay and keep him company. Similar in tone is Felix Dale's *Six Months Ago* (Olym. July 1867), wherein Edwin, rather bored, welcomes Jack Deedes, an old friend of his bachelor days, and so angers his wife that she decides to sue for a divorce. This course of action is prevented only by Edwin's sudden realisation that he loves her truly and cannot bear the thought of parting. Ben Webster, author of *A Novel Expedient*, may be noted as among the more prolific comic writers of his time: witness his *Giralda; or, The Miller's Wife* (H. Sept. 1850) with its gay Spanish intrigue and its management of a confusing set of criss-cross affections.

Another writer who deserves some attention is J. B. Buckstone. His career, of course, falls mainly in the first half of the century,[1] but he carried on his activities into the fifties. In *Leap Year; or, The Ladies' Privilege* (H. Jan. 1850) Flora Flowerdew is a widow who has to take a second husband if she is not to lose her late spouse's money. Her friend, Miss O'Leary, tries hard to get her suited, bringing forward in turn Sir Solomon Solus, Captain Mouser and Mr Dimple; the buxom Flora, however, discovers that she really loves

[1] See *E.N.D.* i, 116–17.

her manservant, William Walker—and he turns out to be the very relative to whom her money would have gone had she remained single. By their marriage it is accordingly kept, most conveniently, in the family. *Good for Nothing* (H. Feb. 1851) displays the more sentimental side of Buckstone's writing. The heroine here is Nan, a hoyden befriended by soft-hearted Tom and Harry. In spite of the fact that she has acquired a most unenviable reputation in the neighbourhood, she succeeds in demonstrating that her heart is kindly and generous; the curtain falls just as she comes in from having saved a poor little child from a watery death in the canal. Equally sentimental, but rather more skilful in technique, is Leicester Vernon's *The Lancers* (P'cess, Nov. 1853) with its fresh treatment of an old theme—the meeting of an aristocrat (Victor de Courcy), disguised as a commoner, with a well-born girl (Estelle Duvernay), dressed as a country lass. Where sentiment is not the dramatist's object, most of these plays veer towards the farcical. J. M. Morton's *The Three Cuckoos* (H. March 1850), in this style, presents a typical example. Set in the year 1691, it deals uproariously with the confusions arising from Pertyn Postlethwaite's entering of Colonel Cranky's house in order to visit the maid, Polly.

This style of play perhaps offers but little to attract us; yet we may recognise the importance, for the building up of the later drama, of this sentimentally humane spirit and of these risible low-comedy elements. In some of the plays written in a kindred manner occasionally there is struck out a really appealing situation or a genuinely comic idea. *The Waiter at Cremorne* (Sur. March 1855) may be trivial in theme, but genuinely comic is the way in which W. E. Suter deals with the distress of Mr and Mrs Muddlebank when, by mischance, they engage a waiter whom both recognise as a familiar servitor at some entertainment gardens and who, they fear, knows of their peccadilloes. A *Meg's Diversion* (Roy. Oct. 1866), by H. T. Craven, may be mostly dull, even though it contains a merry Meg and a comically solemn Jasper Pidgeon. We are, however, in the true realm of laughter when Jasper, the uneducated, proudly boasts that he has been studying in order to make himself worthy of Meg. "Ah! your remarks are French polished—a cut above me that", he says, and then adds with feigned indifference, "though this morning I partly translated a Scotch song into Latin." Pressed to produce his effort, he explains:

Well, I saw in a book that *corpus* was Latin for "body", so it immediately occurred to me to adopt it to music. (*sings*)
"Gin a corpus meet a corpus, coming through the rye,
Gin a corpus kiss a corpus, need a corpus cry."

CHAPTER IV

ROBERTSON AND BYRON:
PLAYS OF THE SIXTIES

1. *The Old School*

THROUGHOUT the whole of this period these earlier styles
remained. They had proved popular in 1840, they still
proved popular in 1860, and even in 1900 they still maintained their appeal with certain audiences. Before the sixties,
however, there had been no formal opposition; sometimes
an individual author such as Boucicault wrested an interest
from material which, in the hands of others, was but imita-
tively conventional, sometimes another playwright caught
a glimpse of wit lighter in texture and more spiritually vivid
than familiarly appeared in the rough-handled farce which
was his model; beyond this, melodrama, burlesque, sentimental comedy and low buffoonery ruled without a rival.
The importance of this decade lies in the facts that for the
first time in the nineteenth century a clear split is discernible
between two distinct schools of playwrights and that, even
before 1870, the influence of the younger group had made itself
widely felt. In thus speaking of older and younger, no suggestion is made that this contest was one between aged
dramatists and more youthful competitors; indeed, some of
the most conservative were the least advanced in years. The
Old School is simply the school of play-writing which looked
to the theatre of 1830–60 for its inspiration; in its ranks it
included both a number of veterans whose greatest achievements belonged to previous decades and several younger men,
recent recruits, who were prepared to march under the same
standard.

How closely the sixties had adopted the popular styles of
the preceding decade is realisable when we compare Planché's

survey of dramatic tastes in *The Camp at the Olympic* (Olym. 1853)[1] with H. J. Byron's similar bird's-eye view in *1863; or, The Sensations of the Past Season* (St J. Dec. 1863). The latter starts in an author's study; the writer is in despair until Fancy "enters suddenly through the panelling" and summons forth the popular successes of the year. First arrives "the Adelphi Ghost of Haunted Man" from *Robert the Devil*, in which the device of Pepper's Ghost was used to add to the thrilling effect.[2] Other supernatural figures are adduced to testify to the popularity of kindred shows at the time. Next comes Bel Domonio and Manfred, the latter of whom complains about the "fickle town":

> Conceived in poet's brain not to be acted,
> It's most extraordinary, I attracted.
> Remorse at heart, dark fancies in my skull,
> Could I be anything but very dull?
> My long soliloquies, though, seldom tired;
> The crowded audience listened and perspired:
> Though 'twas two hours full ere I'd talking done,
> I still had breath for a tremendous *run*.
> My scenery drew too, which the fact denotes,
> The public must be *canvassed* for their votes.

"At the time when *Society* was performed"—two years later than this, in 1865—wrote T. Edgar Pemberton,[3] "the English theatrical world...was in a parlous state." At Drury Lane Phelps was appearing in a short-lived production of *King John*; the Princess's had Reade's *It's Never too Late to Mend*; at the Adelphi Jefferson was acting in *Rip Van Winkle* and Fechter was at the Lyceum in *The Watch Cry*. The plays were most poor in workmanship and antiquated in technique; the playgoers were apathetic.

During these years, the ancient uniform settled with a not uneasy grace on the shoulders of Byron,[4] an author as prolific as the older Planchés and Dibdins. Byron's efforts were various. Farce, sentimental comedy, extravaganza, burlesque

---

[1] *Supra*, p. 82.   [2] *Supra*, p. 42.
[3] *John Hare, Comedian, 1865–95* (1895), pp. 10–15.
[4] P. Wrey, *H. J. Byron* (*London Society*, xxvi, 1874).

—all came readily from his pen, and this very variety renders his work thoroughly representative of the popular tastes in his time. He never reached very high, but he did succeed in descending to almost unbelievable depths. Perhaps at the start it may be convenient to select two characteristic pieces, one typical of the lower levels and the other of his more ambitious flights. *The Garibaldi "Excursionists"* (P'cess, Nov. 1860) may stand for a number of one-act farces, based on simple themes and depending entirely on absurd situation. Here the absurdities arise from the quandary of Fitzbosh and Poldoody when, forced to join the militia, they fancy they are being shipped off to Italy for the purpose of aiding Garibaldi's insurrection. There is no wit here and no idea behind the plot.

In other plays, however, Byron aimed at something more. When this mood comes to him, an almost problem-drama atmosphere is called into being and sentimentalism rules. Of this kind is *Cyril's Success* (Glo. Nov. 1868). Therein Byron very deliberately tried to accomplish more than the writing of a merely popular piece. Clearly, in the dedication to Shirley Brooks, does he indicate his desire to reach beyond the farcical and the melodramatic. "I have endeavoured", he says,

in *Cyril's Success* to write a Play that would be effective in performance, and not altogether unworthy perusal; and, although it is to a certain extent "classy", I can assure those critics who think London and provincial audiences care only for coarse sensation and extravagance, that having been played a hundred nights in London it "went" (to use an actor's phrase) with very remarkable effect, both as regards interest and applause, in some small provincial towns, where the audiences were principally of the humbler classes, and it entirely eclipsed in attraction two of my melodramas which were played during my country tour.

And now you naturally ask—why write and print this? Simply because I am somewhat tired of being termed a "droll", a "punster", and so on; and, as a mere piece of self-justification—self-assertion it may be termed—beg to remind any one who may care to recollect the fact, that *Cyril's Success* is original, and a comedy—and, even in these vicious dramatic days—in five acts! *There!*

The main character in the drama is Cyril Cuthbert, a novelist, who, because of his success, comes to neglect his wife. She believes that he has been unfaithful to her and leaves him. His success, however, proves but a bubble reputation, and, himself neglected by the world, he remains in abject loneliness until the wife, touched by pity, returns and comforts him. Comedy is provided, alongside this serious theme, by Titeboy, Pincher and Miss Grannett (a schoolmistress, really Pincher's wife). Read in the light of present-day standards, *Cyril's Success* may seem rather a poor production, spiritually separated by aeons from the work of, say, Strindberg though chronologically removed therefrom only by some twenty years. Yet, far-off though it may be in conception of character and plot, such a play as this is to the sixties in England what *Comrades* was to the Scandinavian eighties.

Where Byron most lamentably fails in his serious plays is in creation of character and inventive power. His dramatic figures are all marred by artificiality of treatment, and a general tendency towards self-repetition becomes painfully apparent to any reader of his work. Thus, for example, the sympathetically conceived aristocratic fool whose heart is pure as gold boringly intrudes into play after play. Sir Simon Simple of *Not Such a Fool as He Looks* (Manchester, Dec. 1868; Glo. Oct. 1869) has many brothers. Sir Simon is a young knight who has been reared by the money-lender Murgatroyd. The latter has a niece, Felicia Craven, and for her Murgatroyd has, as it were, nourished this supposed scion of a noble race. Unfortunately for his hopes, however, Felicia shows herself to be a lady of individual spirit; loving, and being determined to marry, a certain Frederick Grantley, she takes Simon into her confidence. Poor Simon now finds himself in an awkward position; deeply stirred by Felicia's story, he takes upon himself the burden of telling Murgatroyd he will not wed her. An enraged outburst from the money-lender and a throwing out-of-doors for Simon are the result; and, more important still, the latter is crudely informed that, far from having aristocratic blood in his veins, his mother is Mrs Mould, the washerwoman. Eventually, in act 5, the

wretched youth in search of a mother discovers that to Mrs
Mould, also, he owes no filial obedience and that his genuine
parents are a certain Mrs Merton and Murgatroyd himself.
In this position he stays put; but one has the uneasy suspicion
that his stability is the result, not of a preconceived climax
in the plot, but simply of the fact that Byron, having exhausted
the permitted number of acts, found himself compelled to
abandon his riot of shifting paternities.

A type much akin to Sir Simon appears in *Old Soldiers*
(Str. Jan. 1873) and *Old Sailors* (Str. Oct. 1874). He does
not boast aristocratic birth or upbringing, but in his noble
simplicity he shows spiritual affinity to the other. *Old Soldiers*
thus introduces a faithful Cassidy who heroically tends the
somewhat stupid but honest-hearted Lionel Leveret and aids
this gentleman, after he has been nearly cheated by Captain
McTavish, to woo, successfully, the desirable Mary Moss.
In *Old Sailors*, the faithful servant is Joe Grill, attending
Lieutenant Lamb, a retired naval officer, and his functions
are the same as those of Cassidy. With these persons associate,
fitly enough, several other purely theatrical types—a brewer
Pollard who loves a wealthy young Millicent Tremaine, an
innocuous gentleman Frank who loves and is loved by an
equally harmless Clara Mayfield, and a rich but caddish
Ravenbill.

The stock roles became even more strongly marked in
Partners for Life (Glo. Oct. 1871) which presents, as its
main figures, Emily and Ernest, a devoted pair who occasionally indulge in a domestic quarrel, and, alongside of these,
Horace Mervyn, a gentleman under the thumb of the villainous
Muggles, Sir Archibald Drelincourt, a selfish philanthropist,
and the old maid Priscilla. More skilfully, similar figures are
moulded into the framework of *Our Boys* (Vaud. Jan. 1875)—
perhaps Byron's best play—but types there too they remain.
Sir Geoffry Champneys, the "County Magnate", Talbot his
son, Perkyn Middlewick, "a retired Butterman", Kempster
and Poodles, the menservants, Violet Melrose, the "heiress",
and Mary Melrose, "her poor Cousin", are as utterly innocent
of individuality as any of the persons in Byron's other plays.

That the public enjoyed such type characterisations, however, is proved by the extraordinary success of this comedy-drama; opening on January 16, 1875, it ran continuously for four years and three months, finally ending its run on April 18, 1879. This popular success alone would make Byron's work worthy of our attention; he had caught better than any of his contemporaries the tastes of the public and in so far stands forward as the most representative dramatist of the sixties and even of the seventies.

Apart from the general weakness in character delineation a manifest paucity of plot material is immediately apparent in his plays. Wealth versus birth, selfishness versus honesty— these form his stock themes. They come into *Weak Woman* (Str. May 1875) which a contemporary critic thought "one of his happiest efforts",[1] and they provide the main theme of *Courtship; or, The Three Caskets* (Court, Oct. 1879). In the latter the principal person is Millicent Vivian, a lady who is pursued by two suitors—Claude de Courcy, a pretended aristocrat in dire financial straits, and Phineas Gubbins, a business man who seeks for a well-born bride. This pair is strongly reminiscent of the similar couple in *Old Sailors*. Millicent's heart goes out to neither of these, for a rather saturnine gentleman farmer, one Edward Trentham, has attracted her attention. Since he is full of the most noble and exalted pride and since the other suitors pester her, she pretends that she has lost all her money. True to contemporary theatrical traditions, Courcy and Gubbins instantly veer off and the fair Millicent is left happily nestling in Trentham's manly arms. Villain and heroine, both cast in conventional patterns, dominate in *The Lancashire Lass; or, Tempted, Tried and True* (Alex. Liverpool, Oct. 1867). This play, cast in the form of a dramatic prologue and three acts (a style inaugurated by Douglas Jerrold), is technically similar to *Blow for Blow* (Holborn, Sept. 1868). The latter first shows us Josiah Craddock arrested for forgery, mainly because of testimony brought forward by John Drummond, a man whose actions are motivated by his unsuccessful love for

[1] J. Knight, *Theatrical Notes* (1893), p. 35.

a fair heroine, Mildred. Thence we move to the main action.
Mildred is dead, but Drummond remains filled with bitter
thoughts of revenge on his enemies and is barely thwarted
as the curtain falls. Sentiment rules here; it rules, too, in
the theatrically set *Prompter's Box* (Adel. March 1870) and
in the rustic *Daisy Farm* (Olym. May 1871). The whole plot
of *Daisy Farm* is governed by the desire and determination
of all concerned to keep a certain item of information from
the heroine, Bridget. Bridget has found a happy second mate
in Andrew Armstrong, when suddenly a Tramp appears
posing as her long-lost former spouse. Armstrong gives him
£400 to go off, but the son of Bridget's first marriage, Charley
Burridge, a wastrel with a few good elements to his character,
robs and thinks that he has killed the Tramp. This, of course,
is the moment for the appearance of a *deus ex machina*—here
a Mr Craven, who, persuading Charley to emigrate to
Australia, generally tidies things up. Equally sentimentally
are circus folk dealt with in *Fine Feathers* (Glo. April 1873),
a play in which Byron returns to a fond and familiar theme—
the lost heir. At first it seems that Harry Greville is heir to
the vast Gaisford estates—Madame Rumbalino assures him
he is the true claimant; then Ethel Carlingford appears as
the favoured of fortune; and finally the dark horse comes
home in the modest person of Ruth, supposed daughter of
Madame. More vital and original is *Bow Bells* (Roy. Oct.
1880). Even if the characters in this comedy-drama are stock
figures, the plot at least has an individual theme. After
a long and busy career within the sound of Bow Bells,
Twinklehorn decides to retire and enjoy the peace of a rustic
existence at Sloshington-le-Willows; he will have with him
only his well-beloved nieces, Effie and Bessie. The country,
however, does not present him with the joys he sought. His
butler is rightly named Boozer, boon companion to Sloggs,
the gardener, while his house is haunted by the adventurer
Captain Basil Bagot and his designing sister, Mrs Percival.
Aid has to come from the city ere poor Twinklehorn is
released from their clutches. As a final example of this
particular style of Byronian drama, which, despite melo-

dramatic incidents and rather poor comedy scenes, reveals potentialities of higher worth, his *Married in Haste* (H. Oct. 1875) may be selected. The main theme here concerns Ethel Grainger who has married Augustus Vere, an artist spoiled by having been made entirely dependent on his uncle Percy Pendragon. Cast off, this couple are shown living in abject poverty. While Augustus amuses himself with another lady, he refuses to allow Ethel to sell the pictures she has painted because he is professionally jealous (again an adumbration of the *Comrades* motif). Eventually Ethel decides to leave him, when suddenly a *deus ex machina* plumps heavily down in the person of Gibson Greene. A reading of this play certainly must convince us that Byron possessed, potentially at least, a real dramatic talent; taking *Married in Haste* and *Cyril's Success* alone, we are inevitably forced to a considerably higher appreciation of his talents than one might form from a perusal either of *Old Soldiers* or of the critiques on his work by Archer and Knight. For Archer, Byron is his "*bête noir* in the dramatic world".[1] These plays, in Archer's opinion, "do not contain a thought worth thinking, a lesson worth learning, a scene worth remembering, or a character worth loving or hating".[2] A more kindly tone pervades the criticism of Joseph Knight, but even he finds very little of value either in this drama, *Married in Haste*, or in Byron's work as a whole:

> When first heard...it leaves the impression of being a clever and almost a good play. Reflection is required before we perceive that the story is artificial and improbable as well as flimsy.[3]

Flimsy, improbable and artificial it may be, but a man who could suggest in 1876 the discussion of two fundamental problems—hasty marriage with its possible consequence and artistic jealousy between husband and wife—is not to be entirely dismissed; and this conviction is strengthened when we recall that Byron, trite as many of his "comic" scenes may be, sometimes brings forth a witty jest almost worthy of Wilde. "I never make mistakes," says Greene, "I could rise to crime, if required; but descend to a mistake—never!"

---

[1] *English Dramatists of To-day* (1882), p. 121.
[2] *Ib.* p. 147.   [3] *Op. cit.* pp. 71-3.

This lighter side of Byron's talent was, of course, much obscured and vitiated by the crudely popular humour of his burlesque. In these he punned and over-punned in a frantic effort to keep funny; in these too he filched unmercifully from his predecessors. *1863; or, The Sensations of the Past Season* (St J. Dec. 1863) takes its conception and even some of its dialogue from Planché's *The Camp at the Olympic* (Olym. Oct. 1853); and it by no means stands alone. Popular as Byron's burlesques proved, they do not show the inventive faculty, the delicacy and the grace so apparent in the work of others. What Planché tries to make fantastic and extravagant, Byron is content merely to debase. His puns are innumerable, but he hardly ever succeeds in striking off an example of this type of humour which seems unpremeditated and yet to the point. The really good pun is a play both on word and on idea; Byron generally is content to dwell merely on a similarity in sound. Where William Brough, in *The Field of the Cloth of Gold* (Str. April 1868), makes Henry VIII, on his return to England after a stormy channel crossing, remark sadly that

> Yesterday all was fair—a glorious Sunday,
> But this *sick transit* spoils the *glory o' Monday*,

Byron rests satisfied with a constant crackling of forced wit which lacks vitality and ease; where Planché's wit soars aloft amid a multitude of fiery sparks, Byron's splutters like a damp squib. His usual style finds fairly typical expression in the following lines from *Aladdin: or, The Wonderful Scamp!* (Str. April 1861):

> Such trifles, perhaps as lace, you might just wring out,
> But good *loud*-pattern'd gowns would make you sing out;
> Plain cotton dresses too would make you wince,
> Fancy a *Princess* scrubbing at the *prints*.
> Talk not of washing, or I fain must scold,
> Remember I'm cast in an *iron mould*;
> Therefore obey your *ryal* father, child.
> —Don't be more vexed, and don't get *father riled*.

or these from *Eurydice; or, Little Orpheus and his Lute* (Str. April 1871):

> He aims so sure, he kills all birds that fly,
> Brings down the heron with un-*heron* eye.

That contempt is commonly expressed for the pun may partly
be attributed to Byron's bad example.

Of Byron's companions there were many. Extravaganzas,
full of similar puns, were common, in both senses of the word.
Fairly typical is *Leatherlungos the Great, how he storm'd,
reigned and mizzled* (Adel. July 1872), by C. S. Cheltnam,
where occur many such passages as:

> *Placidorus.* I hope you think our ballet-girls are pretty?
> *Decollatessa.* Their legs, I dare say, are extremely witty;
> For more than dancing, nothing, on the whole,
> Leads to such elevation of the *sole*.

Alongside of the extravaganzas came the familiar mixed
comedies. The setting forth of fixed types in a serio-comic
setting, as in Wybert Reeve's *Won at Last!* (Ch. X. Oct.
1869), proved the easiest of dramatic tasks, and most dramatists took the path of least resistance. In these "straight"
plays a purely conventional view of life was (with a few
exceptions) adopted; this too was the easiest way, for interpretation and criticism imply the exercise of thought. Of
such plays, Thomas J. Williams' *Who's to Win Him?* (Lyc.
Jan. 1868) is typical. Here Cyril Dashwood is shown in
search of a wife; Sylvia, Minuetta, Musidora and Arabella
all seek to capture his fancy, but in the end he chooses poor
little modest innocent Rose. We are bound to suppose, one
must believe, that contemporary audiences did not stop to
consider the implications of the last words spoken by this
blushing maid:

> *Arabella* (*aside*). My deep-laid scheme entirely thrown away!
> (*to girls*) To think that Mr Dashwood should have preferred
> a *little girl.*
> *Sylvia* (*angrily*). Bewildering!
> *Minuetta* (*ditto*). Unheard of!
> *Musidora* (*ditto*). Incomprehensible!
> *Rose* (*to girls*). Nay, not so, my dear friends, 'tis easily explained;
> young as I am, I know that we all disdain that which is within
> our reach, and prize most that which is most difficult to obtain;

so, (*to audience*) young ladies, whenever you fall in love with a gentleman, pray don't *tell* him so; let him alone; and ten to one, he'll fall in love with *you*—a too evident partiality only defeats its own object, while maidenly reserve cannot fail, in the long run, safely to decide the all important question,

"Who's to Win Him?"

A merciful "*curtain*" hereupon descends on this nineteenth-century Pamela.

Farcical situations pleased others. J. P. Wooler uses a highly improbable device in *A Winning Hazard* (P.W. April 1865) and drags out his piece with impossible lies and intrigues, based on the idea that, to win a legacy, it is the object of Dudley and Jack to get Aurora and/or Coralie to accept their hands in marriage. The familiar *deus ex machina* (here a Du Graylock) appears in the same author's *Laurence's Love Suit* (Str. Jan. 1865) which deals with the time-honoured theme of a dependent ward (Eva Carlton) who rejects a young gentleman (Laurence Vane) because he is rich. So far as plays of this kind are concerned it would seem as if half the women pursued men on account of their wealth and the other half occupied their leisure in refusing them for the same reason. Absurd caricatures of various kinds fill these pieces. For many it was sufficient to invent the most flimsy of situations and build upon that foundation a ridiculous series of situations. In *A Return Ticket* (St J. Aug. 1862) by George Spencer and Walter James (it actually required two authors to compose this one-act piece) the authors conceive of an old gentleman, a *virtuoso*, who is so infatuated by recent mechanical devices that he will have none but inventors for his sons-in-law; the way in which two lovers disguise and make fools of themselves provides the questionable fun of the farce. This for its absurdity of situation and, say, C. S. Cheltnam's *Mrs Green's Snug Little Business* (Str. Jan. 1865) for its absurdity in characterisation (Mrs Green, Bung the Beadle and Mr Rapps the Policeman) may serve as representative of a thousand others.

2. *The Reform of Robertson*

Against work of this kind Tom Robertson rebelled. The position that Robertson occupies in the history of the English drama is, of course, one a trifle difficult to define exactly. That he was an innovator is certain; yet it is equally sure that his work found its basis in the efforts of his predecessors and that he made free use of melodramatic devices. "Robertson", wrote Boucicault in 1868, "differs from me, not fundamentally, but scenically; his action takes place in lodgings and drawing-rooms—mine has a more romantic scope",[1] and his judgment is absolutely just. Indeed, he might have gone further, for he himself had already experimented in the dramatic treatment of real life; and even before his time Lytton had made a plea for a serious comedy which should be a mirror of contemporary conditions. In presenting to the public a volume of his *Dramatic Works* in 1841 the author of *Money* clearly showed that he realised the needs of his age. "The comedy of a time", he wrote,

must be faithful to the character of the time itself. In our age men are more earnest than in that of the old artificial comedy. No matter in what department, the essence of the drama is still the faithful though idealising representation of life; and in 1840 we know that all life at least is *not* a jest. In the old comedy there is a laugh at everything most serious. But in that day...the fashion in real life ran in the same direction. In Shakespeare the dishonour of a husband is the material for revenge and tragedy; in Congreve and Wycherley it is the most fruitful food for ridicule and burlesque. But these last writers as artists have their excuse; they are not writing for the pulpit or the academy, but for the stage, and they must embody the manners and morals that they observe around them. It is precisely because the present age is more thoughtful, that Comedy, in its reflection of the age, must be more faithful to the chequered diversities of existence and go direct to its end through humours to truth, no matter whether its path lie through smiles or tears. All that can fairly be asked of comedy for the maintenance of its genuine character is, that the pathos it admits of should not be derived from tragical sources—that it should spring naturally from the comic incidents and comic agencies in which its general spirit must exist.

[1] *Mr and Mrs Bancroft on and off the Stage* (1889), p. 118.

The kind of comedy here adumbrated is tentatively tried in Lytton's own *Money*; an approach is made to it, with melo-dramatic trappings, in some of Boucicault's plays; Tom Taylor has it in his mind when he writes on themes taken from contemporary life; even Byron endeavours to find expression for it in *Cyril's Success* and *Married in Haste*. Others, such as Edmund Falconer, one of Robertson's most interesting predecessors, went even further. Sometimes this author writes cheaply and shallowly. *Next of Kin* (Lyc. April 1860) may be taken as an example of his more mediocre efforts; this, although styled a comedy-drama, deals farcically with a certain Timothy Chump, who is found to be heir to a great fortune, and with a rascally lawyer named Grubton. Equally poor is the comedy entitled *Does He Love Me?* (H. June 1860) which presents an old-fashioned story of Miss Vandeleur, the heiress, who changes places with her cousin, Miss Melrose, and of Lord Mowbray, who similarly exchanges identity with Everton Leigh. The only vitality visible here is in the creation of the amusing "Physical and Mental" Bubble. In *Extremes; or, Men of the Day* (Lyc. Aug. 1858), however, Falconer displays more interesting material. Though sentimental, this is a well-written serious comedy in the Lytton style; and, in view of its realism, there is interest in observing that the play has been dedicated to the author's "Lancashire Friends" —indeed, we might perhaps say that this is the first of the long line of local dramas which, half a century later, introduced as material the provincial life of England; Falconer thus becomes a true ancestor of Stanley Houghton. His main theme, certainly, is an old one, involving the use of the heavily barnacled will, through which Lucy Vavasour and Frank Hawthorne find themselves forced to marry if they are to hope for an inheritance—a convention of which time must be weary. Yet Falconer does succeed in giving this ancient theme life. Interestingly he develops his duel of love and pride, until, when Frank refuses to marry her, Lucy decides to give him her hand. Low comedy is provided by such doubtful comedy matter as the slippery aspirates of James, the butler, but the main object—the writing of a genuine serious (or sentimental) comedy of character—has been realised.

What, then, we may ask, did Robertson really bring to the theatre? Lytton's critical remarks might almost have been framed as a preface for the *Dramatic Works* of Robertson himself, and about 1860 such a man as Falconer was producing plays which bore a marked resemblance to the genuine Robertsonian comedies. In seeking an answer to this question, we must, it seems, look both within and without; for Robertson's contribution consists both in the spirit of his drama and in his stage reforms.[1] To interpret this contribution aright we must bear in mind that, when Robertson came to write, "realism", in the words of Thomas Purnell, was "wanted".[2] Now, various approaches had been made towards that realism, but the steps taken had been somewhat hesitant and faltering. The introduction of a real lamp-post and a real cab may have been thrilling; such procedure may have made a distinct break with the conventional tradition of the past; yet little attempt had been made to harmonise these real objects with the spirit of the plays or with the methods of production.[3] Boucicault thus mixes freely in his dramas matter of a purely artificial kind and material gathered directly from life. What Robertson did was to emphasise clearly the necessity of securing a complete harmony in performance, and of emphasising what may be termed spiritual reality. In this he was aided by the support of Marie Wilton (Lady Bancroft). Under her management of the Prince of Wales's Theatre, which opened in 1865, an endeavour was made so to polish and refine the performances as to make them artistic unities instead of merely virtuoso entertainments. Sharing his ideals,

[1] Konrad Grein, *Thomas William Robertson (1829–1871). Ein Beitrag zur Geschichte des neueren englischen Dramas* (Marburg, 1911).

[2] *Op. cit.* pp. 80–93.

[3] On this see F. Rahill, *A Mid-Victorian Regisseur* (*Theatre Arts Monthly*, xiii, 1929, 838–44); D. Harrison, *Tom Robertson* (*The Contemporary Review*, cxxxv, March 1929, 356–61); T. E. Pemberton, *The Life and Writings of T. W. Robertson* (1893); *The Principal Works of T. W. Robertson. With a Memoir by his Son* (2 vols. 1889); *Thomas William Robertson and the Modern Theatre* (*Temple Bar*, xliv, 1875); W. Wilding Jones, *Robertson as a Dramatist* (*The Theatre*, N.S. ii, July 1879, 355–60).

Marie Wilton allowed Robertson to direct his own plays, and the care which he devoted to this is amply indicated even in the abbreviated acting texts of his comedies.

It is not, of course, that Robertson was a revolutionary from the beginning of his career. In *The Star of the North* he demonstrates that he was simply carrying on accepted forms. All the persons in this silly treatment of Catherine and Peter are cast in the stock terms hallowed by time; the "Lead, Light Comedian, Character Role, Walking Gentleman, Juvenile and Soubrette", as listed in the printed text, strut and fret their shadowy parts on an uninspired stage. Knowing Robertson's later achievements, one finds surprise and interest in such early works as *The Half Caste; or, The Poisoned Pearl* and *Birds of Prey; or, A Duel in the Dark*. Both of these are melodramas, and at first glance we might say that they offer nothing which might remove them from the familiar run of similar contemporary pieces. Awareness of what Robertson was later to accomplish, however, leads us to detect in both elements of a prophetic kind. In *The Half Caste* the eccentric wit of Lord Falconer and the Hon. Augustus Fitznoddleton suggests later comedy scenes, while the general theme of *Birds of Prey*, vaguely suggesting the mood of *Les corbeaux*, gives a faint suggestion of the purposeful flavour which appears in his more familiar plays. This sketch of pretended aristocrats battening upon fools provides a serious outline to what otherwise would have been merely a play of exciting incident.

Robertson's efforts in realism are adumbrated in *David Garrick* (P.W. Birmingham, April 1864; H. April 1864). The apparatus which accompanies the printed text is revealing. First comes a section on the scenery, with plans for two sets and elaborate description of the arrangements in the rooms. "Closed in", we read,

Curtains to window, L. 2 E., and open doorway (wide), R. 2 E.; door, L. 1 E., practicable. A is a lacquer-work sideboard; B, B, B. are large China jars on stands; L. side there are smaller vases, and East Indian curiosities, arranged for effect, C. is a backing to R.U.E. opening; pictures on flat are, among others (all very dingy), a pair of portraits, lady and gentleman, period James I or Charles II; hearth-rug; carpet down; statuette on table, L.C., front, with small books; books on table, R., with one folio Shakespeare. All the furniture having chintz cloths on; bell-pull, R. 1 E.; picture on set, R. 1 E.; high up, looking-glass over mantel; fire in fireplace, to burn; ornaments on mantel.

This is followed by an equally elaborate description of the costumes. Throughout the play itself, moreover, Robertson has indicated, in precise manner, both the gestures of his characters and their relative positions on the stage. These directions naturally become still more extended in the plays which he later penned for the same management. Thus, in *Society* (P.W. Liverpool, May 1865; P.W. Nov. 1865), the space devoted in Act II to the setting and action at the "Owl's Roost" is almost as great as that devoted to the dialogues. That Robertson did not confine himself entirely to "doorknobs" is already proved by contemporary record. Certainly, he wanted a room to look like a room, and he was determined to see that it should contain the kind of furniture and ornament which such a room would have in real life; but more important for him was the sense of spiritual reality to be conveyed by means of his actors. "I look upon stage management, as now understood," declared W. S. Gilbert, "as having been absolutely invented by him."[1]

This reform Robertson was able to undertake at the Prince of Wales's, partly because of the sympathetic direction of that theatre, partly also because social conditions had so altered as to allow an evening's performance to be made up with one single play and to permit that play to run for many weeks.[2] So long as three pieces had to be given on one night and so long as there was constant change in repertoire, there could be but little hope of securing such attention to detail as Robertson demanded. The long-run system may have done much harm, but for Robertson's work it was indispensable; only by time and care might his effects be realised. Spectators could now come to the theatre and feel that they were looking on a genuine domestic interior; many indeed expressed some

---

[1] See *supra*, p. 32.   [2] See *supra*, pp. 55.

surprise that audiences would pay to hear "what they hear in their own houses".[1]

This reference to "hearing" brings us to the inner contribution of Robertson. When care could thus be devoted to the set and the actors, opportunity was offered for a greater realism in dialogue and in theme. Robertson made us, as a contemporary noted, carry "our fire-side concerns to the theatre with us".[2] So far as dialogue is concerned, Robertson, while perhaps not adding anything to what had already appeared in the work of his predecessors, contrived to get a more even flow, a greater semblance to reality, than any of his predecessors had done. Sentimentality there is in his plays, and his moral purpose makes him indulge in passages which are obviously far removed from common parlance. These artificial passages undoubtedly fix themselves more firmly upon our minds than they once did, and, as a result, we are sometimes inclined to overlook the genuine ease and skill of his style. When, however, we are able to shake ourselves free, we realise that, not only has he been sufficiently skilful to adapt his language to the requirements of his several persons but he has the power of evoking a comic spirit distinct from the farcical and burlesque experiments of his companions. It is peculiar, and perhaps unfortunate, that Robertson's deliberately expressed jokes are often trite, obvious and futile, while his plays abound in sly little hits and comments which, because of their appositeness, are excellent theatre. "I would have existence all like Tennyson," sighs a young lady in *Play* (P.W. Feb. 1868), "instead of which, it's nothing but butchers' bills!"

This varied and skilfully modulated dialogue accompanies a fresh treatment of dramatic characters. The drama of the period 1800–60, both serious and comic, had been dominated by type portraits. These type portraits were either of conventionally conceived figures (such as hero and villain in melodrama) or of grotesque eccentricities so absurd as to be utterly impossible. The range of parts was thus definitely

---

[1] Thomas Purnell, *op. cit.* p. 93.
[2] M. Morris, *op. cit.* pp. 165–87.

limited, and any deviation from the commonly accepted roles was rare and unfavourably frowned upon. It is to Robertson's credit that he restored once more the individually conceived character, and that this was the result of conscious effort and deliberate aim is shown by his continued progress as a dramatist. Such an early play as *David Garrick* (H. 1864) contained a collection of types—Ingot, the familiar old "father", Squire Chivy, the equally familiar "huntsman" with his "Yoicks", Araminta, the typical "bluestocking". Something of this style still remains in *Society* (P.W. 1865); it has practically vanished in *Caste* (P.W. April 1867).

On one other thing does Robertson's reputation rest. In spite of its propensity for sentimental moralisings, English comedy prior to 1860 was largely innocent of any larger sense of purpose. Lytton's *Money* is one of the very few plays of the early nineteenth century wherein may be discerned a desire to introduce something more than a mere collection of type characters involved in a conventional series of intrigues. Put in another way, we may declare that these plays rarely, if ever, paid thought to theme as distinct from plot. This conception of theme value, it is true, is apparent in some of Byron's dramas, but, with hardly an exception, such plays belong to a date after and not before the production of Robertson's *Society*. There can be no doubt that Robertson it was who first in the modern English drama realised the desirability of introducing a central purpose into his comedy dramas. Of this realisation testimony remains in the titles he gave to his plays—*Society*, *Caste*, *Play*, *School* and *War*. Still further, Robertson's aim lay, not merely in presenting a problem or a moral truth, but in surveying this problem impartially. Looking at the Chodds in *Society*, one may be tempted to aver that it was Robertson's aim to ridicule the vulgarities of common life; but a deeper glance shows us that Lady Ptarmigant and her aristocratic companions are correspondingly ridiculed. It was Robertson's virtue that he endeavoured to present a view of the whole life of his time— its complete *Society*. Instead of Byron's rude juxtaposition of well-born pride and the vulgar honesty of the middle-classes, Robertson welded a unified whole from the teeming life of his day.

His skill in plot construction hardly need be insisted upon. It is apparent even in *David Garrick* (H. 1864); indeed, this quality alone gives distinction to that improbable tale of the eighteenth-century actor's noble magnanimity. The same skill carries him successfully through the complexities of the plot used in *Society* (P.W. 1865). Sentimentality rules in both of these, a sentimentality interspersed with patches of comic matter in the "Tom and Jerry" style; but such sentimentality is atoned for by the directness and firmness of the "Owl's Roost" scene in the latter play. Here Robertson displays both a keen power of observation and an acute sense of the theatre. To us its effect may be somewhat cheapened by imitation, but the "five-shillings" episode is cleverly designed:

SIDNEY (L.). I find I've nothing in my portmonnaie but notes. I want a trifle for a cab. Lend me five shillings.

TOM. I haven't got it; but I can get it for you.

SIDNEY. There's a good fellow, do. (*Returns to seat.*)

TOM (*to* MAC USQUEBAUGH, *after looking round*). Mac, (*whispering*) lend me five bob.

MAC U. My dear boy, I haven't got so much.

TOM. Then don't lend it.

MAC U. But I'll get it for you. (*Crosses to* BRADLEY—*whispers*) Bradley, lend me five shillings.

BRAD. I haven't it about me; but I'll get it for you. (*Crosses to* O'SULLIVAN—*whispers*) O'Sullivan, lend me five shillings.

O'SULL. I haven't got it; but I'll get it for you. (*Crossing to* SCARGIL—*whispers*) Scargil, lend me five shillings.

SCARG. I haven't got it, but I'll get it for you. (*Crossing to* MAKVICZ—*whispers*) Doctor, lend me five shillings.

DR M. I am waiting for chaange vor a zoveren; I'll give it you when de waiter brings it me.

SCARG. All right! (*To* O'SULLIVAN) All right!

O'SULL. All right! (*To* BRADLEY) All right!

BRAD. All right! (*To* MAC USQUEBAUGH) All right!

MAC U. All right! (*To* TOM) All right!

TOM (*to* SIDNEY). All right!

Similarly does *Caste* (P.W. 1867), in spite of its Victorian sentiment, make theatrical use of life. The results of George

D'Alroy's marriage to Esther Eccles, the haughty disdain of the Marquise de St Maur, the jollity of Polly Eccles, the honesty of her jo, Sam Gerridge, and the charming kindliness of Captain Hawtree—all are combined to create a definite whole. Even in our modern days, when *Caste* was revived at the Old Vic, its sentimentalities were forgotten in the genuine interest it aroused.

Play (P.W. Feb. 1868) is less entertaining—perhaps because Robertson was a trifle out of his depth in his delineation of the rascally Chevalier Browne, the romantic Rosie and the fervent Frank Price. In passing it may be noted how prone Robertson was to linking his plot up with some legendary narrative material. Here it is a German myth; in *School* (P.W. Jan. 1869) it is the familiar tale of Cinderella. The first act of the latter play starts with a retelling of the fairy tale by Bella, while the other girls listen and pass comments, these comments finally destroying the narration as the ever-important theme of love is introduced:

NAOMI. Go on, Bella, The prince fell in love.

CLARA. What is love?

MILLY. You stupid thing!

TILLY. Such ignorance!

HETTY. That stupid Clara!

CLARA. I don't believe any of you know; not even you big girls.

TILLY. Everybody knows what love is.

CLARA. Then what is it?

NAOMI. Who's got a dictionary? You're sure to find it there.

TILLY. My eldest sister says it's the only place in which you can find it.

HETTY. Then she's been jilted.

MILLY. My pa says love is moonshine.

NAOMI. Then how sweet and mellow it must be.

MILLY. Particularly when the moon is at the full.

NAOMI. And there's no eclipse.

TILLY. It seems that nobody knows what love is.

HETTY. I despise such ignorance.

CLARA. Then why don't they teach it us? We've a music master to teach music, why not a love master to teach love?

NAOMI. You don't suppose love is to be taught like geography or the use of the globes, do you? No, love is an extra.

And it is Robertson's business in the play to show how little Naomi discovers this extra and meets her prince. In a similar fashion, the second scene of *Play* introduces Rosie's retelling the legend "of the beautiful lady in Grey"—a legend which also has its bearing on the action of the comedy. While the device is fairly obvious, it does aid in giving to Robertson's plays a broader foundation and in early focusing the attention of the audience upon the main theme.

School in many respects is a much more interesting and a better written comedy than *Play*. With a fairly deft touch Robertson treats of the love of Lord Beaufoy for Bella and that of Jack Poyntz for Naomi Tighe, and he succeeds in giving individual life to Dr Sutcliffe and his schoolma'am wife. The end is frankly artificial, but we must not condemn it unless we are prepared to condemn a precisely similar device in the last act of Shaw's *Heartbreak House*:

FARINTOSH. A true lady.

DR SUTCLIFFE. So many things are required for the composition of the real thing. One wants nobility of feeling.

FARINTOSH. A kind heart.

DR SUTCLIFFE. A noble mind.

FARINTOSH. Modesty.

DR SUTCLIFFE. Gentleness.

FARINTOSH. Courage.

DR SUTCLIFFE. Truthfulness.

FARINTOSH. Birth.

DR SUTCLIFFE. Breeding.

MRS SUTCLIFFE (*coming between them*). And above all—School.

As a final example of Robertson's work, we may select his *War* (St J. Jan. 1871). No better understanding, perhaps, may be gained of his ability than a comparison of this play with Carpenter's *Love and Honour* (Sur. 1855), written on a similar theme.[1] In the latter is an entirely melodramatic plot; there is a pure heroine; an equally pure hero finds himself confronted by a black and cowardly villain. Robertson's play has a different cast. A melodramatic tinge colours its action, certainly; and the situations are frequently dealt with in a sentimental manner. On the other hand, we

---

[1] See *supra*, p. 95.

recognise immediately that the dialogue here has a naturalistic ease which sharply differentiates it from Carpenter's effort. The very first lines strike a novel note:

> BLANCHE (*heard without*). Never mind; I'll find her in the garden.
> JESSIE (*heard outside*). Don't trouble yourself; I'll find them.
> (*Enter* BLANCHE *from* D. *in flat, and* JESSIE *from* D. *at back. They look about the stage as if searching for someone. Suddenly they meet each other face to face, and start.*)
> BLANCHE. Oh!
> JESSIE. Oh!
> BLANCHE. Jessie!
> JESSIE. Blanche!
> BLANCHE }
> JESSIE   } (*together*). Is that you?
> BLANCHE. You took away my breath.
> JESSIE. And you've made my heart beat.
> BLANCHE. Did you think I was a young man?
> JESSIE. No, but—
> BLANCHE. But what?
> JESSIE. I—I don't know.

This opening gives the tone of the whole play:

> KATIE. I know all about it. The fact is, that because Lotte's papa is a German—
> BLANCHE. Now, don't tell us that, because we know that as well as you.
> JESSIE. Yes, we all know as well as each other.
> BLANCHE. Girls, I have an idea. As we all know, and all want to tell, let's all tell each other.
> THE GIRLS. Yes, yes, yes, yes!
> BLANCHE. Well, you know, in Germany it is the custom to call a young lady a bride—
> JESSIE. As soon as she is engaged.
> AGNES. Just so; and everybody congratulates them—I mean the bride and bridegroom, just the same as if they were married.
> JESSIE. How nice! I should like to be a bride.
> BLANCHE. And I should like to be a bridegroom.
> KATIE. And I should like to be both bride and bridegroom, too.
> JESSIE. Oh, how selfish!
> AGNES. Katie wants everything.
> BLANCHE. And what a bridegroom!
> JESSIE. An officer.

AGNES. A soldier.
KATIE. More—a horse soldier.
BLANCHE. And more—a French horse soldier.

This may be regarded merely as a dramatist's trick, a convenient method of concealing the provision of necessary information; but, even though it be a trick, the device is novel and indicates in itself one of Robertson's contributions to the playwright's craft.

A second matter attracts our attention. *Love and Honour* was a pure melodrama, evil brother and all. *War* may occasionally recall the transpontine thrills, but it lacks the familiar vulgar trappings, and, in particular, we note that the villain has vanished. Robertson essays to write, not in terms of theatrical black and white, but in those of life where grey is the predominant shade. The conflicts in his plays are not so much conflicts of moral opinions as the clash and confusion of social forces. Impartially he views *Society*; and with unprejudiced judgment he delineates the racial hatred of French and Germans.

This introduces us to the final and essential difference between *War* and *Love and Honour*. *Love and Honour* exists for a story and its component situations; *War* exists for an idea. It is the very theme of war which dominates the dramatist's mind as he traces the love of Oscar de Rochevaunes and Lotte Hartmann, as he dwells sympathetically on the peace-loving German father. At one step we have moved from an old world into a new, from an exploiting of sensationalism to a deliberate attempt, through the medium of art, at dealing significantly with the major problems of the day. Antiquated though *War* may be to-day, it is definitely and demonstrably modern in its essential conception.

"Of the playwrights of yesterday," says William Archer, "the first in point of merit and influence is undoubtedly Mr T. W. Robertson."[1] A more reasoned view of dramatic development during the nineteenth century must be forced to place Tom Robertson not first in merit among the playwrights of the past but first in time among the dramatic writers of the present.

[1] *English Dramatists of To-Day* (1882), p. 21.   9-2

CHAPTER V

GILBERT AND ALBERY: PLAYS OF THE SEVENTIES

1. The Fantastic and Satiric Comedy

DURING the gradual but determinedly certain progress of this naturalistic style a few men murmured of revolt. The forces of rebellion, however, were weak and ill-armed; nor may we feel surprised that, confronted at once by the naturalistic pioneers and by the popular exponents of melodrama, they failed to achieve either immediate power or future influence. Among their ranks only one attained a position of pre-eminence, and that rather because of his association with a composer than because of his own unaided dramatic efforts.

William Schwenk Gilbert is a peculiar but a by no means unexplainable figure in the grey shadows of the Victorian stage.[1] Born in 1836, he started his dramatic career at the

---

[1] On this period generally see *The Eighteen-Seventies* (1929), with an article by Sir A. W. Pinero, *The Theatre of the Seventies*. Gilbert's relations with the drama of his time are dealt with by M. Ellehauge, *The Initial Stages in the Development of the English Problem-Play* (*Englische Studien*, lxvi, March 1932, 373–401). On Gilbert generally see Sidney Dark and Rowland Grey, *William Schwenk Gilbert, his Life and Letters* (1923), A. C. Wilson, *W. S. Gilbert* (*Manchester Quarterly*, li, 1925, 277–97) and Peyton Wrey, *Mr W. S. Gilbert* (*London Society*, No. 157, Jan. 1875). An excellent bibliography has been prepared by T. Searle (1931). There are, of course, many books and articles on the operas: see particularly P. Fitzgerald, *The Savoy Opera* (1894), F. A. Cellier and C. Bridgeman, *Gilbert, Sullivan and D'Oyly Carte* (1914), H. Walbrook, *The Gilbert and Sullivan Opera* (1922), H. A. Lytton, *The Secrets of a Savoyard* (1922), A. H. Godwin, *Gilbert and Sullivan* (1926), I. Goldberg, *The Story of Gilbert and Sullivan* (1929), E. A. Browne, *W. S. Gilbert* (1907). Of special interest are C. Lambton, *Gilbertian Characters, and a Discourse on W. S. Gilbert's Philosophy* (1931). On Gilbert's 'philosophy' and on the type of comedy he made his own, particularly interesting are the following: A. F. Marshall, *The Spirit of Gilbert's Comedies* (*The Month*, lv, 1885, 254–62), Max Beerbohm, *Mr Gilbert's Rentrée* (*The Saturday*

age of thirty with a piece called *Dulcamara* (St J. Dec. 1866) and proceeded prolifically to turn out a series of farces and extravaganzas which, although marked by a neater turn of phrase and a more delicate wit, are akin to scores of similar pieces produced between 1830 and 1860. The school to which he belongs is clearly shown; from Planché he derives his original inspiration and thus he stands as the boon companion of the brothers Brough and of H. J. Byron.[1] This indebtedness to Planché was noted in his own time, and has been duly emphasised by both Harley Granville-Barker[2] and Dougald MacMillan.[3] There can be no doubt about it; Gilbert would not have been, had Planché not turned out his long series of pleasant extravaganzas. Again and again may we demonstrate—demonstrate specifically with due citation of act and scene—how many witticisms, quips and cranks the author of *Patience* filched from the author of *Success*. Yet Gilbert's genius was not merely an imitative one. From Planché he may derive much, but he both gives new use to what he borrows and informs his plays with a spirit distinctively his own. As Davenport Adams noted, he "was the first to apply systematically to extravaganza the spirit and method of Topsy-turveydom".[4] That spirit and method found its earliest clear expression in *The Palace of Truth* (H. Nov. 1870).

The Palace of Truth is a blank verse "fairy comedy", a new type of play which we must associate directly with Gilbert's name. The fairy comedy that Gilbert exploited was no pretty-pretty piece peopled by tripping Oberons and

---

Review, xcvii, May 1904, 619–20), W. Sichel, *The English Aristophanes* (*The Fortnightly Review*, N.S. xc, Oct. 1911, 681–704), H. Rowland Brown, *The Gilbertian Idea* (*The Cornhill Magazine*, lii, April 1922, 503–12), Edith Hamilton, *W. S. Gilbert* (*Theatre Arts Monthly*, xi, Oct. 1927, 781–90), and A. E. du Bois, *W. S. Gilbert, Practical Classicist* (*The Sewanee Review*, xxxvii, Jan.–March 1929, 94–107).

[1] W. Davenport Adams, *The Silence of Mr Gilbert* (*The Theatre*, N.S. xxiv, Dec. 1894, 286–9).

[2] H. Granville-Barker, *Exit Planché—Enter Gilbert* (*The London Mercury*, xxv, March and April 1932, 457–66, 558–73).

[3] *Planché's Early Classical Burlesques* (*Studies in Philology*, xxv, July 1928, 340–5) and *Some Burlesques with a Purpose* (*Philological Quarterly*, viii, July 1929, 255–63).

[4] *Loc. cit.*

coquettish Titanias; indeed, the term "fairy" hardly does true justice to the form. A more just title would be "fantastic comedy", and this would have the advantage of being applicable to those many plays of Gilbert's which, while not introducing the fairy characters, share in the general atmosphere of poetic fancy which was peculiarly his own. *Engaged*, though written in prose about contemporaries, is intimately related to *The Palace of Truth*.

Gilbert's Palace of Truth is a mysterious mansion entering which all persons are compelled, without realising what they are doing, to utter aloud their inmost thoughts. Thither go King Phanor and his court, with the result that the seeming cold Princess Zeolide becomes passionate, the gushing Prince Philamir grows blasé and cold, the Diogenes-like Aristaeus develops into quite a genial gentleman. Perhaps the atmosphere of the play may best be represented by the scene where the artful coquette Azema tries to entrap Prince Philamir, revealing as she does so all the tricks of her trade:

AZEMA.   Are you Prince Philamir?
CHRYSAL. (C.). Not I, indeed, fair lady. This is he—
         The most conceited coxcomb in the world.
         (*With an elaborate bow to* PHILAMIR, *who starts
            angrily*).
         No thanks—indeed 'tis true.
AZEMA (*to* CHRYSAL). Then go your way—
         I don't want you! I only want the prince.
         'Twas Philamir I came to captivate.
CHRYSAL. Here's candour, if you like!
AZEMA.   Oh, leave us, sir!
         Find some excuse to go, that he and I
         May be alone together.
PHILAMIR.   Leave me, sir.
         I'll give your tongue a lesson ere the night!
CHRYSAL. How has my tongue offended?—Oh, I see—
         Exactly—don't explain! (*Aside*) Poor Zeolide!
                                          Exit, L.U.E.

PHILAMIR. Insolent scoundrel! (*following him*).
AZEMA.   (R.).   Oh, don't follow him.
         I want you here alone. You can begin—
         I am not shy, thou I appear to be.

Indeed, I entered here ten minutes since;
Because I heard from those outside the gates,
That you, Prince Philamir, had just arrived.

PHILAMIR. (L.). Then you're a stranger here?

AZEMA.   I am, indeed!
The people told me any one was free
To enter.

PHILAMIR. Yes, quite right. Did they say more?

AZEMA.   Oh, yes, much more. They told me, then, that you
Received but sorry treatment at the hands
Of Princess Zeolide. They told me too,
That your betrothal might ere long collapse;
(*With extreme modesty*), So, thought I, as I am
    beyond dispute
The fairest maid for many a mile around—
And as, moreover, I possess the gift
Of feigning an enchanting innocence,
I possibly may captivate the Prince,
And fill the place once filled with Zeolide.
(*Sits R.—her dress is disarranged.*)

PHILAMIR. The Princess has a candid enemy!
I beg your pardon, but the furniture
Has caught your dress.

AZEMA (*re-arranging her dress hastily*).
                  Oh, I arranged it so;
That you might see how truly beautiful
My foot and ankle are.
(*As if much shocked at the expose.*)

PHILAMIR.   I saw them well,
They're very neat.

AZEMA.   I now remove my glove
That you may note the whiteness of my hand.
I place it there (*near* PHILAMIR) in order that
    you may
Be tempted to enclose it in your own.

PHILAMIR. To that temptation I at once succumb.
(*Taking her hand—she affects to withdraw it angrily.*)

AZEMA (*struggling to release herself*).
                  Go on! If you had any enterprise
You'd gently place your arm around my waist
And kiss me.

PHILAMIR.   It might anger you!

AZEMA.   Oh, no!
It's true that I should start with every show

Of indignation, just in order to
Maintain my character for innocence—
But that is all.

PHILAMIR (*puts his arm round her and kisses her*).
There, then—'tis done!

AZEMA (*starting, with a great show of rage*).
How, sir?
I think it's time that I should take my leave.
(*Very indignantly*) I shall be in the Avenue of Palms
At ten o'clock tonight. I mention this
That you may take the hint and be there, too.

The spirit of *The Palace of Truth* is ironic and satiric, but in his next important poetic play, *Pygmalion and Galatea* (H. Dec. 1871), Gilbert showed that his fancy could move as easily in serious as in comic realms. The irony may still be there, but it is now an irony which approaches the tragic impression. Bringing Galatea to life, Pygmalion is cursed with blindness by his jealous wife, Cynisca. Greatly loving, Galatea, in a spirit of self-sacrifice, voluntarily turns herself once more to stone. Such is the bare theme of the piece; this, however, is enriched, not only by the introduction of several subsidiary characters such as the wealthy patron Chrysos and his wife Daphne, but by a tremulous poetic expression which shows Gilbert capable of greater and more serious things than one might, judging from his other works, have imagined. In this play, inspired though it may have been by *Les filles de marbre*,[1] he proves himself something more than the jester and indicates that his genius contained an emotional as well as an intellectual quality. This seriousness is reflected in a different way in *Randall's Thumb* (Court, Jan. 1871), a peculiar drama amidst this fantasy. The thumb of the title is one under which Buckthorpe is firmly held. Forced to serve the villain's purposes, this hero is saved only by the love of a sentimentally conceived heroine. Such a milieu, however, could not hold Gilbert long. More typical of his genius is the "musical fairy tale" entitled *Creatures of Impulse* (Court, April 1871) which, with the score of Alberto Randegger, anticipates the Savoy operas to come. The witch who

---

[1] See *supra*, p. 97.

FANTASTIC AND SATIRIC COMEDY 137

has power to charm and ensnare is characteristic, and even some of the verse reads as if it came, not from this early work, but from one of the famous later series:

> *Sergeant.* A soldier of the King's Hussars,
> Although a gallant son of Mars;
> To no one may he be gall*ant*,
> Except his mother and his aunt!
>
> *Pipette.* A very proper rule indeed,
> And one that surely should succeed.
>
> *Peter.* But don't you find it rather slow—
> Monotonous, in fact?
>
> *Sergeant.*   Oh no!
> Each warrior who joins our corps,
> Can count his mothers by the score;
> And as for aunts—as I'm alive—
> Each grenadier has thirty-five!
>
> *Peter.* I shouldn't like to serve with him,
> One's aunt's are elderly and grim.
>
> *Pipette.* One's mothers too, as facts will show,
> Are always aged dames.
>
> *Sergeant.*   Oh no!
> The grimmest aunt in all our corps,
> Is seventeen—or little more;
> The oldest mother's age may be,
> A little short of twenty-three!

The intellectually serious predominates once more in *The Wicked World* (H. Jan. 1873), and a comparison of the tone of this play with that of *Pygmalion* is not uninstructive. Sometimes we get the impression in Gilbert's work that he is genuinely afraid of life. He has the seeing eye of the artist, and what he sees makes him terrified. To conceal that terror and to find escape he turns to his topsy-turvy fantasy. In *The Wicked World*, lightly as the theme is dealt with, this is amply apparent. The fairy world here is a replica, in refined form, of a human world below. From the latter, two men, Sir Ethais and Sir Phyllon, are drawn upwards, and through them love is introduced into the fairy realms. At first this love intrigues the gossamer creatures of the upper air, but gradually horror and dismay enter their hearts. In fear they banish the two humans, and banishing them, they cast off the emotion of love. Nature, as Gilbert sees her, is a monster of fair proportions and awesomely cruel spirit. Gilbert himself is the jester who mocks and grimaces lest his own being break under the strain of life and lest his hatred of worldly vices issue forth in terms anti-social and lunatic.

Another aspect of his cynicism, thus born of his peculiarly individual conception of human existence, is to be traced in *Sweethearts* (P.W. Nov. 1874). The first act of this takes place in the year 1844. Here we see an ardent lover, Spreadbarrow, vowing eternal devotion to Jenny Northcott. Brokenhearted at her apparent indifference, he leaves for India after having planted a small sapling before her drawing-room window. In the second act the scene is unchanged, save that thirty years have passed by. The old house is there, but no longer as a solitary mansion, for the city has spread its octopus arms around it; and the tiny sapling has now become a great spreading tree. Spreadbarrow enters, an elderly man, and meets Jenny without recognising her. In an adroit piece of dialogue it is made clear that while he has come to regard his boyish passion as a mere folly, while he even makes a mistake in Jenny's name, she, who had affected indifference, has all this time been living devotedly on his memory. This is sentimentalism, if you like; but it is sentimentalism worn with an intellectual difference. *Sweethearts* is as clever a bit of play-making and as atmospheric a drama as the nineteenth century had, so far, produced.

The quiet sorrows of life, against which naught may prevail, dominate throughout *Broken Hearts* (Court, Dec. 1875). The scene is a lonely island, where dwell in seclusion a group of girls who, injured by the world, have fled here for safety and rest. The only man in their company is a servant, Mousta, an ill-shapen dwarf. The essential tone of the play Gilbert suggests in his very first lines, "*A tropical landscape*" forms the setting, "*in the distance, a calm sea*". Quietly a fountain plays and in the foreground is "*an old sun-dial formed of the upper part of a broken pillar, round the shaft of which some creeping flowers are trained*".

MOUSTA, *a deformed ill-favoured dwarf, hump-backed and one-eyed, is discovered seated R. of fountain, reading a small black-letter volume.*

MOUSTA (*reads*). "*To move a mountain.*" That will serve me not,
    Unless, indeed, 'twill teach me how to lift
    This cursed mountain from my crippled back!
    "*To make old young.*" Humph! I'm but forty-two—
    But still, I'll mark that page—the day will come
    When I shall find it useful. Ha! What's this?
    "*To make the crooked straight; to heal the halt;*
    And clothe unsightly forms with comeliness."
    At last! At last!

The contrast of physical misshapenness and natural beauty, made the more poignant by the entry, immediately afterwards, of the lovely young Vavir, is typical Gilbert's mood. The book which Mousta has is a magic volume belonging to Prince Florian who, possessing the power to make himself invisible, has succeeded in landing on the island. There he finds these broken-hearted girls, each of whom has taken some object on which she may lavish her pitiful devotion—one adores the sun dial, another the fountain. And as the play thus opens with Mousta's pain, so it ends with Vavir's death:

VAVIR (*very feebly*). Weep not; the bitterness of death is past.
    Kiss me, my sister. Florian, think of me.
    I loved thee very much! Be good to her.
    Dear Sister, place my hand upon my dial.
    Weep not for me; I have no pain indeed.
    Kiss me again; my sun has set. Good night!
    Good night!

Without possessing that sternness of character out of which the tragic dramatist is made, without showing any tendency towards that self-superiority from which the satirist takes his being, Gilbert assumes certain qualities of each and frames them in a mood of abject hopelessness. His world is the world of the world-weary and of the disillusioned. "Years afterward, Gilbert told Miss Anderson there was 'more of me' in *Broken Hearts* than anywhere else."[1]

---

[1] Sidney Dark and Rowland Grey, *op. cit.* p. 54.

In *Broken Hearts* he reaches the most poignant expression of this temper. Joseph Knight's criticism was just when he said that whereas in *The Wicked World* Gilbert was a satirist and in *Pygmalion* a humorist, in this he proved himself a poet.[1] But having become a tragic poet, he suddenly throws off his despair and seeks with a laugh to see the universe, not as a cruel prison and torture-chamber, but as a hall of most ridiculous folly. From this mood spring *Tom Cobb* (St J. April 1875) and, more importantly, *Engaged* (H. Oct. 1877). *Engaged* is a light comedy and it deals with persons who, outwardly at least, are ordinary humans; but in essence its spirit belongs to the spirit which produced the pathetically serious poetic dramas of imaginary characters. From them it takes its pervasive colouring; from them is derived that peculiar laughter which, free though it may be and based on incidents of an almost farcical kind, yet assumes at times a poetic flavour and remains always beyond the reach of farce. Gilbert's own preliminary note is important. "It is absolutely essential to the success of this piece", he says,

that it should be played with the most perfect earnestness and gravity throughout. There should be no exaggeration in costume, make-up, or demeanour; and the characters, one and all, should appear to believe, throughout, in the perfect sincerity of their words and actions. Directly the actors show that they are conscious of the absurdity of their utterances the piece begins to drag.

Technically, this is the cleverest thing which Gilbert had yet done. It starts with a new device, the surprise exposition, a device which has so frequently been employed by more recent dramatists. The play opens with what seems a perfectly simple bucolic love scene between Angus and Maggie. Then enters Maggie's mother, Mrs Macfarlane:

MRS MACFARLANE. Why, Angus—Maggie, what's a' this!
ANGUS. Mistress Macfarlane, dinna be fasht wi'me; dinna think worse o'me than I deserve. I've loved your lass honestly these fifteen years, but I never plucked up the hairt to tell her so until now; and when she answered fairly, it was not in human

---

[1] *Theatrical Notes* (1893), pp. 83–8.

nature to do aught else but hold her to my hairt and place one kiss on her bonnie cheek.

MRS MACFARLANE (R.). Angus, say nae mair. My hairt is sair at losing my only bairn; but I'm nae fasht wi' ee. Thou'rt a gude lad, and it's been the hope of my widowed auld heart to see you twain one. Thou'lt treat her kindly—I ken that weel. Thou'rt a prosperous, kirk-going man, and my Meg should be a happy lass indeed. Bless thee, Angus; bless thee!

Immediately after this apparently sentimental-emotional opening comes the shock of the following:

ANGUS (C., *wiping his eyes*). Dinna heed the water in my 'ee—it will come when I'm over glad. Yes, I'm a fairly prosperous man. What wi' farmin' a bit land, and gillieing odd times, and a bit o' poachin' now and again; and what wi' my illicit whusky still—and throwin' trains off the line, that the poor distracted passengers may come to my cot, I've mair ways than one of making an honest living—and I'll work them a' nicht and day for my bonnie Meg!

MRS MACFARLANE (*seated*, R.). D'ye ken, Angus, I sometimes think that thou'rt losing some o' thine auld skill at upsetting railway trains. Thou hast not done sic a thing these sax weeks, and the cottage stands sairly in need of sic chance custom as the poor delayed passengers may bring.

MAGGIE. Nay, mither, thou wrangest him. Even noo, this very day, has he not placed twa bonnie braw sleepers across the up-line, ready for the express from Glaisgie, which is due in twa minutes or so.

This clever device gives the tone to what follows. Ingeniously Gilbert proceeds with the fortunes of Maggie and her Angus, and pursues the susceptible Cheviot Hill through his amazing jungle of amatory adventures, getting him into and out of engagements with extraordinary dexterity until, in the end, he abandons him to the arms of Miss Treherne with whom, it is discovered, he has unwittingly contracted a Scots marriage.

Already, however, by the time when *Engaged* was written Gilbert had discovered another medium of expression—one which was destined to bring him and his collaborator, Arthur Sullivan, endless fame, but which, precisely because of its success, served to deviate his attention from the ordinary drama. With *Trial by Jury* (Roy. March 1875), we may say, the Savoy operas were born; and the realm of poetic drama and of irresponsible comedy lost one of its most promising supporters. These Savoy operas, of course, do not mark any radical change in Gilbert's attitude or in his fundamental method; they too are "fairy comedies". Topsy-turvydom is as prominent here as in the earlier plays; satire at human follies, an undercurrent of pathetic seriousness and an inimitable fund of wit have combined to give them their peculiar popularity, and just such a combination rules in *The Palace of Truth*. In *Trial by Jury* we are introduced to a world in appearance like our own but unlike in thought. The Judge brings to a fitting conclusion the lyrical case:

> All the legal furies seize you!
> No proposal seems to please you,
> I can't stop up here all day,
> I must shortly go away,
> Barristers, and you, attorneys,
> Set out on your homeward journeys;
> Gentle, simple-minded Usher,
> Get you, if you like, to Russ*her*;
> Put your briefs upon the shelf,
> I will marry her myself!

Even more alike to *The Palace of Truth* is *The Sorcerer* (O.C. Nov. 1877), with its eccentric Sir Marmaduke Pointdextre and Lady Sangazure confronted by John Wellington Wells, of J. W. Wells and Co., Family Sorcerers. So soon as this last-mentioned character speaks we recognise, too, how closely Gilbert is allied to one who, had he not been stopped by an officious censorship and so forced to write *Tom Jones*, might have been the Gilbert of the eighteenth century. Gilbert is another Henry Fielding with less robustness and a greater wealth of poetic expression. Compare, for instance, these words of Wells with the auction in *The Historical Register* (H.² 1737):

MR WELLS. Yes sir, we practise Necromancy in all its branches. We've a choice assortment of wishing-cups, divining-rods, amulets, charms, and counter-charms....Our penny Curse—one of the cheapest things in the trade—is considered infallible. We have some very superior Blessings, too, but they're very little asked for. We've only sold one since Christmas—to a gentleman who bought it to send to his mother-in-law but it turned out that he was afflicted in the head, and it's been returned on our hands. But our sale of penny Curses, especially on Saturday nights, is tremendous. We can't turn 'em out fast enough.

Thus speaks Mr Wells; and here is Fielding's Mr Hen:

> Gentlemen and Ladies, this is Lot 1. A most curious Remnant of Political Honesty. Who puts it up, Gentlemen? It will make you a very good Cloke, you see its both Sides alike, so you may turn it as often as you will—Come, five Pounds for this curious Remnant; I assure you, several great Men have made their Birthday Suits out of the same Piece—It will wear for ever, and never be the worse for wearing—Five Pounds is bid—no Body more than five Pounds for this curious Piece of Political Honesty, five Pound, no more—(knocks) Lord Both-Sides. Lot 2, a most delicate Piece of Patriotism, Gentlemen, who bids? Ten Pounds for this Piece of Patriotism?...I assure you, several Gentlemen at Court have worn the same; its a quite different thing within to what it is without....You take it for the old Patriotism, whereas it is indeed like that in nothing but the Cut, but alas! Sir, there is a great Difference in the Stuff. But, Sir, I don't propose this for a Town-Suit, this is only proper for the Country; Consider, Gentlemen, what a Figure this will make at an Election—Come, five Pound—one Guinea—Put Patriotism by.

The one passage may owe nothing directly to the other, but the operation of mind is the same and the technical means used for securing the satirical effect are almost identical.

A slightly different field Gilbert turned to conquer in *H.M.S. Pinafore; or, The Lass that Loved a Sailor* (O.C. May 1878). Here the whole navy is upside down and the Captain greets his crew in recitative:

> CAPTAIN. My gallant crew, good morning.
> ALL (*saluting*). Sir, good morning!
> CAPTAIN. I hope you're all quite well.
> ALL (*as before*). Quite well; and you, sir?
> CAPTAIN. I am in reasonable health, and happy
>   To meet you all once more.
> ALL (*as before*). You do us proud, sir!

A still greater verve, a still easier flow of ridiculous rimes and eccentric ideas, have come to the author; nothing quite so good as Sir Joseph's "When I was a lad I served a term" had he introduced into any of his work. Perhaps striving to capitalise on his success Gilbert's next effort was again a sea story, *The Pirates of Penzance; or, The Slave of Duty* (O.C. April 1880), but this suffers from the comparison. Ruth's "When Frederick was a little lad" is not so fine as Sir Joseph's frank self-revelations.

With *Patience; or Bunthorne's Bride* (O.C. April 1881) a new door is opened. The caricature of certain poetic tendencies of the time is magnificently done, and an even cleverer use of rhythmic devices becomes evident:

If you're anxious for to shine in the high aesthetic line as a man
    of culture rare,
You must get up all the germs of the transcendental terms, and
    plant them everywhere.
You must lie upon the daisies and discourse in novel phrases of
    your complicated state of mind,
The meaning doesn't matter if it's only idle chatter of a transcen-
    dental kind.
    And everyone will say,
    As you walk your mystic way,
"If this young man expresses himself in terms too deep for *me*.
Why, what a singularly deep young man this deep young man
    must be!"

Patience was followed by *Iolanthe; or, The Peer and the Peri* (Savoy, Nov. 1882), in its title indicating the close connection which bound Gilbert to earlier writers of extravaganza, and in its settings—"An Arcadian Landscape" and "Palace Yard, Westminster"—showing how equally close was its connection with his own fairy plays. In *Princess Ida; or, Castle Adamant* (Savoy, Jan. 1884) the fantastic spirit has taken complete command, only to suffer a transmutation in *The Mikado; or, The Town of Titipu* (Savoy, March 1885). Deservedly *The Mikado* has become a favourite among the Gilbert and Sullivan operas. A free fancy riots here in a maze of intricated and varied measures. From the lyric movement

of "A wandering minstrel I" through the grotesque narrative
of "Our great Mikado, virtuous man" and the satirically
lively "As some day it may happen that a victim must be
found" to the delightfully inane "On a tree by a river"
and the grotesquely ridiculous "There is a beauty in the
bellow of the blast" the author moves with undiminishing
ease and skill.

The manner in which Gilbert sought to avoid self-imitation
is indicated by the production of *Ruddigore; or, The Witch's
Curse* (Savoy, Jan. 1887) and *The Yeomen of the Guard; or,
The Merryman and his Maid* (Savoy, Oct. 1888). The latter,
too, shows clearly enough the serious element which, given
the slightest excuse, was prepared to rise above Gilbert's
eccentric jesting. The figure of Jack Point may be related
thus to little Vavir in *Broken Hearts*; Vavir's dying speech
has a definite relationship to Point's last song ere he falls,
insensible, on the stage:

> It is sung to the moon
> By a love-lorn loon
> Who fled from the mocking throng, O!
> It's the song of a merryman, moping mum,
> Whose soul was sad, and whose glance was glum
> Who sipped no sup and who craved no crumb,
> As he sighed for the love of a ladye!

Jack Point may be a jester and his words may have a comic
ring; but again the merriment is born of a universal sadness.

The Gondoliers; or, The King of Barataria (Savoy, Dec.
1889) came next, and here the laughter has regained its sway
in a world where

> Lord Chancellors were cheap as sprats,
> And Bishops in their shovel hats
> Were plentiful as tabby cats—
> In point of fact, too many.

Then once more a return in *Utopia Limited; or, The Flowers
of Progress* (Savoy, Oct. 1893), an opera in which Gilbert
reveals clearly what may be called the philosophic basis
of his work. The state where "a Despotism tempered by

Dynamite provides—the most satisfactory description of a ruler" is not merely a joke; it is the logical creation of Gilbert's thoughts on humanity. "Properly considered," says the King, "what a farce life is, to be sure!

> First you're born—and I'll be bound you
> Find a dozen strangers round you.
> "Hallo," cries the new-born baby,
> "Where's my parents? which may they be?"
> > Awkward silence—no reply—
> > Puzzled baby wonders why!
> Father rises, bows politely—
> Mother smiles (but not too brightly)—
> Doctor mumbles like a dumb thing—
> Nurse is busy mixing something—
> > Every symptom tends to show
> > You're decidedly *de trop*—
>
> You grow up and you discover
> What it is to be a lover.
> Some young lady is selected—
> Poor, perhaps, but well-connected,
> > Whom you hail (for Love is blind)
> > As the Queen of fairy kind.
> Though she's plain—perhaps unsightly,
> Makes her face up—laces tightly,
> In her form your fancy traces
> All the gifts of all the graces.
> > Rivals none the maiden woo,
> > So you take her and she takes you!
>
> Ten years later—Time progresses—
> Sours your temper—thins your tresses;
> Fancy, then, her chain relaxes;
> Rates are facts and so are taxes.
> > Fairy Queen's no longer young—
> > Fairy Queen has got a tongue.
> Twins have probably intruded—
> Quite unbidden—just as you did—
> They're a source of care and trouble—
> Just as you were—only double.
> > Comes at last the final stroke—
> > Time has had his little joke!

Like this King, Gilbert, who saw so clearly the follies and the miseries of the world, always liked "to look on the humorous side of things".

With *Utopia Limited*, as expressing the inner mood from which Gilbert's fantastic conceptions proceeded, we may take our leave of him—by far the greatest writer whom the English stage had attracted throughout the entire course of the nineteenth century. That his genius was a peculiar one, that he stands apart from the prevailing realistic movement of his time and that he abandoned the ordinary stage for the stage of comic opera, cannot in any wise take from his importance. His influence, if directly it proved but slight, indirectly was enormous. From his work sprang the new comedy of manners, and in particular the eccentric Wildian comedy, during the last ten years of the century. Nor has his power entirely waned. New York, in *Of Thee I Sing*, *As Thousands Cheer* and *Let 'Em Eat Cake*, recently witnessed a revival of musical satire which owed not a trifle to Gilbert's example.

2. *The Continuance of the Realistic Drama*

During the years that Gilbert was thus opening up fresh vistas for the comic dramatist, the realistic movement continued on its steady course towards an impossible goal. A very few authors, mostly members of the earlier extravaganza school, endeavoured to vie with him in producing comedies, but, lacking his grace and wit, they all miserably failed. One example here will suffice. Gilbert à Beckett[1] essays a fairly clever theme in *The Last of the Legends; or, The Baron, the Bride, and the Battery* (Ch. X. Sept. 1873). Introducing a number of characters supposed to belong to the Middle Ages, he contrasts these with another person who is a tourist of the year 2100 come to view some medieval ruins. The story is quite in the Gilbertian manner (and since this play appeared two years before *Trial by Jury* we get another indication of the way in which Gilbert was influenced by his contemporaries), but the ingenuity both in intrigue and in

[1] On him see Arthur à Beckett, *Gilbert Abbott à Beckett as a Dramatist* (*The Theatre*, N.S. ix, March 1887, 146–53), A. W. à Beckett, *The à Becketts of Punch* (1903).

juxtaposition of conflicting thoughts is almost entirely absent. Where Gilbert's work has the immediate touch of authentic genius, à Beckett's is laboured and forced. All we may say is that, in such works as *In the Clouds: A Glimpse of Utopia* (Alex. Dec. 1873), à Beckett proved himself a link uniting the extravagant world of Planché and the fantastic realm of Gilbertian opera.

Within these ten years from 1870 to 1880 the old melodrama still continued to make its pristine appeal, and the lesser houses of entertainment revelled in their bold bad villains and their impossibly virtuous heroines. How incredibly poverty-stricken in style were many of those pieces cannot be appreciated save by those who have waded through the volumes of *Lacy's Acting Edition* or the manuscripts in the Lord Chamberlain's collection of plays, many of which never saw the light of day in printed form. At the Grecian, audiences revelled in such dismalities as Paul Meritt's *Glin Gath; or, The Man in the Cleft* (Grec. April 1872); in the provinces spectators groaned under works such as T. A. Palmer's *East Lynne* (Nottingham, Nov. 1874). The latter is interesting both for its wretchedness of dialogue and for its method of adaptation; Palmer has seen fit to put in brackets after many of his speeches page references to the novel, from which, of course, his plot is taken, as thus:

LEVINSON (*leaning over her chair*). His wife, ah, Isabel, there is the bitterness in reflection, that you *are his*; had we listened to our hearts in those days we might have been happier now, you and I were created to love each other, and (ISABEL *rises*) I would have declared the love that was consuming me, but—....I know the fault was mine, I might then have won you and been happy. (165).[1]

Many of the plays, even those given at more important theatres, were, like G. C. Herbert's *Our Bitterest Foe: An Incident of 1870* (Glo. April 1874), incredibly stupid in theme and execution. Even at the Court, where Gilbert was serving his apprenticeship, audiences could delight in such a work as H. T. Craven's *Coals of Fire* (Court, Nov. 1871), a silly

---

[1] Act I, scene ii.

drama which tells how Wilfred Jormal jilts Ella for Edith, how his father is discovered to be a swindler, how Edith falls in love with Ella's brother and how Ella thus has her revenge. We may remember, too, that it was this decade which produced Leopold Lewis's famous melodrama of *The Bells* (Lyc. Nov. 1871), for long Irving's most famous instrument.

This kind of drama, on the other hand, was, in the main, moving towards newer things. In such a play as *Gilded Youth* (T.R. Brighton, Sept. 1872) by Sir C. L. Young, although the basis is melodrama, it is melodrama chastened and striving towards a fresh goal. The tone is modern, and the actions are provided with a psychological basis. Still further, the farcical underplot which was the almost constant accompaniment of the older plays of this type has here been replaced by a tone of bantering light comedy. The same development may be observed in other works by this writer, such as the "dramatic sketch" *Yellow Roses* (High Wycombe, Jan. 1878), and the comedietta *Petticoat Perfidy* (Court, May 1885). The latter is particularly interesting since it carries a stage further the social comedy element introduced into *Gilded Youth* and achieves some real success in character-drawing with its Mrs Montrevor and its Mrs Jones. The latter, suspecting that the former has robbed her of the affections of Lord Fabian, dupes her into sitting in an opera-box with a tailor. To gain vengeance, Mrs Montrevor causes her maid Juliette to pose as a Russian princess and so puts Mrs Jones completely to shame. In the end both are discomfited, for it is discovered that Juliette is the real flame of Lord Fabian.

The work of Sir Charles Young, although forgotten to-day, has considerable historical interest. In *Shadows* (P'cess, May 1871), for example, he tries an interesting experiment. The action is contemporary, but in order to demonstrate the links which connect generation with generation the author has introduced a prologue set in 1660. The device is similar to that used in reverse wise by John Drinkwater in *Mary Queen of Scots*. Of all this writer's work only one play is at all remembered now. In *Jim the Penman* (H. April 1886) is told the story of apparently respectable and philanthropic James Ralston, who in reality is a swindler leagued with Baron Hauteville. This rogue's security is threatened by the arrival of Louis Percival, a former dupe, and shattered by the testimony of his wife. *Jim the Penman* is a purposeful melodrama not unworthy to stand beside Taylor's *The Ticket-of-Leave Man* and Jones's *The Silver King*.

The old melodramatic devices might remain, but the essential spirit, as here, was changing. C. H. Hazlewood was thus impelled, in *The Lost Wife; or, A Husband's Confession* (Brit. Aug. 1871), to introduce, amidst a series of improbable adventures which end among the bushrangers of New South Wales, a fully motivated villain similar to Luke the Labourer.[1] Jonas Fletcher here pursues Sir Michael Saxilby with his vengeance, but he has been sufficiently wronged to become more than a stock evildoer. Thus, too, in George Roberts's *Behind the Curtain* (Holb. April 1870), although the technique is old, a certain freshness of spirit is evident in the handling of the subject. The author shows his indebtedness to the past by falling back, at the close of his play, upon those lengthy stage directions which had so pleased a Fitzball and a Dibdin:

BOLTON *makes a feint of taking notes from his pocket, while* TWIST *does the same with respect to will, when* BOLTON *suddenly turns upon him, and after a short struggle throws him,* L.—*as* BOLTON *is kneeling on* TWIST *and takes will,* OLIVE *rushes forward and snatches it from* BOLTON—*picture*—ALL *advance from doorway*—BOLTON *turns upon* OLIVE—*short struggle*—OLIVE *throws* BOLTON *off,* C.—POLICE *enter down steps whom* D'ARCY *has called on*—*they seize* BOLTON—*he struggles, throws them off and rushes into chamber,* R. 3 E. *followed by* OLIVE—*a pause*—*report of pistol heard,* R.—GRACE *and* POLLY *scream*—*music throughout.*

In spite of this, the theme has a certain vitality and the choice of a stage world for milieu is something new.[2]

---

[1] *E.N.D.* i, 116–17.

[2] Incidentally may be noted the popularity of stage material during this time, as in *Behind a Mask* (Roy. March 1871) by B. H. Dixon and A. Wood, and of police themes, as in Wybert Reeve's *The Dead Witness; or, Sin and its Shadow* (Sheffield, Nov. 1863). *Masks and Faces* and *The Ticket-of-Leave Man* no doubt had much to do with the exploitation of these themes.

During this time the more important works of the contemporary realists in Paris were gradually becoming known, and through this influence the already awakening spirit of the English drama was being impelled still further along fresh lines. Campbell Clarke proved in this sphere an able intermediary. In *Awaking* (Gai. Dec. 1872) he takes the *Marcel* of J. Sandeau and C. A. de Courcelle, and, even though he does alter, succeeds in retaining the more important elements of the original play. The general idea has been preserved intact and the drama remains, what it was, a study in psychology, not without its adumbrations of Pirandellesque methods. The story tells how Victor Tremaine, who has accidentally killed his child several years before, suffers from an obsession, believing that his wife hates him bitterly. The wife, Dr Merridew and his brother Harold decide on an experiment. They bring Victor back secretly to his house and surround him with newspapers and other objects belonging to the time when the accident occurred. The endeavour has for its object, of course, the preparing of the man's mind for the quiet reception of his wife. Less successful was Clarke's version of the *Monsieur Alphonse* by Dumas *fils*. In this play, which he entitled *Love and Honour* (T.R. Birmingham, June 1875; Glo. Aug. 1875), the English adapter, no doubt influenced by contemporary popular taste, has completely altered the essential theme of the French play. In the hands of Dumas, *Monsieur Alphonse* essays to do what Kotzebue tried in *Menschenhass und Reue*—the preparing of such a plot and the creation of such characters as might render a plea for forgiveness of adultery appreciated by an ordinary audience. Clarke, however, evidently feeling that this would not be immediately palatable in a London theatre, has taken away all guilt from the heroine through the introduction of a sham-marriage episode. As a result, the essential basis of its action is completely cut away and any interest we might have had in the plot vanishes. Unquestionably, this version is a failure; but it did serve to introduce something new, and the very cause of its failure gives it considerable historical interest.

The development of the new note in drama is, perhaps, to be seen most clearly in the change almost everywhere observable throughout the realm of light comedy. Already this new note has been commented on in connection with the work of Sir C. L. Young, but to him it is by no means confined. Fred W. Broughton shows something of it in *Withered Leaves* (Sheffield, April 1875) while *Ruth's Romance*, albeit somewhat hackneyed in theme, captures the same mood. The heroine here is a bright and sprightly Ruth, a young lady of fashion who has been forced by her father's will to spend some weeks in the country engaged in farm pursuits. With her lives her sister and her brother-in-law, but this pair, because of the brother-in-law's (Captain Wilton's) debts, remain incognito and as obscure as may be. With Ruth, Jack Dudley falls in love, but, ere the course of his passion may run smooth, he has to surmount various obstacles—the most important being due to the fact that, hearing Ruth and Wilton in private conversation, he believes they are lovers and imagines the worst. The easy dalliance of Broughton's dialogue, though William Archer failed to see it, was to be of profound value for the later theatre.[1]

The increased technical skill of these dramatists of the seventies is shown, too, by such a play as Walter Lisle's *The Love Test* (Gai. June 1873) where a half-hour of badinage is kept up, uninterruptedly and without action, by two characters only. For a playwright of 1830 such a task would have been a hard one, but Lisle succeeds here in keeping our interest intent on his lively Mrs Leslie and his honest Captain Beaumont. *The Love Test* is only one of many such single-act comediettas which, introducing only two characters, sought to concentrate attention on character and dialogue instead of on action. Most of them, certainly, like S. Theyre Smith's *Happy Pair* (St J. March 1868), simply ring the changes on domestic infelicities;[2] but the commonness of themes and persons should not conceal from us the very important training ground they provided for those later dramatists who,

---

[1] See W. Archer, *English Dramatists of To-day* (1882), pp. 87–94.
[2] On Smith see W. Archer, *op. cit.* pp. 328–33.

abandoning the swift movement of the melodramatic stage, were determined to evoke dramatic excitement out of ordinary thoughts and commonplace motives. In two respects particularly did these plays thus give assistance towards the building up of a new drama. When only two characters appear on the stage throughout the course of a play, obviously that play, if it is to have any hope of success, must be dominated by an idea. It may be simply the idea of a wife's revolt, as in *Happy Pair*, or that of elderly love-making, as in *The Love Test*; but, however vague and however trite, there has to be introduced something of which most of the earlier farces were entirely innocent. Secondly, in such plays the dramatist must concentrate on style. His dialogue has to have verve, logical development and point. Again, when we turn for comparison to the older plays, we find that frequently a playwright, feeling his dialogue grow weak, took the easiest course and allowed horse-play to make up for his lack of wit. Of this expedient the new dramatists refuse themselves permission to make use; they are willing to restrict themselves to a bare interior, a couple of chairs and two persons who, if they move at all, do so only to settle in their chairs again. The light easy style, as exemplified in the plays mentioned above, in C. M. Rae's *Follow the Leader* (Ch. X. April 1873) or in J. W. Jones's *On an Island* (Bradford, March 1879), where Jack and Mildred, accidentally abandoned on an island in Windermere, patch up an old quarrel, has triumphed over farcical incident.

As yet, of course, comedy had not been able to cast over the sentimentally rosy colouring which had rouged its cheeks since the eighteenth century. A new light comedy was unquestionably coming into existence; but so far it remained heavily trammelled by that sickly emotionalism which had been passed down from Cumberland and Kelly. The union of the two qualities is well to be seen in the work of James Albery.[1] Everyone knows the title at least of his most famous play, *Two Roses* (Vaud. June 1870), a drama second to none

[1] See *The Dramatic Works of James Albery*, ed. by Wyndham Albery (2 vols. 1939).

in this period both for influence and for popularity. So far as plot is concerned, Albery here is content to follow along time-worn lines. The central figure, if not the hero, is Digby Grant, a decayed gentleman who has not been too proud to accept presents from Jenkins and loans from Jack Wyatt. Suddenly, however, he finds himself—or thinks he finds himself—the possessor of an income totalling £10,000 a year, and at once he breaks off the engagement between Jack and his daughter Lotty. Fortune in comedy has usually a trick in store for persons who act in this wise, and, by the time the third act is reached, Grant discovers to his dismay that the £10,000 a year income really belongs to the poor, rejected Caleb Deecie, a blind youth who has been passionately devoted to Grant's other daughter, Ida. The story, as will be realised, is a tissue of episodes, each one of which had been consecrated by frequent use; any claim Albery may have cannot rest on his theme. This theme, however, has associated with it a number of figures interestingly drawn. Digby Grant has personality, even if that personality is of a somewhat unenviable sort. Similar characters have been introduced in a variety of plays from 1870 on to our own day—sometimes, as here, he is a decayed gentleman living on his social position, sometimes he is an impoverished artist, living on his reputation for genius—but, whatever his actual status may be, he displays the familiar contempt of money and willingness to sponge on others. Save when such a character is presented in a new light, we have become a trifle tired of his eccentricities now, but again we must remember that in 1870, so far as the stage was concerned, he had all the virtues of novelty. He represented an entirely fresh comic type, and it must be confessed that Albery has succeeded in wresting from him a number of scenes which, even to-day, still possess comic vitality. Jenkins, too, is an individuality and a creation; while, if the one lover, Jack Wyatt, is somewhat conventional, the other, Caleb Deecie, has an engaging and sympathetic presence. One of Albery's great assets clearly lay in his power of drawing character.

In addition to this, he shared with others of his time a new skill in the writing of dialogue. When Mrs Cupps, Grant's landlady, presents him with her bill, that gentleman airily waves her aside. "And yet", says Mrs Cupps, "you pay away money without occasion. Last night you gave my pot-man sixpence to fetch you a cab—but I must go without!" To this Grant replies:

> Mrs Cupps, you do not understand the feelings of a gentleman. I cannot be under obligations to a potman—absurd! Your case is different. There's your account—I acknowledge the debt—I do not dispute it, or attempt to deduct overcharges, or take off a discount for cash like a common cad. If you bring it to me next year, I shall still acknowledge it; I can do no more—I am a gentleman, I can do no less.

There is evident here a nice sense of values—character values as well as those that appertain to dramatic rhythm and comic purpose. A disciple of Robertson, Albery makes marked advances and definitely leads the comic stage towards the plays of Wilde.

With these two essential qualities, it may seem strange that Albery did not succeed in doing more for the stage than he actually succeeded in accomplishing. The reason of his failure lay, first of all, in that weakness of plot-constructing power to which reference has been made. Throughout the whole of his dramatic career this weakness is evident and possibly because of it Albery turned so freely to the French for his later themes. *The Spendthrift; or, The Scrivener's Daughter* (Olym. May 1875) thus might have been a really good comedy had it not been marred by the introduction of a series of utterly impossible and improbable situations. The second defect lay in the lack of unity in Albery's aims. Throughout Gilbert's writings we may trace a consistent progress; pathos may predominate in one, satire in another, light jesting in a third—but the pathos, the satire and the jesting are all demonstrably the varied expressions of one man's personality. Personality it was that Albery lacked. At one moment he is penning sentimental comedy of *Two Roses* type; next he is trying to pursue Gilbert with poetic fantasies like *Oriana* (Glo. Feb. 1873) and *The Will of Wise King Kino* (P'cess,

Sept. 1873), showing in this how far he fell below Gilbert's easily attained eminence; next he turns to French sources and out of *Les dominos roses* he fashions that play, *The Pink Dominos* (Crit. March 1877) which seemed so *risqué* to the society of its day, and in which the sentimental comedy is laid aside in favour of a rather mawkish cynicism; next again we have him turning to the serious plays of Sardou and Augier, making a *Crisis* (H. Dec. 1878) out of *Les Fourcham-baults*. Lack of a central purpose and not creative versatility explains this strange variety. "Most undisciplined" of the better dramatists of his day, Joseph Knight considered him,[1] and the criticism is just. William Archer expressed a similar opinion about his work. "I should like," he wrote,

in conclusion, to sum up Mr Albery's literary character in a neatly rounded paragraph, but it somehow does not lend itself readily to neatly-rounded treatment. It is too full of contradictions and paradoxes. His mind has so many different veins and strata that a whole case-full of specimens would be necessary to present an adequate sample of it.[2]

In this his talent proved but a reflex of the spirit of his age. The theatre was in a state of transition. New ideas were germinating; new devices were being tried out; new experiments were being made in choice of theme and of character; but so far there was but little sense of conscious direction. The audiences had increased and, as all contemporaries noted, fresh interest was being taken in things theatrical, but the spectators' tastes were mixed and no one could clearly diagnose what they would desire. The raw material, as it were, had been prepared for the modern drama, but the modern spirit had not yet come to form that raw material into the finished fabrics, the comfortable and uncomfortable woollens of the problem play, the delicate silks of the new comedy of manners.

[1] *Theatrical Notes* (1893), p. 37.
[2] *English Dramatists of To-day* (1882), pp. 85–6.

CHAPTER VI

JONES AND PINERO: PLAYS OF THE EIGHTIES

1. *The Turn of the Tide*

IN the year 1882 appeared a remarkable volume. William Archer was at that time a young enthusiast for the theatre and *English Dramatists of To-day* was his first published book. So many works of kindred sort have succeeded this essay of 1882 that maybe we shall be apt to overlook its real significance unless we bear firmly in our minds the thought that it was the only study up to that date which deliberately attempted to provide a critical survey of contemporary dramatic writing. There had been, of course, hundreds of volumes written on stage affairs, but almost all of these were either biographical and anecdotal (lives of actors and the like) or historical. The only predecessors of Archer's series of critical estimates were the collected reviews of men like Hazlitt and Leigh Hunt, and those, while they succeeded in presenting a clear and vivid picture of the contemporary stage, did not have the same comprehensive aim as he held before himself in the composition of his work.

The publication of *English Dramatists of To-day*, therefore, marks a distinct level reached by the theatre of the early eighties; it reflects the new living interest which had been awakened among thinking people in the fortunes of the English drama. This living interest may be amply traced, too, in the periodical writings of the day. From 1850 to 1870 the newspapers and journals had tended monotonously to echo those complaints concerning dramatic decline which had been so piteous in earlier years.[1] In 1871 Tom Taylor was engaged in shedding many tears over the poor dejected stage

---

[1] *E.N.D.* i, 58–77.

of his time.[1] Long runs, show and machinery induced his severest comments and, characteristically, he contrasted present with past unfavourably. "Till the present generation", he opined, "the theatre was pre-eminent among amusements, and commanded attention and interest from all classes, the most instructed and cultivated, as well as the most high-bred." Even at the very close of this decade there were men still prepared to praise the "palmy" days of English drama between 1800 and 1825.[2] "With the rapidity of a whirlwind," wrote another, forgetting earlier complaints, "and with much of its wildness, a sudden passion has arisen, to run down our English Theatres, our Managers, and our actors in a breath."[3] H. F. Hyde, a few years later, referred to the repeated "remarks on the dearth of dramatic authors",[4] a fact accepted as unchallenged in *The Theatre* for 1877.[5]

Archer's book and the periodical writings of the eighties introduce us to something new, to an entirely fresh approach. For Archer the terms "yesterday" and "to-day" mean, not "flourishing" and "moribund", as they had done for earlier critics, but "outworn" and "vital" respectively. Suddenly men came to the realisation that the dramatist's worth was beginning to be appreciated and that "men of the mightiest intellect" were coming to devote themselves to the stage.[6] That "the attitude of Literature towards the stage" was "now more friendly than it used to be" was recognised by Henry Morley in 1880,[7] and, speaking thus at University College, London, he drew attention to the fact that, on the

[1] Article by Tom Taylor in *Dark Blue*, discussed in *The Era*, xxxiii, Aug. 27, 1871, 11.
[2] *The Theatre*, N.S. ii, June 1879, 296–300.
[3] *The Era*, xxxiii, Aug. 20, 1871, 12.
[4] *Id.* xxxvii, May 2, 1875.
[5] N.S. i, July 1877, 343–4, where the long run is held responsible. Other references of a similar kind may be found *id.* N.S. ii, Feb. 1879, 1–4 and 14–17; March 1879, 71–5 and 107–8; *The Era*, xli, Jan. 26, 1879, 12–13.
[6] *The Era*, xli, Feb. 9, 1879, 12; xlii, Nov. 2, 1879, 12. W. S. Gilbert, in a letter to *The Times* (Feb. or March 1879) declared that it was "most unfair" to require authors of established reputation to submit their plays "in a complete form" (that is to say, in a matinée production). A new attitude is apparent in his remarks.
[7] Cf. *The Era*, xlii, Jan. 11, 1880, 3.

night of his lecture, there were nine original plays being acted in London as against six taken from the French. This, he observed, was "a change and an improvement upon the state of things two years ago".[1] As yet, of course, there was no general agreement concerning a genuine dramatic revival, and some persons continued to murmur either against the literary men of the time or against the supposedly unfair conditions which prevented these literary men from giving their best to the stage. Writing to *The Times* in January 1880, Henry Irving deemed the "dearth of good dramatists" to be "unquestionable", proposing as the reason that "although many people are anxious to write for the stage, few will take the trouble to study the technique which is essential to an acting play".[2] In this judgment he was supported by J. Palgrave Simpson who thought that "it is not dramatists who are needed...but dramatists who...know their business",[3] but countered by F. C. Burnand who declared that

there's no dearth of authors, but there's a deuce of a difficulty in getting them to write. Those who get their living by it...are all hard at work from year's end to year's end, not only at plays, mind you, but at half-a-hundred other things—essays, articles, magazines, books. The current literature of the day takes it out of them, so to speak, and leaves them small time for really important work.

By 1883, however, the "remarkable improvement in the condition of the English drama", the beginnings of which had been traced by Henry Morley, had become indisputable.[4] "The British Drama," he said,

is no longer written by Frenchmen; and no longer are plays presented as New and Original which are not adapted, only taken, from the French.... It seems as though the English dramatist instead of stealing the Frenchman's plays ready-made, has rather

---

[1] In the same year (*The Era*, xlii, Aug. 22, 1880, 3) Frank Freeland took up Gilbert's complaint and emphasised the fact that while managers were prepared to take the work of known authors, the untried dramatist (unless he had money to put his play into matinée performance) was doomed to silence. See *supra*, pp. 59.

[2] See *The Theatre*, N.S. i, Jan. 1880, 1–11.

[3] *Id.*

[4] *The Saturday Review*, lxi, Nov. 3, 1883, 364.

awakened to the greater advantage of borrowing the Frenchman's tools and of using them to make his own. The recent raising of the general level of the contemporary British drama is due to the adoption of French methods and customs.

The passing of but a few seasons during these adventurous years wrought strange marvels. "The extraordinary number of new plays produced" was noted by *The Saturday Review* in its comprehensive survey of the season 1887–8;[1] this was regarded as evidence of an increased "dramatic literary industry", warranting employment of the phrase "Renaissance of the Drama".[2]

In viewing this advance, of course, we must bear in mind two facts—first, that, while a fresh technique was entering in and while some revolutionary experiments were being made, the old guard continued to hold its own with the greater public, and, secondly, that many critics, championed by Clement Scott, did their best to stem the rising tide.[3] The results of a competition organised by *Truth* in the summer of 1884 are, in this connection, highly illuminating. The popular favourites were duly graded, and the voting provided the following list. Three men came in the "50" class— H. J. Byron (57), T. W. Robertson (56) and W. S. Gilbert (51); four were in the 40's—W. G. Wills (48), Tom Taylor (47), Lord Lytton and Dion Boucicault (both 45); two in the 30's—G. R. Sims (36) and Charles Reade (33); and two in the 20's—J. Albery (24) and F. C. Burnand (23). Nothing could indicate more clearly the general tastes of the public. On the other hand, the playbills of these years tell the story of advance. The season 1887–8 saw the appearance of Mrs Beere's productions of F. C. Grove's *As in a Looking Glass* and Mrs Praed's *Ariane*, and of Olga Nethersole's production of *The Dean's Daughter* by Sydney Grundy and F. C. Philips.[4] The following years witnessed the appearance of A. W. Pinero's *The Profligate* (Gar. 1889), H. A. Jones's *Wealth* (H. 1889), and *The People's Idol* (Olym. 1890), wherein

[1] *The Saturday Review*, lxvi, Aug. 4, 1888, 147.
[2] *Id.* lxvi, Dec. 8, 1888, 676.
[3] See *supra*, p. 23.
[4] On these see *The Theatre*, N.S. xxiii, May 1894, 239–47.

W. Barrett and V. Widnell dealt with the question of capital and labour, a theme likewise taken up by W. Bourne in *Work and Wages* (Hanley, 1890; Pav. 1890) and by W. J. Patmore in *Capital and Labour* (Pav. 1891).[1] About the same time L. N. Parker treated the theme of illicit love tragically in *The Sequel* (Vaud. 1891) and W. Jones discussed hereditary insanity in *The Scapegoat* (Glo. 1891). It was all of this which made Clement Scott feel it his bounden duty to speak out boldly. "I can see no value", he said,

in a play that only provokes disgust—no pity, no love, no charity, no mercy, no tenderness, no nobility—only cowardice, meanness, and horror.[2]

Such plays, he thought, were ruining the stage.

2. *Henry Arthur Jones*

If we refer back to the *Truth* competition, it will be observed that of the eleven favourites recorded there William Archer dismissed five in a single chapter devoted to the "dramatists of yesterday"—Robertson, Taylor, Lytton, Boucicault and Reade. His own catalogue includes sixteen playwrights, among whom appear the other six from the 1884 competition. This leaves ten whom, although not voted for heavily by the readers of *Truth*, Archer would place among the "dramatists of to-day". Some of these we have already encountered as representative dramatists of the seventies—Broughton, Meritt and Smith; the others are Sydney Grundy, Bronson Howard, H. A. Jones, H. C. Merivale, A. W. Pinero, Robert Reece, Alfred Tennyson and W. G. Wills.

Whatever shortcomings Archer may have had as a critic, his youthful acumen is ably demonstrated by his inclusion of Jones and Pinero among his company of major writers, for neither had, before 1882, done much to merit such a choice. Cleverly and keenly Archer sensed their potentialities.

[1] On this subject of labour and strikes see *The Theatre*, N.S. xxi, Feb. 1893, 99. George Moore's *The Strike at Arlingford* appeared at the Opera Comique in 1893.

[2] *Why do we go to the Play?* (*The Theatre*, N.S. xi, March 1888, 117–26).

"Though neither long nor eventful," he wrote, "the career of Mr Jones as a dramatist has been promising",[1] and this promise gave him hope for the future. Up to that time Jones had given to the stage *Hearts of Oak* (Exeter, May 1879), *Harmony Restored* (Grand, Leeds, Aug. 1879), *Elopement* (Oxford, Aug. 1879), *It's Only Round the Corner* (Exeter, Dec. 1879), *A Clerical Error* (Court, Oct. 1879), *An Old Master* (P'cess, Nov. 1880), *His Wife* (S.W. April 1881), and *Home Again* (Oxford, Sept. 1881).[2] Of these, Archer knew only three—a couple of comediettas and the dramatisation of a novel by Anthony Hope; yet, from such limited knowledge, he divined what we, with our advantage in time, recognise as among Jones's most valuable assets—"a good deal of culture and a great deal of earnest aspiration".[3]

Two forces moulded Jones's apprentice efforts—the influence of Robertson and the less tangible influence of contemporary melodrama, and of these perhaps the latter is the more important. Throughout the whole of his career he found that the serious theme provided him with the greatest opportunity for the expression of his dramatic interests. True, he could on occasion turn out a comedy-farce like *The Deacon* (Shaft. Aug. 1890) and a comedy of manners such as *The Liars* (Crit. Oct. 1897), but these were not his most characteristic plays; his early work is best represented in *The Silver King* (P'cess, Nov. 1882) and his later in *Michael and his Lost Angel* (Lyc. Jan. 1896).

In his youth Jones was thus trained in the melodramatic tradition. *Hearts of Oak* (Exeter, May 1879) moves along a path trodden by countless feet since the beginning of the nineteenth century. The large legacy concealed in an ancient manor had served many another dramatist, and Jones makes no more startling use of it than his companions had done.

---

[1] *Op. cit.* p. 220.
[2] On Jones's dramatic work see R. A. Cordell, *Henry Arthur Jones and the Modern Drama* (1932), D. A. Jones, *The Life and Letters of Henry Arthur Jones* (1930), P. Shorey, *Henry Arthur Jones* (1925), and W. A. L. Bettany, *The Drama of Modern England as viewed by Mr H. A. Jones* (*The Theatre*, N.S. xxii, 1893, 203–9). His plays are, of course, discussed in all volumes dealing with the "dramatic renaissance".
[3] *Op. cit.* p. 225.

Grandfather Prettyjohn, cynically wise though he be, is a
stock character; the love of Kitty Prettyjohn for the ne'er-
do-well Ned Devenish runs roughly in conventional manner;
and the villain, Mr Cornelius, differs from other villains in
nothing save that he has the grace to show faint twinges
of conscience. *The Silver King*, written in collaboration with
Henry Herman, belongs to the same school; it certainly would
never have been composed had Tom Taylor not penned
The Ticket-of-Leave Man in 1863. This, of course, does not
mean that *The Silver King* possesses no merit. It is, indeed,
a well-constructed and interesting play of its kind; but its
kind is that of melodrama. Wilfred Denver, like the hero of
Taylor's play, is cast among evil companions and barely
succeeds in escaping the clutches of the law. Eventually he
finds himself in America and returns to England as a wealthy
man to wreak vengeance on his foes and relieve the distress
of his poverty-stricken wife. Dark villainy, sentimental pathos
and a dash of comedy are employed here to build up an
atmosphere which, although it bears the semblance of reality,
is demonstrably theatrical.

   The Silver King presents to us two of the qualities destined
to be the most clearly marked in Jones's later writings—
a desire to treat certain social problems seriously and a tendency to infuse into this treatment much of an artificial and
melodramatic flavour. Of these, *Saints and Sinners* (Margate,
Sept. 1884; Vaud. Sept. 1884) may be taken as an example.
The preface to this play clearly indicates the author's desire
to enlarge the sphere of dramatic material and to bring to the
drama of his time a sense of artistic and philosophic purpose.
In so far, Jones was doing, earlier than Pinero, what the
latter accomplished in *The Second Mrs Tanqueray* (St J.
1893). Indeed, he went further, for whereas Pinero restricted
himself to purely social problems and to the delineation of
character, Jones here made a plea for the introduction into
the theatre of larger problems still, of questions not concerned
with man's relation to man but of those where man's relation
to God was the object of enquiry. Bold as this endeavour
was, however, Jones failed in two ways. First of all, here as

elsewhere, he was apt to interpret religious problems in a material way. His interest is not in faith and pious rapture but in sectarian conventions and the outward manifestations of piety. The beliefs of a particular church concern him little; his mind is mightily occupied with the social results of the clash between church and chapel. Secondly, because of his training in melodrama, Jones constantly falsifies and makes artificial both his situations and his characters. *Saints and Sinners*, which, to be effective, ought to have been etched in delicate shades, becomes monotonously crude with its violent contrasts. The story tells of Jacob Fletcher, Minister of the Bethel Chapel, Steepleford. This man's daughter, Letty, a good-natured girl weary of her daily round of dull respectability, is entrapped by the villain, Captain Eustace Fanshawe. With the aid of George Kingsmill, Letty's faithful lover, Jacob succeeds in releasing her; but in the meantime rumours of her escapade have been bruited abroad. At his chapel Samuel Hoggard, a sanctimonious money-grabber, stands out against Jacob and gets him hounded out of his position. The last scene shows Letty miserably dying. The play is unquestionably an interesting one, but its effect becomes weakened because of its emphasis on social conventions and because of its sentimentally melodramatic colouring. "If ever there was a devil on the face of this earth," says Leeson, Fanshawe's servant, "it's Captain Eustace Fanshawe!" and that gentleman himself thus soliloquises:

And I might have been a good man, I suppose—if I could have chosen my own father and mother, and if everything and every creature I've met, from my cradle upwards hadn't pushed me to the bad. If, instead of meeting that other woman ten years ago, I had met with Letty Fletcher—What's the good of wishing? After all, there's a great comfort in being out-and-out wicked—it's like being soaked through, you can defy the elements.

No black-whiskered villain of 1830 could have expressed himself with greater assurance. Indeed, had we met with this speech out of its context, we should hardly have guessed that it came from a play which may be regarded as one of the first of modern English problem dramas.

The sentimentalism which underlies *Saints and Sinners* finds even clearer expression in a number of plays written about this time—notably in *Sweet Will* (New Club, C.G. March 1887). Here Will Darbyshire loves Judith Loveless, but refuses to reveal his adoration because he has to go to a fever-infested district of the Orient in order to provide an income for his old mother. Just as our feelings are at the point of being hopelessly harrowed, a *deus ex machina* (in the shape of a Chicago friend) makes a gesture, if not an appearance, by sending him a present of 50,000 dollars. Joy in his heart, sweet Will tells Judith he loves her and wedding bells begin to peal in the distance. It is all very pretty and all very absurd.

But if one part of *Saints and Sinners* finds exaggerated expression in *Sweet Will*, another, and a more important part, is carried to extremes in Jones's strangest play, *The Tempter* (H. Sept. 1893)—a still more courageous effort to establish a new verse drama. The effort proved futile and even disastrous, yet nevertheless by making it Jones showed that he had a vision beyond that of Pinero. Where the latter reached a culmination of artistic striving in the naturalistic social drama, Jones, in spite of his often petty and querulous girding at Ibsen, proved himself anxious to get further than mere naturalism might carry him and devise a medium of expression richer and more profound than the imitation of real life could offer. The very setting of *The Tempter* is interesting—fourteenth-century life with the Devil in a physical embodiment drawing Prince Leon from the love of Lady Avis to that of Lady Isobel. The attempt was surely a noble one for the year 1893, and the attack on realism in the critical preface sounded a note rarely heard in those years. Again, however, Jones failed—failed partly because he was not poet enough to master such a theme, partly because his mind was too little to grasp the implications of that theme, partly because of his own overweening self-confidence. A very great leader he might have been; instead of which he made himself an exceedingly lonely figure. Striving to bring religion into drama, he professed to despise religion; striving to get beyond a narrower naturalism, he turned foolishly and besottedly against Ibsen; striving to reform the stage, he bitterly attacked William Archer. "For many years", he wrote in answer to some of Archer's criticisms, "I have been in great peace about the future of my soul. I am in equal peace about the quite minor question of my future place in the English drama." By the narrowness of his outlook and the pettiness of his nature, Jones ruined whatever chances he had of guiding the drama of his time in new directions.

That is not to say he did not do important work; it implies only that he might have done greater. His own mind could not keep pace with his dreams. In concept he imagined the theatre of Strindberg and Andreev; in actuality he could do little more than write unsuccessful essays like *The Tempter* or pursue the common path of contemporary realism, with a strong flavour of sentimental ideality. Of the latter style *The Masqueraders* (St J. April 1894) provides a good example. Dulcie Larondie is his heroine here—a girl of breeding who, having lost her money, is forced to serve as a barmaid. At the inn, a kiss from her is auctioned and Sir Brice Skene gains it against her true, if somewhat morose, lover David Remon. Sir Brice proposes marriage and she accepts; but soon their domestic felicity is ruined by the fact that Brice runs through all his money. Remon aids her and at last gambles for her against her husband. After he has won, he confronts her, but goes off on a scientific expedition in sentimental exaltation, leaving her unstained and "pure". The story here is a rather foolish one, and, although Jones has succeeded in making a fair portrait of Remon, his characters generally do not have sufficient life to conceal from us the violent creaking of his plot.

Passionate adoration of an ideal sort fascinated Jones. He would have been in his true element had he been born a companion of Dryden and so been permitted to pen dramas in the Almansor style. Perhaps his leaning towards melodrama is the result of this, for melodrama was the nineteenth-century bastard of seventeenth-century love-and-honour tragedy.

The Physician (Crit. March 1897) displays him essaying another plot not dissimilar to that of *The Masqueraders*. Dr Carey is a famous nerve specialist who, when the curtain rises, is in the uncomfortable mood of feeling that nothing matters simply because his friend Lady Valerie Camville has light-heartedly thrown him over. A new vision, however, comes to him when Edana Hinde steps into his consulting room. Not for herself has she come; her business is to beg him to cure her fiancé Walter Amphiel, a temperance reformer. For her sake Carey consents and to his horror discovers that the temperance reformer is in reality a secret drunkard subject to violent attacks of delirium tremens. What he is to do, is the question. Magnanimously he conceals from Edana both the fact that he loves her and the fact that Amphiel is a drunkard. Of course, she succeeds in penetrating to the truth, Amphiel conveniently dies and the curtain eventually falls as Edana sinks gracefully and lachrymosely into the doctor's arms. His great self-sacrifice is being suitably rewarded. Again we recognise here the attempt at something genuinely significant, and again we realise that the something significant has become of little account precisely because of Jones's lack of subtlety. His play professes to be a play of character, but his persons are all stock types—the familiar clergyman's daughter, the drunken villain who has ruined a village maiden, the noble hero, one after another they thrust their familiar visages across the footlights. Everything is old and tawdry except perhaps Carey's appreciation of suffering as the basis of self-knowledge, and that intrudes as a kind of extraneous conception imposed on, instead of developing from, his personality.

More interesting in many ways, since less pretentious, is *The Rogue's Comedy* (Gar. April 1896). Had the treatment been a trifle lighter, this might have proved an excellent play. The main character is a certain Bailey Prothero, a rogue who finds it lucrative to pretend to occult powers. Aided materially by his wife, "Miss Jenison" (who gives him necessary information), he hoodwinks many persons in society by revealing to them supposed secrets of their past, and luck aids him by

leading him to make excellent prophecies regarding several
stocks which rise in value. Gradually he is surrounded by
a flock of believers, with only two dissentients, Lady Clarabut
and George Lambert, a barrister. Lambert, although he
does not know it, is really Prothero's son and his opposition
to the latter is dictated largely by the fact that he dotes on
Nina Clarabut. Gradually Prothero rises in power till eventually he heads a great South African company. At this
moment an old companion of his named Robert Cushing
makes his appearance. Vainly his wife counsels him to leave
London; instead he sets up palatial quarters in Park Lane.
Inevitably disaster overtakes him, and, forced by Cushing
and by his own son Lambert, he is compelled to abandon
his projects. Many artificialities there are in this play, but
on the whole it shows excellent treatment. The drawing-room
scene in Act I and the dramatic climax of Act III when
Prothero points out to his restive dupes that they must sink
or swim with him are boldly managed. *The Rogue's Comedy*,
in one way, displays Jones at his best, for, when he forgot
his philosophic purposes, he manifested a theatrical skill
superior to almost anything which his period had to offer.

Michael and his Lost Angel (Lyc. 1896) presents his serious
style at its best. Ambitious in scope, it aims at setting forth
fundamental principles in dramatic form, and we must agree,
with some necessary qualifications, that in this aim Jones has
succeeded. In Michael, the clergyman who falls from grace
through his love of Audrie, he presents a study bolder and
more complex than anything he had hitherto attempted. To
take as dramatic hero a man of the church who, after forcing
a girl to confess her sin publicly before the congregation,
finds himself seized by an all-consuming love and actually
declares that he feels no sorrow for his defection, was an
endeavour sufficiently temerarious in the nineties, and the
choice of theme indicates how determined Jones was to
permit no outside considerations to thwart him in his aims.
Yet *Michael and his Lost Angel* somehow fails to convince
us. The weakness may be due to the fact that Jones by
inclination would have been a tragic dramatist whereas in

talent he was capable of giving expression only to the serious problem note. The utter disaster of *The Tempter* tells its own tale; Jones had not the slightest spark of poetry in his nature, and something of poetic abandon is, perhaps, necessary if such a theme as he had here chosen were to find adequate dialogue. In reading *Michael and his Lost Angel* we ache for an infusion of that trembling rhythm, that unsought vision, which, even in translation, is never absent from Ibsen's scenes. Bernard Shaw imagined that the play required a different ending, that Michael ought to have trumpeted abroad his new-found glory of love; maybe some such conclusion might have been given to the plot, but it is not from this that our inner dissatisfaction arises. That dissatisfaction comes from a discrepancy between the essential aim of the drama and its actual execution.

An indication of those qualities which Jones lacked is provided by an earlier play, *The Dancing Girl* (H. Jan. 1891). Popular in its own time because it gave all the thrill of novelty without raising those awkward thoughts which the plays of Ibsen persisted in raising, it reveals itself to us as a prime example of dramatic falsity. Fundamentally it is untrue, because the author is incapable of rising to the level of thought he desires to attain. This story of a young Quaker girl (Drusilla Ives) who goes to London, becomes famous as a dancer, lives with the Duke of Guisebury as his mistress, and finally suffers poetic justice by dying miserably in New Orleans was intended to be a kind of problem plot, but the poverty of Jones's intellect forbade it from being anything save a rather tawdry tale of *The Girl's Friend* variety. Jones, of course, declared that he was not writing here a play with a moral, but the declaration rings false; in this, as in so many other of his dramas, his whole conception was based on a moral idea, and the treatment of his characters was determined by a definite point of view, not of a theatrical but of a social kind. Unfortunately, much as he thought about life and much as he prided himself upon the importance of his own ideas, his mind was narrow and conventional; "I am still in favour of what is called bourgeois morality", he stated once, and the confession is self-revealing. His interpretation of Drusilla Ives and of her adventures rises not one whit above the commonest opinions of the most common among the many persons who flocked to see *The Dancing Girl* in 1891. In a pure melodrama we do not seek for anything beyond common standards; our dissatisfaction with Jones arises from the fact that he considers himself somewhat superior to this level and consequently raises expectations which, because of his intellectual inferiority, he cannot satisfy.

So far as the new drama is concerned, Jones's contribution was therefore indirect rather than direct. He awakened the desire for something that should stimulate thought even although his own plays remained bound by a middle-class morality innocent of thought or vision. For this we may be grateful to him, and in this tendency we may readily see the beginnings of that movement which later produced such social plays as those of Galsworthy on the one hand and, on the other, of Somerset Maugham. Besides this, Jones proved himself an able craftsman. *The Dancing Girl* owed its success partly at least to a most effective situation handled with genuine theatrical skill at the close of the second last act. The same skill gives life to many of his plays, and in its finest expression provides the magnificent cross-examination scene in *Mrs Dane's Defence* (Wyndham's, Oct. 1900). This scene we could not imagine treated in any more adroit manner; every line has its purpose and we are held breathless watching the conflict of forces in an episode essentially theatrical. *Mrs Dane's Defence* has the same weakness as *The Dancing Girl*, but that it is magnificently planned we cannot deny.

In addition to this power of creating impressive and dramatically thrilling scenes, Jones possessed one other quality which, although somewhat obscured by his over-serious aims, gives to his plays a genuine value. He was—strangely enough when we consider his solemn demeanour and his melo-dramatic training—a master of a certain kind of satirical humour, blunt but occasionally very effective. The best parts of *The Rogue's Comedy* are those wherein the whims of society are depicted; even more markedly is this power of humour exhibited in *The Triumph of the Philistines, and how Mr Jorgan preserved the Morals of Market Pewbury under very trying Circumstances* (St J. May 1895). In Jones resided something of the spirit of Dickens; much as he fancied himself as a seriously minded contemplator of life, his best work was done when he remained contented with the grotesque delineation of common follies. His touch, perhaps, may be somewhat heavy, but, however broadly his colours are laid on, he was clearly fashioning here the body of a new comedy. A vicious attack on the "smug and banal ideals" of the English forms a rather unsatisfactory preface for this play; after all, Jones was the last person on earth to indulge in criticism of ideals of such a kind. No doubt the comedy springs from a recognition of the absurdities consequent upon the intrusion of a liberated morality into a sphere of conventional existence; but whatever of virtue there is in *The Triumph of the Philistines* arises, not from a sense of conscious purpose, but essentially from the merely observing and recording eye of the dramatist. The attitude of Jorgan and his associates when they endeavour to banish Alma Suleny from their community is dealt with vividly and vivaciously; Sally Lebrune is drawn to the life; and the complications which ensue when the amoral Sally winks to Sir Valentine Fellowes and maliciously entangles Jorgan are followed through with a genuine sense of fun.

The same good humour gives grace to *The Liars* (Crit. Oct. 1897), wherein Jones presents a real contribution to the newly developing comedy of manners. At times the dialogue takes on the refinement of real wit as when, in the first act, Dolly addresses Mrs Crespin:

Oh, my dear, you don't expect me to remember *all* the things that are inconvenient to you. Besides, other people don't wrap up. Jessica is out on the river with absolutely nothing on her shoulders—

and Mrs Crespin replies:

Is it not a physiological fact that when our hearts reach a certain temperature our shoulders may be, and often are, safely left bare?

But the special flavour of this play is formulated, not by witty conversation, but by a delicate treatment of character and of situation. The story of Falkner's love of Lady Jessica, wife to Gilbert Nepean, becomes informed by a true sense of humorous observation. The serious purpose which, because not profound enough, marred Jones's other plays is here avoided and all his best qualities—his theatric skill and his ability to see and, seeing, to depict—are permitted free play.

Jones's contributions to the stage of his time are important, and that importance we must duly recognise even while we discern that his value as a dramatist is considerably less than was once imagined. That he failed to introduce any deep thought is certain, for deep thought was beyond him; but his very attempt to produce plays in which an idea—particularly an idea of a religious kind—assumed a major role aided the stage in shaking itself free from the innocuous and stupid farces which hitherto had been the rage. Jones undoubtedly did much to assist the audience towards the rediscovery of fields of dramatic interest long left barren and neglected. During the Elizabethan period all that interested man was material for the playwright, but, during the later centuries, the subject-matter permitted to the dramatist had become narrowed down to a few set themes. Jones showed, in *Saints and Sinners*, in *The Tempter* and in *Michael and his Lost Angel*, that religious convention, if not religious conviction, might form as effective a theme as wooing and marriage; in *The Physician* he presented what was a real problem, however sentimentally he himself dealt with it; while in *The Liars* he pointed out the way for a new social comedy. For these things unquestionably he deserves to be remembered. Just is the summary of Richard Cordell:

Henry Arthur Jones found the contemporary English drama insignificant, puerile; he left it respected, flourishing, and mature. That he alone is responsible for the renascence is contrary to fact and reason; that to him belongs a generous share of the credit for restoring the drama in England to its rightful position as a civilized and civilizing art is indisputable.[1]

[1] *Op. cit.* p. 253.

3. Sir Arthur Pinero

In his criticism of Jones, William Archer had but two or
three plays on which to build a judgment; hardly more had
been provided by Arthur Pinero by the year 1882.[1] Available
for Archer, indeed, were only a few short pieces—*The Money-
Spinner* (P's, Manchester, Nov. 1880; St J. Jan. 1881), *Imprudence* (Folly, July 1881) and *The Squire* (St J. Dec. 1881)—
all plays which, although they may contain work potentially
interesting, can hardly be rated as masterpieces.[2] In each one
of these Pinero was clearly trying his hand at dramatic composition, and the prentice touch is often painfully apparent.
Even then, however, such apprentice efforts indicated a certain primitive originality, and Archer, again acutely, recognised that his

manner is not that of Mr T. W. Robertson, nor of Mr Gilbert,
nor of Mr Byron, nor of Mr Burnand. His style is his own, and
his effects, if not in themselves novel, are procured in a more or
less original fashion. Even his construction, though it is his
weakest point, shows an effort at something better than the
ordinary invertebrate pulpiness of "original comedies".[3]

Already, too, a decided versatility had been shown in these
early adventures. *Imprudence* was a farce, *The Money-Spinner*
a kind of melodrama, and *The Squire* an essay in a real study
of character. To select a theme which definitely posed a
problem such as is introduced into the last-mentioned play
indicates at once how sincere Pinero was at the start of his
dramatic career and how determined he was to relate the
characters of his imagination to the social life of his day.
The Squire points forward unmistakably to *The Second Mrs*

[1] On Pinero see Hamilton Fyfe, *Arthur Wing Pinero* (1902) and *Sir
Arthur Pinero's Plays and Players* (1930); W. Stöcker, *Pineros Dramen.
Studien über Motive, Charaktere und Technik* (Marburg, 1911); Dutton
Cook, *The Case of Mr Pinero* (*The Theatre*, N.S. v, 1882, 202–4); R. F.
Sharp, *A. W. Pinero and Farce* (*id.* N.S. xx, 1892, 154–7); *Mr Pinero and
Literary Drama* (*id.* N.S. xxii, 1893, 3–8).
[2] Before this date Pinero had also written *Two Hundred a Year* (Glo.
Oct. 1877), *Two can play at that Game* (Lyc. 1878), *La Comète* (Croydon,
April 1878), *Daisy's Escape* (Lyc. Sept. 1879), *Hester's Mystery* (Folly,
June 1880) and *Bygones* (Lyc. Sept. 1880).
[3] *Op. cit.* p. 277.

Tanqueray (St J. 1893) and to *Mid-Channel* (St J. Sept. 1909). As Archer observes:

In the course of the very curious and interesting controversy which raged for some time after the production of "The Squire", Mr Pinero published the memorandum in his note-book which formed the germ of the drama. It ran as follows: "The notion of a young couple secretly married—the girl about to become a mother—finding that a former wife is still in existence. The heroine amongst those who respect and love her. The fury of a rejected lover who believes her to be a guilty woman. Two men face to face at night-time. Qy—Kill the first wife?"[1]

By this we realise the essential problem from which Pinero's conception of plot and character was evolved. His play differs from the majority of contemporary efforts in its purpose; and, as it were, he goes back to the stage which Robertson had reached, resolute to advance still further than that dramatist had done. For this he was qualifying himself excellently. Not only had he the advantage denied to Robertson of many models provided by the newer school of French playwrights, he showed himself possessed of a power over both the realm of serious emotional situation and that of light comedy. In the one Robertson was restricted by prevailing standards in melodrama and in the sentimental play, and in the other by lack of experience in handling light social conversation. Being a pioneer, he was forced to create his own medium; Pinero came at a time when, through the efforts of men such as Gilbert, Albery, Theyre Smith and Young, the requisite medium had been shaped and adjusted to dramatic requirements.

How far this medium as it was applied to light comedy aided Pinero is to be seen when we glance at the farces and comedies which he wrote between *The Squire* (St J. 1881) and the problem plays of the nineties. Of these *The Magistrate* (Court, March 1885) proves one of the most interesting. Here the weakness in construction, which Archer had seen as one of his greatest faults, has disappeared. In a series of growing crises Pinero carries us onward from one ridiculous

[1] *Op. cit.* pp. 282–3.

situation to another, indulging in the impossible certainly—
for such is the way of farce—but retaining always a lively
sense of theatrical values. The magistrate who gives his title
to the play is one Posket, married to a widow who, in order
to conceal her age, declares that her nineteen-year-old son
Cis is really only fourteen. To her dismay news comes that
the lad's godfather, Lukyn, is arriving home from India and
off she proceeds to warn him of her deception. Meanwhile,
in her absence the mice (Posket and Cis) decide they can
safely play. They, too, set off on a jaunt and by farcical
coincidence all find themselves in the same hotel. Fortunately
for the plot, there is a police raid, in the course of which
Lukyn and Mrs Posket are arrested. This pair are then brought
up in court before Posket himself, who is so utterly dazed
that he permits his clerk to persuade him into giving them
seven days hard. A solution is finally reached when a brother
magistrate, Bellamy, reopens the case and releases the prisoners
with an admonition.

Not so skilfully constructed as *The Magistrate*, but none
the less interesting as a specimen of the work through which
Pinero gained his training, *The Schoolmistress* (Court, March
1886) deals with adventures in the Volumnia College for
Daughters of Gentlemen, managed by a certain Miss Dyott
who has married an impoverished gentleman, Queckett. To
obtain money for the satisfying of his somewhat luxurious
tastes, she plans to take part in an opera bouffe planned for
the Christmas vacation. During her absence, the girls and
Queckett decide to have a spree, the main object of which is
to celebrate the secret marriage of Dinah Rankling to Reginald
Paulover. Admiral Rankling, by an error, arrives at this
party and, as one may imagine, there are many confusions,
until in the end Miss Dyott returns home and proceeds to
exercise her authority.

One other specimen of this farce may be mentioned—
Dandy Dick (Court, Jan. 1887)—perhaps, on the whole, the
best of them all. The Very Rev. Augustin Jedd is the chief
figure in this; arrested in suspicious circumstances, this poor
gentleman suffers a series of doleful adventures. Easily and

with dramatic interest the plot develops, while the characters are well conceived and nicely balanced. The horsy Georgiana Tidman is thus well contrasted with the Dean, and an air of liveliness is provided by means of Jedd's precocious daughters, Salome and Sheba, who succeed in marrying Major Tarver and Mr Darbey. An excellent comic butler, Blore, completes a group skilfully blended to draw the last ounce of merriment from a ridiculous situation.

The value of these farces for the development of Pinero's art rests in the experience they gave him in the building of plot and the requirements of stage speech. That they make no pretence to mirroring life naturalistically matters not at all; their importance is definitely theatrical. Through them Pinero learned the use of his chosen instrument.

In the midst of this world of laughter, however, Pinero did not forget the serious purpose which had inspired him to write *The Squire*, and in *The Hobby-Horse* (St J. Oct. 1886) he turned aside to pen a social comedy. The general atmosphere here was one which he was to exploit in a number of plays—the satirising of social follies without the vigour and intellectual passion of the pure satirist. Philanthropy in *The Hobby-Horse* gains Pinero's contempt, and this he exposes in the scheme of Spencer Jermyn for a decayed jockeys' home and in that of his wife for an orphanage. In the interests of her cause Mrs Jermyn goes off as "Miss Moxon" to the East End of London, and there the Rev. Noel Brice falls deeply in love with her. She and her husband are shown thoroughly rid of their philanthropic predilections by the fall of the final curtain. This play well illustrates a weakness which mars much of Pinero's work during the eighties and nineties. First of all, he often mixes his styles in these plays, so that unity of impression is hopelessly lost. When Jermyn is conversing with the unregenerate Shattock and Pews we are wholly in the realm of farce; when Brice is making love to "Miss Moxon" we are in that of the lachrymose drama. Shattock is a figure who might have appeared in *Dandy Dick*; Brice is the familiar unhappy lover who, his day's work ended, is allowed to fade away into a melancholy

gloom. This in itself, however, is not the chief failing of
The Hobby-Horse. Satire springs from an intellectual disgust
at human stupidities. The satirist thus laughs at and lacerates
the miser or the astrologer's dupe because intellectually he
views their actions as being beneath human dignity. Pinero's
satire is not of this kind; it does not build itself out of a feeling
of superiority. The true satirist never sneers, for a sneer
implies that the object sneered at is subconsciously conceived of as a superior object. Jonson satirises follies beneath
him; the lesser man simply sneers at those above. *The Hobby-
Horse* and some of its companion pieces might, then, more
reasonably be called sneering comedies than comedies of
satire. No high intellectual ideal inspires them and drives
them forward.

This judgment is true of many plays by Pinero. In *The
Weaker Sex* (Manchester, Sept. 1888; Court, March 1889)
he turns on the movement for women's rights just as he
had turned on philanthropy in the other drama. Technically
this comedy-drama is good; but its theme is handled in
a manifestly shallow manner. The story deals mainly with
Lady Vivash who had loved and quarrelled with Philip Lyster.
Lyster has since made a great name for himself as Ira Lee,
the poet, and, meeting Lady Vivash's daughter, Sylvia, has
fallen madly in love with her. On discovering who Sylvia
really is he departs out of their lives. Into this circle the
author thrusts Mrs Boyle-Chewton, the leader of the women's
movement. With rather futile sneering, he makes her farcically
believe that a member of Parliament, Mr Bargus (who has
associated himself with her cause only to serve his own
ambition), is making her a proposal of marriage when in
reality he is merely presenting a report. The treatment here
seems as weak as that of *The Hobby-Horse.* The struggle for
women's rights was one that might have been dealt with in
an entirely farcical manner for the sake of such merriment
as it might provide or in an entirely serious manner. Between
these two there could be no dramatically effective middle
course.

A third example of this style appears in *The Times* (Terry's,

Oct. 1891). The object against which Pinero here tilts is social aspiration, and again we recognise that his method is spiritually lacking in power and in sympathy. The scheming of a self-made parvenu to enter the sacred portals of society may quite legitimately lead towards farcical episode; equally legitimately it may be dealt with seriously, either from the point of view of society as a whole or from that of the individual. Pinero again contents himself with sneering. Percy Egerton-Bompas he presents as a man who, grown wealthy, dreams of naught save higher social life; quite naturally this man is overjoyed when he learns that his daughter Beryl has become engaged to Lord Lurgashall, and quite naturally, too, he is dismayed when he discovers that his son, Howard, has been inveigled into marrying his landlady's daughter. Trimble, a social tout who, for considerations, aids him in his social advances, advises him to conceal the *mésalliance*, to educate his son's wife and her mother and to bring them before society under changed names. Various complications arise, and in the end Egerton-Bompas has to confess, brokenheartedly, that he has lost. The treatment of this theme, however, leaves Beryl and Lord Lurgashall in the air, and that, of course, would never do, so, after the latter has departed from the parvenu's house, back he comes to whisper sentimentally in Beryl's ear that he loves her still, that he will overlook her father's vulgarity and marry her just the same. The combination of this sneering and this sentimentality takes from *The Times* any virtue it might otherwise have possessed.

Happily, however, Pinero by no means confined his attention to themes of this kind and to this atmosphere. Pure sentimentality he exploited in *Sweet Lavender* (Terry's, March 1888) where, as one reviewer enthusiastically declared, he gave

an admirable retort witty to the disciples of Zola and "*naturalisme*" who think a play cannot be healthy without being insipid. In "Sweet Lavender" the dramatist introduces us to good women and honest men, and withal the play is as brilliant as a flash of light.[1]

[1] *The Theatre*, N.S. xi, May 1888, 263.

Even if we cannot share in this enthusiastic acclamation, we may admit that *Sweet Lavender's* sentimentality provides more pleasing theatrical qualities than the sneers of *The Times*.

Something of the same mood he introduced into *Lady Bountiful* (Gar. March 1891), wherein Camilla Brent is shown maintaining her uncle Roderick Heron and his son Dennis, whom she loves. The latter thinks of nothing but hunting, and this much distresses Camilla, but when he learns that he and his father have been living on her bounty he immediately leaves the house and takes a job as riding-master at the stables of honest John Veale. There Margaret Veale falls in love with him and out of pity he marries her. Later she dies and Dennis returns to find Camilla just about to wed old Sir Richard Philliter. On seeing Dennis she faints and the wedding is postponed. The plot is a trifle stupid, but Pinero's sincerity of purpose may be acknowledged.

In these plays love acts a major role, love that is faithful and true and devoted, love that is tortured and misled and weak. Sentimentally it is dealt with, yet the sentimentalism has a quality of its own which may be genuinely esteemed. Here Pinero was on surer ground than when he was writing his sneering comedies. And out of these sentimental pieces grew one drama of real significance—*Trelawny of the "Wells"* (Court, Jan. 1898). In *Trelawny* may be viewed a symbol of the renascent English drama. Something of the refashioned farce had gone to its making, something too of the newer sentimentalism. It is a period piece in which an endeavour is made to present a picture of the young Tom Robertson and his times; Robertson becomes viewed partly as a figure of the past, partly as the master of the then modern style. Thirty years have gone by since he was stirring theatrical audiences by his revolutionary methods, and those methods, like many things revolutionary, have settled down to become common practice and daily convention. The people talk, not as Robertson would have made his own characters talk, but in the manner of 1890, which simply means that their dialogue is nearer to the real green-room chatter of the sixties than to the more formal (and yet for its time naturalistic) speech put into the mouths of Robertson's own stage figures. Here the style of *Caste* is seized upon, fondly analysed and made more vivacious in content.

That Pinero had a gift for the writing of comedy *Trelawny* amply testifies; additional testimony comes from *The Princess and the Butterfly; or, The Fantastics* (St J. March 1897) which is a truly excellent sentimentalised comedy of manners. The Princess Pannonia has here returned to London after the death of her old husband. Middle age is beginning to creep upon her and upon a friend of hers, Sir George Lamorant, whom she is about to marry. Suddenly, however, she falls violently in love with a serious-minded youth named Edward Oriel, and Sir George experiences an equally violent infatuation for the Princess's adopted child, the bright-spirited Fay Zuliani. Through the mazes of this situation the characters drift in a whirl of fashionable gaiety. Their artificiality and the contrast between that artificiality and natural impulse provide Pinero with material of which he makes good use. Nearly does he succeed in his attempt to enter that dream world which Charles Lamb saw in the comedy of Congreve. "Are you sane, all of you—any of you?" cries Lady Ringstead at the close of the play. "Are you real? To me, you appear like dream people—fantastic creatures", and the answer to her questions comes in the form of a Hungarian dance, "Love is Ever Young". *The Princess and the Butterfly* has the theme of *The Vinegar Tree* presented without the sophistication of that modern comedy and with a delicate sense of fantastic values.

Through these plays Pinero made many important contributions to the stage of his time; but their historical value becomes of minor importance when they are placed beside *The Second Mrs Tanqueray* (St J. May 1893). "On May 27, 1893," wrote a reviewer in *The Theatre*,[1] "a day long to be remembered in the annals of the English stage, *The Second Mrs Tanqueray* was produced at the St James's Theatre, and Mr Pinero was hailed unanimously not only as one of the

[1] N.S. xxii, July 1893, 3–8.

greatest of living dramatists, but as the author of a play which is also a piece of literature." With this drama, as *The Theatre* reviewer recognised, the long-desired union of literary excellence and of dramatic skill had become an accomplished fact; and from that union he prophesied not only the further cultivation of the theatre by men of letters but the arising of a new style in theatrical criticism. "In the days to come when the production of a new play by a leading dramatist shall be regarded not as a theatrical fixture, but as an important event in the world of art and letters, masterpieces will not be dismissed in hastily scribbled paragraphs, but will be discussed soberly and thoughtfully by men of culture and intelligence." "I wonder", wrote William Archer,[1] "if Mr Pinero himself quite realises what an immeasurable advance he has made in *The Second Mrs Tanqueray* on all his former works?...It is not merely the seriousness of the subject that distinguishes this play from its predecessors.... Here we have a positively good play. Here, without raving, we can praise almost without reservation....In brief, the play is modern and masterly." By modern Archer meant that this drama aimed at the closest possible approach to naturalism. In it, Archer imagined, the author had "thrown to the winds all extrinsic considerations, compromises, superstitions, and...set himself, for his own personal satisfaction, to do the best work that was in him". From it Archer looked for the inauguration of a new period of creative productivity, and rightly he prognosticated that after times would find it "epoch-making".

To-day, of course, we see the weaknesses of this drama more clearly than contemporaries saw them. We recognise in it a certain sentimentalism; we detect a spurious literary quality in the dialogue; we are not so rapturously prepared to recognise in the characters masterpieces of psychological delineation. Yet, with all this recognition of its failings, none of us may deny the fact that in *The Second Mrs Tanqueray* the English drama at the close of the nineteenth century first surely found itself. It did not spring full-formed like Minerva

[1] *The Theatrical "World"* for 1893, p. 128.

out of Jove's forehead; much work in the theatre had gone
to its making. It did not face facts so boldly as many imagined.
It did not even provide such a fine technical model as some
other plays of the same period. To it more than to any other
drama of its time, however, the English stage owed its later
prevailing tendency towards the naturalism of daily life. The
fantasy of Gilbert was forgotten; the artificiality of Wilde
was neglected; and the strange poetic quality of Ibsen's work
was interpreted in terms of common daily life.

With *The Second Mrs Tanqueray* and with *The Notorious
Mrs Ebbsmith* (Gar. March 1895)[1] Pinero succeeded in doing
something more important than all Henry Arthur Jones had
accomplished. His theatrical skill is as assured as Jones's;
and he brings to his themes some at least of those qualities
which make for tragedy—conviction, deeper thought and
fine sympathy. Here the sneering tone which vitiated the
spirit of his other plays has been laid aside and he re-intro-
duces to the stage that noble pity which had found hardly
any exponent since the seventeenth century. It is a strange
fact that whereas Jones, brought up in the melodramatic
tradition, seemed to reach his finest achievement in *The
Rogue's Comedy* and in *The Liars*, Pinero, whose training
had been in farce, discovered his real strength in a kind of
tragic drama.

4. *Other Dramatists of the Eighties*

Necessarily, in dealing with the work of Pinero and of
Jones, we have carried our survey to the end of the century.
Most of their important work, as will be realised, came after
and not before the year 1890, and consequently the influence
of their styles is but little to be traced in this particular
decade which is at present under our consideration. Apart
from their plays, these ten years have not much to offer us.
Farce of a violently exaggerated and almost unbelievably
inane kind mightily pleased the public. C. H. Hawtrey's
The Private Secretary, based on *Der Bibliotheker* of von

---

[1] See H. Schutz Wilson, *The Notorious Mrs Ebbsmith, A Study* (1895).

Moser, appeared obscurely at the Theatre Royal in Cambridge, was brought to the Prince's in March 1884 and settled down to an extraordinary run. This piece, coldly regarded in the script, seems utterly beneath contempt, although, as may be realised by its success, it formed a not entirely despicable medium for farcical interpretation. That such was its only object is shown by dialogue and stage direction:

CATTERMOLE. Oh dear! oh dear! (*he turns chair round with a howl. She shrieks and runs away*). My good woman, go and play! go and run up and down! (*gag*).

MRS STEAD. And he never goes out—always, etc. etc.

It is these "gags" and "etceteras" rather than the actual written dialogue which give interest to this piece in the theatre. Of like kind is *Charley's Aunt* (Bury St Edmunds, Feb. 1892; Roy. Dec. 1892) by Brandon Thomas; and only a trifle more foolish are the American farces of Harry Pleon. *Dutch Justice; or, Up before the Magistrate* (Gai. Birmingham, July 1888) may be taken as a fair specimen. Described as "A Funny Melange of Magisterial Errors", it utterly baffles us in its unbelievable stupidity. Only the fact that audiences of to-day roar with merriment over the sillinesses of the Ritz Brothers can make us credit the following as having once been laughable:

Well, here's a go! I was standing where I was, and running as fast as I could, and all of a sudden I slipped and fell over myself, and slipped, just as a fourwheeled hansom cab run over me. I shouted hands off, and he nearly took my feet off. But anyhow I found this note (*Shows one*) And it says the beak is too ill to go to court to-day. So I'm going to take his place and lock everybody up, and cop all the fines myself. I shan't know what to say, but I suppose it will be all right. Whatever foolish things I say it will be in my favour, because then I shall be like a many of our Judges, full of silly and unfair sentences.

(*Song, if required, and exit.*)

The song, I fancy, we do not require. Equally poor are all Pleon's works—*Muldoon's Picnic* (M'bone, Nov. 1886), and *Peck's Bad Boy* (Brit. June 1891) are both "nonsensical pieces of absurdity" without the slightest grain of true wit or humour. Some farces, it is true, reach a trifle higher, but the trifle must be duly emphasised. J. Wear Gifford's *Supper for Two; or, The Wolf and the Lamb* (P'cess, Glasgow, Nov. 1883) is fairly representative of such plays. This shows Quilldriver, an attorney, coming to an inn and there meeting one Horatio Blazer. Blazer, to display his courage, wishes to pick a quarrel with someone not very formidable, and poor Quilldriver finds himself in an awkward predicament. Happily, however, the waiter, Joseph, endeavours to make capital out of the two of them; overstepping himself, he finds Blazer and Quilldriver leagued against him. The theme, though slight, is at least superior to that of any among Pleon's pieces. Similar in character are the farces of Alfred Maltby, once noted as a prolific writer of burlesque, extravaganza and would-be amusing sketches; *Taken by Storm* (Aven. Nov. 1884) in which "Dick" (Captain Richard Shye) captures his Gertrude, presents a fair specimen of his style.

The eighties abound also in melodramas which rarely proceed beyond the forms established earlier in the century. G. R. Sims and Henry Pettitt turned out a variety of these. *The Harbour Lights* (Adel. Dec. 1885), written in collaboration, may be selected for mention here. The hero is a bold and frank-faced lieutenant; the villain a wicked squire who ruins an innocent girl and then attempts to steal the fair heroine's money. Through trial and torment move the good characters until, just before the final curtain, the squire is shot by the honest lover of the girl whom he had dishonoured. Plays of this kind, mostly with domestic settings, flourished, for spectators were still attracted by melodramatic simplification of human character and emotion. Stories could please such as that presented in Brandon Thomas's *The Colour-Sergeant* (P'cess, Feb. 1885), where we are told how a retired sergeant has disowned his son and sits at home all alone and desolate, when suddenly the son returns—dressed up all gloriously in a sergeant's uniform too. Even a man like Westland Marston could traffic in these things. His *Under Fire* (Vaud. April 1885) deals mainly with a stereotyped Lady Fareham who has a dread secret known only to a Mrs Naylor.

Lady Fareham's daughter Carrie is truly loved by Guy Morton who is forced to resign his pretentions in favour of a more showy Charles Wolverley. In the end, of course, Wolverley's worthlessness is demonstrated and Guy, the hero, returns in triumph. To proceed more deeply into the niceties of the plot were needless.

At the same time, various efforts were being made in the direction of the newer drama and, although few of them reached even a faint measure of literary success or escaped, even temporarily, from sentimental mawkishness, these demonstrate that the forces of the "moderns" were increasing. In *Human Nature* (D.L. Sept. 1885), for example, by Henry Pettitt and Augustus Harris, we can easily trace the infiltration of the new style of ideas into the melodramatic form. The old type villain is here, in the person of a rascally lawyer, and by his side is the stock villainess, a wily scheming woman. This pair, acting in concert, poison Captain Temple's mind and make him doubt his wife's virtue. The villainy is antiquated, but the application of the villainy is new. Melodramas of this sort come fairly close in spirit to the mood of the English adaptations of such French problem-dramas as Octave Feuillet's *Péril en la demeure*[1] and Victorien Sardou's *La maison neuve*. The latter was rendered into an English form, as *Mayfair* (St J. Oct. 1885), by A. W. Pinero. Although condemned by some contemporaries because, in their opinion, its theme of a wife tempted by a lord's advances after she hears of the infidelities of her husband was not "British", *Mayfair* comes within approachable distance of *Human Nature*, an essentially British production.

Some of the melodramas, too, developed a kind of propagandist tone—another straw in the rising wind. G. R. Sims's *The Last Chance* (Adel. April 1885), in spite of its confused Russian adventures among impossible Nihilists, thus has a certain serious note, as has Mark Quinton's *In His Power* (Alex. L'pool, Sept. 1884; Olym. Jan. 1885), a drama which

[1] In the version by G. W. Godfrey as *The Opal Ring* (Court, Jan. 1885). An earlier adaptation had been made by Tom Taylor as *The House or the Home?* (Adel. May 1859).

mingles a theme of bigamous marriage unwittingly entered into with another theme of diplomatic secrets and devious espionage.

Besides such plays, of course, there were other more determined efforts in the direction of the newer styles; sometimes these were accomplished with a faint measure of success, more commonly the play of ideas and the posing of problems were dealt with in a spirit mawkish and uninspired. Jerome K. Jerome, for example, shows himself impelled towards the modernist movement in *Sunset* (Com. Feb. 1888). Based on Tennyson's *The Sisters*, this one-act piece has value in demonstrating the increased skill which the dramatic renaissance had brought with it. The story is a simple one—telling how Lois loves Lawrence, how Lawrence has become infatuated with her sister Joan whom he has met while on holiday without knowing who she is, and how Lois, in self-renunciation, gives him up—sentimental unquestionably, yet revealing a poignancy of which the old sentimentalism was utterly ignorant. Just as the one-act comedies of manners demonstrated the growing power of the dramatists in their handling of character, situation and dialogue, so such a play as *Sunset* shows clearly how much deeper these dramatists could strike at the basis of human emotion and how infinitely more skilful they were in dealing with episodes in which the dramatic interest arose, not from an outer conflict as in the melodrama, but from the clash of nature with nature, or of thought with thought.

CHAPTER VII

WILDE AND SHAW: PLAYS OF THE NINETIES

1. The Success of the Reformers

THE eighties had achieved something quite definite, but only in the last decade of the century was absolute surety reached. These ten years opened well. Between 1890 and 1891 audiences were able to witness the first productions of *The Pharisee* (Shaft. 1890) by M. Watson and Mrs Wallis, H. A. Jones's *The Dancing Girl* (H. 1891), C. Haddon Chambers's *The Idler* (St J. 1891), A. W. Pinero's *Lady Bountiful* (Gar. 1891) and *Beau Austin* (H. 1890) by W. E. Henley and R. L. Stevenson. Apart from these—all notable plays—the works of Ibsen came freely before the public. *A Doll's House*, which had been originally presented at the Novelty in 1889, was revived at Terry's in 1891, and English audiences saw for the first time *Rosmersholm* (Vaud. 1891), *Ghosts* (Roy. 1891), *Hedda Gabler* (Vaud. 1891) and *The Lady from the Sea* (Terry's, 1891). While the season of 1891-2 was, perhaps, not so satisfactory, it counted in its repertoire J. M. Barrie's *Walker, London* (Toole's, 1892) and Oscar Wilde's *Lady Windermere's Fan* (St J. 1892), besides welcoming the early performances of the Independent Theatre Society and a number of revivals at the Olympic and the Lyceum—notably Irving's *Henry VIII*. The great event of the next season was the production of Pinero's *The Second Mrs Tanqueray* (St J. 1893), an enormous success; less popular in appeal but of no less importance were the performances of George Moore's *The Strike at Arlingford* (O.C. 1893) and G. B. Shaw's *Widowers' Houses* (Roy. 1892). The old melodrama and comic opera, as contemporaries observed, were ceasing to have their earlier appeal; the public was now clamouring for realism. So great had been the progress that one writer, in comparing conditions in 1894 with those in 1878, could speak of the latter as "prehistoric".[1]

A lull came in the years 1894–5, causing some to lose heart. Malcolm Watson noted that playwrights were falling into ruts and that there was a boring run of dramas dealing with women of whose pasts public opinion was doubtful.[2] The annual review of the stage presented by *The Theatre* in 1897 was despairing.[3] Musical farce, it was noted, had taken a new lease of life and "no new playwright" had "been discovered to help on that 'renascence' of which we heard so much two years ago, and those with established reputations" had "done little or nothing to add to them". The only encouraging feature seemed to be "the revival of interest...in the romantic drama, and especially in Shakspere".[4] Once more the pessimists seized their chance to complain. The managers were attacked for their "shrinking from anything new" and for their "timidity as to incurring any chance of failure".[5] "The efforts made in the past to stimulate the production of original plays", notes *The Theatre*,

have been extremely feeble, and have had poor results. The Independent Theatre is practically the only working organisation that has professed such an aim, and the original English pieces which it gave were in about the same proportion to its foreign productions as was Jack Falstaff's halfpenny worth of bread to his "intolerable deal of sack". The Dramatic Students' Society contented itself with the revival of old plays....The British Society of Dramatic Art declared a part of its mission to be the affording to young and deserving authors a chance of getting their feet upon the ladder, but it went the wrong way to work, and came to an untimely end.[6]

[1] *Our Stage To-day* (*The Theatre*, N.S. xxiv, Sept. 1894, 89–96); cf. *id.* N.S. xxi, Feb. 1893, 115. On this period generally see Holbrook Jackson, *The Eighteen-Nineties* (1923).
[2] *The Turn of the Tide* (*The Theatre*, N.S. xxvii, Sept. 1895, 134–7).
[3] N.S. xxix, Jan. 1897, 1–3.
[4] On the revivals sponsored by Forbes-Robertson, Beerbohm Tree, Irving and Alexander see *A Boom in Shakespere* (*The Theatre*, N.S. xxx, Sept. 1897, 115–17).
[5] *Id.* N.S. xxix, April 1897, 205–10.
[6] *The Dearth of Dramatists* (*id.* N.S. xxix, May 1897, 268–74).

It is interesting to observe that these were the years that saw the appearance of Pinero's *The Notorious Mrs Ebbsmith* (Gar. 1895) and *Trelawny of the "Wells"* (Court, 1898), H. A. Jones's *The Masqueraders* (St J. 1894), *The Triumph of the Philistines* (St J. 1895), *Michael and his Lost Angel* (Lyc. 1896) and *The Liars* (Crit. 1897), all of Oscar Wilde's brilliant comedies, C. Haddon Chambers's *The Tyranny of Tears* (Crit. 1899), J. M. Barrie's early plays, and Shaw's *Arms and the Man* (Aven. 1894), *Candida* (S. Shields, 1895), *The Devil's Disciple* (Bijou, 1897), *The Man of Destiny* (Grand, Croydon, 1897), and *Caesar and Cleopatra* (Newcastle, 1899).

A decade which gave birth to all of these—especially when we compare it with any decade since those wonderful opening years of the seventeenth century—need not feel ashamed of itself. Looking back, we can only smile now at such a statement as that which appeared in *The Pall Mall Gazette* for 1893:[1] "at present," wrote the critic, "English dramatic art is sick unto death, and the signs of her rejuvenescence attenuated to the dimensions of the mathematical point". Thus does time have his revenges.

It was, of course, still an age of transition, so that the poor dramatist stood, as Robert Buchanan said, "bewildered... certain of execration from one side or the other, sure that if he secures the approval of Mr Bernard Shaw he will earn the contempt of Mr Clement Scott" until he drifted "aimlessly from one experiment to another" or sat "paralysed at his desk".[2] To one who truly recognised the spirit of the time, however, there could be no doubt. Max Beerbohm divined aright that the main dramatic current of the time was that "of realistic modern comedy and tragedy".

Regret it as you may, modern realism is the only direction in which our drama can really progress....Every decade has brought us perceptibly nearer to something fine.[3]

He thought "that in sixty years at the present rate of progress", the theatre should have achieved its final aims in this kind.

[1] lii, April 8, 1893, 3.
[2] *A Word on the Defunct Drama* (*The Theatre*, N.S. xxviii, Oct. 1896, 208–10).
[3] *The Saturday Review*, xc, July 28, 1900, 112.

2. *The New Comedy of Wit*

The two plays which Oscar Wilde wrote in the eighties—
Vera; or, The Nihilists (printed 1880) and *The Duchess of
Padua* (printed 1883)—could hardly have led anyone to presage the later contributions to the stage which this author
was to make. *Salomé* (Paris, 1896) belongs to their tradition,
but not that exquisite set of four dramas—*Lady Windermere's
Fan* (St J. Feb. 1892), *A Woman of No Importance* (H. April
1893), *An Ideal Husband* (H. Jan. 1895) and *The Importance
of Being Earnest* (St J. Feb. 1895). With these entered into
the theatre once more a grace and a refinement which long
it had lacked. Jones was usually too serious; Pinero, if sincere,
wanted polish; Wilde brought to the drama qualities distinct
from each. "I took the drama," he declared in *De Profundis*,
"the most objective form known to art, and made of it as
personal a mode of expression as the lyric or the sonnet;
at the same time I widened its range and enriched its characterisation"—and the self-judgment bears with it an element
of truth. Jones and Pinero both wrote of society, but society
they had come to know only after they had won a certain
measure of success. Wilde was of the élite from the very start,
and all his career is coloured by his passion for style; an
attitude for him was more important than a moral truth. No
external considerations prevented his appreciation of mannered gesture; indeed, the mannered gesture became for him
the most desirable thing in life. He did not need to sneer,
as Pinero did; he permitted others to do the sneering. He
felt no call to preach, as Jones did; for preaching to him
remained hopelessly outside the sphere of art. It is this
quality of fashionable ease which represents his greatest
contribution to the stage.[1]

Lady Windermere's Fan has at first sight a definite kinship

---

[1] See Frank Harris, *Oscar Wilde, His Life and Confessions* (2 vols.
1916); Arthur Ransome, *Oscar Wilde* (1912); Stuart Mason, *Oscar Wilde,
Art and Morality* (1912); André Gide, *Oscar Wilde, a Study* (1905);
L. C. Ingleby, *Oscar Wilde* (1907). For his writings consult Stuart Mason,
A Bibliography of Oscar Wilde (1914).

with *Mrs Dane's Defence* and *The Second Mrs Tanqueray*;
this "play about a good woman" seems as obvious an essay
in the delineation of social life as any of the other plays about
women not so good. A further glance, however, soon convinces us of the falsity of such a judgment. Wilde takes delight
in choosing a theme which may be likely to interest contemporary audiences, but in the moral implications of the
theme he has simply no interest. Many an episode to which
Pinero and Jones would have devoted infinite care, endeavouring to make them as life-like as possible, are hastily hurried
over. A good example comes at the end of the first act, where
Lady Windermere thus soliloquises:

How horrible! I understand now what Lord Darlington meant
by the imaginary instance of the couple not two years married.
Oh! It can't be true—she spoke of enormous sums of money paid
to this woman. I know where Arthur keeps his bank book—in
one of the drawers of that desk. I might find out by that. I *will*
find out. (*Opens drawer.*) No, it is some hideous mistake. (*Rises
and goes* C.) Some silly scandal! He loves *me*! He loves *me*!
But why should I not look? I am his wife, I have a right to look!
(*Returns to bureau, takes out book and examines it, page by page,
smiles and gives a sigh of relief.*) I knew it, there is not a word of
truth in this stupid story. (*Puts book back in drawer. As she does
so, starts and takes out another book.*) A second book—private—
locked! (*Tries to open it, but fails. Sees paper knife on bureau,
and with it cuts cover from book. Begins to start at the first page.*)
Mrs Erlynne—£600—Mrs Erlynne—£700—Mrs Erlynne—£400.
Oh! it is true! it is true! How horrible! (*Throws book on floor.*)

Here Wilde is using an old technique—a technique, moreover,
which he, skilled as he was, must have known to be antiquated
and which easily he could have replaced by another. The fact
seems to be that he simply did not wish to make this scene
more life-like; he has chosen his theme, not in order to create
a sense of illusion, but simply as a basis for something else.
That something else was his wit. The value of *Lady Windermere's Fan* does not rest in its story but in its dialogue. Finely
polished, his prose has a metallic ring lacking in the less
refined accents of Jones and Pinero. Once more Wilde carries
us into the realm once dominated by Etherege when gentlemen

conversed in epigram and gaily tossed similes to one another as in some spiritual battledore and shuttlecock.

This style reaches its finest expression in *The Importance of Being Earnest*. No inharmonious thoughts of life and morality intrude here, for the plot is given the same filigree grace as the language itself. Shot through with the best flowers of Wildian epigram, it maintains easily its settled plan and style. "My dear Algy, you talk exactly as if you were a dentist. It is very vulgar to talk like a dentist when one isn't a dentist. It produces a false impression"—"The amount of women in London who flirt with their own husbands is perfectly scandalous. It looks so bad. It is simply washing one's clean linen in public"—"You don't seem to realise that in married life three is company and two is none"—"Algy, you always adopt a strictly immoral attitude towards life. You are not quite old enough to do that"—one after another these epigrams keep crowding in upon us, harmonising in their artificiality with the wholly artificial spirit of this eccentric comedy. From the first interlude with Lane, the butler, to Jack's final "Gwendolen, it is a terrible thing for a man to find out suddenly that all his life he has been speaking nothing but the truth. Can you forgive me?" we are in a world of delightful make-believe where effervescent wit and swift surprise in situation keep us constantly in mental alertness.

This perhaps is the only comedy written by Wilde wherein he fully achieves complete harmony in aim and achievement. *A Woman of No Importance* is serious without conviction and *An Ideal Husband* seems to veer between the problem note of Pinero and the delicately absurd. That the latter play has a successfully developed and interesting plot cannot be denied; but there may be experienced a slight sense of dissatisfaction when Lord Goring throws off his air of polite inefficacy and becomes a business-like and energetic man of the world. It is as if Earnest suddenly revealed himself as a capable stockbroker or Algernon displayed a dully solemn interest in stamp-collecting. On the other hand, here as in *Lady Windermere's Fan* Wilde showed how the fashionable

society of his time could be used for the purposes of comedy
and in so far he re-established a true comedy of manners
which, during the twentieth century, was to develop in the
hands of Somerset Maugham and of Noel Coward. His
success stimulated others in his own time—Pinero and Jones
particularly; and we recognise that, quite apart from his own
plays, the English theatre of the last few years of the century
would have proved much less lively and much less stimulating
had Wilde not been there to give it ease and grace.

3. *George Bernard Shaw*

To emphasise the importance of Bernard Shaw were
obviously otiose; that has been done sufficiently by himself
and by others.[1] This importance derives from the fact that
here a great genius, with an essentially dramatic talent, came
to the stage and seized from each of the various forces of his
time those elements which were of greatest value and significance. To compare Shakespeare and Shaw may be a trifle
foolish, for such comparisons of persons far removed in time
from one another savour of the purely academic; but, provided we maintain our sense of proportion and balance, the
parallel may yield material for critical evaluation. Shakespeare
was born in 1564 and came to the theatre in the early nineties
of the sixteenth century; Shaw was born in 1856 and had his
first play produced in 1892. When Shakespeare joined a
company of London players he found a renaissant drama
which as yet had not realised its own destiny. Lyly had
provided a new model in mythological fantastic comedy;
Gascoigne had experimented in translations from the Italian
commedia erudita; a strange romantic style was being exploited
by Greene and a peculiar romantic revenge drama had attracted the attention of Kyd; above all, Marlowe was plumbing

[1] The library of critical works on Shaw has not yet assumed the pro-
portions of the Shakespeare library; but then Shakespeare died over
three hundred years ago. The standard biography is that of Archibald
Henderson (new edition, 1933). The studies by Holbrook Jackson, H. L.
Mencken, G. K. Chesterton, Edward Shanks, John Palmer, Joseph
McCabe, A. Hamon and D. A. Lord survey various aspects of his work.

the depths of a new tragedy and displaying the full powers
of blank verse rhetoric. Shakespeare's virtue it was, not
merely to bring a still further outstanding genius to the stage,
but to seize from Lyly and Greene and Kyd and Gascoigne
and Marlowe just such material as might be regarded most
valuable and to weld these into one harmonious whole.
Marlowe's verse and high tragic conception he made his own,
and combined with that the subtlety of *The Spanish Tragedy*;
to the Italian wit as reflected in Gascoigne he added Lyly's
over-delicate grace and Greene's romantic robustiousness.

Shaw's position is by no means dissimilar. From Jones
and Pinero he learned much, and still more did he learn from
Ibsen. To Wilde he went for some of his skill in quip and
epigram, and many a device he borrowed from dramatists
whose very names maybe are now forgotten. In our excitement over all that seemed so novel and so startlingly thrilling
in Shaw, we often forget that when he was a young man of
twenty or thirty he frequented the theatres and eagerly
watched performances of all the good old plays from earliest
melodramas to Jones's *The Silver King*, from Lytton's *Money*
to Robertson's comedies and Byron's latest successes. His
dramas, so far from being new, are a tissue of reminiscences
of earlier work; just as Shakespeare's plays are broadly based
upon the foundations laid by his predecessors. One of the
most surprising things about drama is that greatness does not
really spring from complete originality. "The thief of all
thieves was the Warwickshire thief" sang David Garrick in
The Jubilee (D.L. 1769), and almost the same might be lilted
of every dramatic genius. Molière found inspiration for his
work in the *commedia dell' arte* as Wycherley found inspiration
in Molière.

Already[1] an example has been given of the way in which
Shaw has seized material from a play by Boucicault; and this
example must be regarded, not as a solitary one, but as
representative of much in the plays pleasant and unpleasant.
Other melodramas find themselves reflected in his work; there
are reminiscences of Lytton's *Money* and of comedies by

[1] See *supra*, pp. 90–1.

Jerrold and Robertson and Byron. This does not, however, by any means imply that Shaw's dramatic genius, any more than Shakespeare's, was merely imitative. The appearance of *Widowers' Houses* in 1892 marked the beginning of a new epoch even as did the appearance of *Love's Labour's Lost* almost exactly three centuries previously.

Shaw's genius consisted in his fusing of different elements in the theatre of his day and in looking towards the future instead of towards the immediate present. Jones's plays were frequently powerful dramatically, but they were apt to be a trifle dull; Wilde's were gay enough but proved, on examination, to be but flimsy things at the best; Pinero could laugh farcically, or superiorly sneer, or write pathetically of the woman with a past, but he had not the all-embracing ability to do more than one of these things at one time. Shaw takes the whole of theatrical emotion as his province and can move easily from one mood to the other while keeping all subordinate to one universal aim. Where Jones and Pinero were single-minded pioneers, he was the accomplished master benefiting from their adventures.

The great Shavian epoch, of course, does not come until the beginning of the twentieth century, but already before 1900 Shaw had fully displayed the extent of his powers. Ten plays in all he wrote in the course of these eight years— *Widowers' Houses* (Roy. Dec. 1892), *Arms and the Man* (Aven. April 1894), *Candida* (S. Shields, March 1895; H.M. Aberdeen, July 1897), *The Devil's Disciple* (Bijou, April 1897), *The Man of Destiny* (Grand, Croydon, July 1897; Com. March 1901), *The Philanderer* (published 1898), *Mrs Warren's Profession* (published 1898), *You Never Can Tell* (published 1898; Roy. Nov. 1899), *Caesar and Cleopatra* (Newcastle, March 1899; Sav. Nov. 1907) and *Captain Brassbound's Conversion* (licensed 1899; Str. Dec. 1900; Court, March 1906). Not one of these before 1900 proved a popular success, yet even in the nineties Shaw's influence was far-spread. Both by these plays and by his dramatic criticisms in *The Saturday Review* he had made himself one of the most dominant theatrical forces in London.

13-2

One thing must be realised if ever we are to understand Shaw rightly; he is not a philosopher, but a dramatist. He himself, of course, has constantly reiterated that the theatre is being used by him merely as a platform, and his reiterations have been taken seriously by most of his critics; but Shaw is no more a prophet than were Shakespeare and Molière. "I am convinced that fine art is the subtlest, the most seductive, the most effective means of propagandism in the world," he declares, and would have us believe that his only interest in the stage lies in the fact that the drama gives him an opportunity of appealing to thousands; "prophet" he styles himself and wishes (or pretends to wish) us to regard him as a purveyor of ideas and not of episodes. Perhaps, so often has he repeated this, Shaw has become convinced in his own mind; but it is certain that the power of keeping his plays alive will be, not their prophetic ideas, but their sheer dramaturgic skill. Essentially a playwright, his comedies are instinct with the life of the theatre.

This, of course, is not to say that he has no literary aim; rather that he, more than any other man of his time, sought for and achieved a significant and harmonious union of literary and theatrical qualities. With a boldness rivalled by none save perhaps Oscar Wilde, Shaw made claim to the appreciation of the literary connoisseur. His plays he issued in a form which made them appeal to a reading public; his prefaces were intended to stimulate this appeal, and by means of his elaborate stage directions he aimed at creating in the study the atmosphere of the stage. From many other literary dramatists, however, Shaw separated himself by frankly accepting those elements in the playhouse which make for popularity; and not a single writer has shown a surer knowledge of stagecraft and of the desires of the audience, or a more subtle and effective use of these elements. He was willing and eager to make full and free employment of physical action on the stage—the eternally exciting appeal of melodrama—and to utilise boldly those conceptions which made the burlesque, the farce and the extravaganza once so popular. Again we realise how much akin he was in 1890 to the young

Shakespeare of 1590. When the latter came to London, he found the playhouses in the hands of crude dramatists who courted attention by rough, tempestuous, melodramatic action or by vulgar and unpolished jests. Instead of condemning these and striving to evolve something new, Shakespeare laid his hands on whatsoever was likely to be of service to him— plots, situations, characters, dialogue—transforming all by the magic of his skill, yet retaining that which formed the basic strength and theatrical value of the material he had chosen. In a manner precisely similar Shaw turned for guidance to the dramatists who were his immediate pre-decessors and laid heavy toll upon them.

That Shaw's plays are not merely reproductions of popular melodrama and farce is obvious; like Shakespeare he created out of what he took from others an art expression individual and distinct. This introduces the question of the kind of theatre which Shaw has produced. Tragedy and gloomily serious drama such as *The Second Mrs Tanqueray* and *Mrs Dane's Defence* he completely avoided; the sphere of comedy it was which he made his own. Shaw's comedy, however, was of a peculiar kind, and clearly our first task should be to determine the precise aim which he had in view when com-posing, say, *Arms and the Man* or *Androcles and the Lion*. To be continually seeking for elaborate classifications in art, of course, may become a very definite critical fault; but, whatever disdain we may experience when we encounter such formal criticism carried to excess, we cannot escape from the fact that some sort of classification is necessary; we could not deal with *Twelfth Night* by comparing it with Sean O'Casey's *The Silver Tassie*. We all recognise, that is to say, certain clearly differentiated types of drama—tragedy, comedy, melodrama, farce. Beyond this, however, we must go. Within the one sphere of dramatic endeavour which we call "comedy", we have to distinguish many diverse forms; indeed, there are some comedies which aim at conveying to an audience impressions which are more nearly allied to the impressions conveyed by some kinds of tragedy than to those aroused, say, by *As You Like It* or *The Way of the World*.

There is a vast measure of difference between the spirit of Jonson's *The Alchemist*, classically bitter, and the enchanted fancies of *A Midsummer Night's Dream*.

Looking at English drama as a whole, it seems that we may trace four main forms within this comic sphere. The first is Shakespeare's comedy of romance, distinguished by its all-pervading humour—a humour which permits the dramatist to mingle together the most strangely varied elements, which allows him to put his fairies alongside his human lovers, to make his clown strut with his kings. In addition to this quality of humour, there is always in Shakespeare's comedy the overshadowing presence of a kindly and dominant Nature. It is Nature that leads the lovers out of the mazy wildernesses of the fairy-haunted forest; it is Nature that makes Don John's machinations, which have hoodwinked the clever, superior and self-conscious aristocrats, revealed through the agency of the dull-witted Dogberry. When Dogberry triumphs, Nature smiles. This, then, is one type of comedy; the second is that of Ben Jonson. Here the aim is directly satirical—satirical, not of social manners but of individual follies. Jonson seizes on particular eccentricities or errors or vices peculiar to certain men, and by the creation of type characters such as his Sir Epicure or his Volpone, throws lurid light on human duplicity. In the comedy of Congreve there is another, and a distinct, aim. Here the dramatist is no longer concerned with individual follies. He has deliberately restricted himself to one small section of society—the courtly circle—a section of society highly conscious of its own rules, conventions and manners, anxious to preserve intact the refinement of social graces and to reveal its intellectually brilliant wit. If Shakespeare is preoccupied with humour, and Jonson with satiric bitterness, Congreve is concerned, above all other things, with a wit that is airy, delicate and flimsily brittle. Finally, we reach what, for want of a better term, we may style the sentimental comedy. In this once more the whole of social life is taken within the playwright's sphere of observation, and his endeavour is to delineate and to discuss certain problems or difficulties which confront man as a social animal. At first, perhaps, only the most immediately obvious problems will be dealt with—duelling, gambling and the like; in the beginning, too, these problems will be discussed, not in a rationalistic and realistic manner, but in a spirit of vague emotional sympathy; but gradually a deeper note will enter in and the purely sentimental comedy will become the comedy of serious purpose.

When we turn from these four major forms of comic endeavour to the plays of Bernard Shaw, we recognise that many of their characteristics are to be found reflected in his work as well. Something of Shakespeare's humour is here. The atmosphere of *Measure for Measure* and, more particularly, of *All's Well that Ends Well*, seems very close to that of *Man and Superman*. Shaw's Life Force is simply Shakespeare's Nature. Many of Shaw's characters are conceived intellectually as types in the Jonsonian manner; yet his comedy as a whole does not reflect the mood established in *Volpone* and *Bartholomew Fair*. To other scenes we turn and find there a pure wit, as delicately expressed as the wit of Congreve; viewing this we feel we are in the presence of comedies cast in the Restoration mould. Yet immediately other scenes attract our attention, scenes in which we discern something of that aim to which, crudely, the sentimental dramatists were seeking to give expression.

This does not imply, however, that Shaw's plays are made up merely by a mingling of devices and moods exploited by earlier dramatists. From his first comedies to his latest, Shaw has exhibited a characteristic quality which has made his work essentially and uniquely individual. Perhaps the clue to this quality is provided by himself. In a conversation some time ago, someone spoke of his wit and humour. "My plays contain," he said, "not so much humour and wit, as fun." This self-judgment gives us our clue. His comedies, as distinct from all the others mentioned above, are comedies of purposeful fun. Herein lies one of his great contributions to the modern theatre. His fun is something peculiar to himself: an effervescing, bubbling-up, eternally youthful and joyous exuberance of spirit. He is continually inverting ideas and poking fun—poking fun at us, at his audiences, at his characters, at ideas. He will take the popular conceptions of certain historic figures—a Napoleon, a Caesar—and, turning them topsy-turvy, will smile good-naturedly at our set ideas. In *Caesar and Cleopatra* he will introduce a secretary for Caesar, a British slave, and he will make this Briton declare to Cleopatra:

> Blue is the colour worn by all Britons of good standing. In war we stain our bodies blue; so that though our enemies may strip us of our clothes and our lives, they cannot strip us of our respectability.

He will make Apollodorus approach Caesar with "Hail, Caesar! I am Apollodorus the Sicilian, an artist." The Briton cries "An artist! Why have they admitted this vagabond?" to be checked by Caesar "Peace, man. Apollodorus is a famous patrician amateur." The Briton bows—"I crave the gentleman's pardon. I understood him to say he was a professional."

The introduction of this character—in spite of Shaw's own note on Britannus—has been condemned; but, as the author well knew, the excuse for his introduction lies, not in arguing that climate produces similar features in all centuries, but in the fact that he is eminently in his right dramatic place. Throughout this play, Shaw is not intent on naturalistically recreating a past period of history; over all he casts the light of his own imagination and that imagination is tinged and irradiated by his inimitable spirit of fun. It is the same with his later dramas. In *Back to Methuselah* Franklyn is introducing his brother to Burge: "I forget whether you know my brother Conrad. He is a biologist", on which Burge suddenly bursts into energetic action and words:

> By reputation only, but very well, of course. How I wish I could have devoted myself to biology! I have always been interested in rocks and strata and volcanoes and so forth: they throw such a light on the age of the earth. There is nothing like biology. "The cloud-capped towers, the solemn binnacles, the gorgeous temples, the great globe itself: yea, all that it inherit shall dissolve

and, like this influential pageant faded, leave not a wrack behind."
That's biology, you know: good sound biology.

The words and the scene are exaggeratedly ridiculous: but
again they do not clash with the serious, imaginative arguments which precede and follow because over all Shaw has
thrown the mantle of his peculiarly dominating sense of
fun, just as Shakespeare cast the radiance of his humour
alike on Dogberry and on Claudio.

The invention and elaboration of this comedy of purposeful
fun forms an important contribution to the theatre; but this
is by no means all. Each one of Shaw's plays contains an
element of fantastic incongruity. True, he has written some
plays in the "realistic" style, but these, in my opinion, may
not be compared with those in which he has allowed free
rein to this imaginative fantasy. It is precisely here that
Shaw's historical position becomes significant. The decade
1890–1900 presented the growing power of naturalism in the
theatre; such naturalism, as we have already seen, was, owing
to the outworn and useless conventions that had been encrusted on the playhouse, both necessary and desirable. This
Shaw saw as clearly as any, and he aided materially in helping
forward those who were intent on introducing these new aims.
But even in his apprentice period, Shaw was always too big
for realism. Even in 1892 he realised that realism was not
enough, that the naturalistic stage was merely a step towards
something beyond. He recognised that plays are definitely
works of art and not merely mirrors of the life we see around
us. From the beginning, then, from *Widowers' Houses*,
through *Arms and the Man*, *Caesar and Cleopatra*, *Man and
Superman* on to *Back to Methuselah*, *Heartbreak House* and
The Apple Cart he has introduced this extra-realist element.

This extra-realist element is to be traced in conception of
situation, and it is equally to be traced in the conception of
character. Some time ago Shaw, in a private letter discussing
his then new play, *Too True to be Good*, referred to "the great
length to which *Too True* carries my practice of making my
characters say not what in real life they could never bring
themselves to say, even if they understood themselves clearly

enough, but the naked soul truth, quite objectively and scientifically presented, thus combining the extreme of un-naturalness with the deepest attainable naturalness. . . . The Shakespearean soliloquy, in so far as it was not merely an 'aside' for the information of the audience, was an attempt at this. The highest drama is nothing but a striving towards this feat of interpretation." Once more this self-judgment is a correct one; and, accepting it, we realise how far removed Shaw was in his scope from the dramatists who were his companions in the nineties.

That his work did not reach absolute perfection during his earliest efforts is, of course, obvious. *Widowers' Houses*, even though it does make a significant contribution to the theatre, clearly has not complete unity of conception, and *The Philan-derer* proves unsatisfactory because in composing it Shaw has been misled by the prevailing naturalism of his day. Perhaps there is another reason for the failure of this latter play. Unquestionably autobiographical in concept, it at one and the same time approaches too near to real life and presents a picture hopelessly artificial. In Charteris we cannot fail to see Bernard Shaw himself, and the fact that this is a kind of portrait of the artist robs the character of those qualities which animate Tanner and Bluntschli. Instead of being above his characters, Shaw sits here in their midst. The essence of Shaw's comedy, moreover, demands an entire absence of emotion. Start feeling for the Elderly Gentleman and you completely misinterpret his role; stir pity in your heart for Androcles and the very spirit of the comedy vanishes. In his letter, quoted above, Shaw stated that his persons were "quite objectively and scientifically presented", and this is true of most of his work; he generally succeeds in standing above his *dramatis personae*. "I am of the true Shakespearean type," he states elsewhere,[1] "I understand everything and everyone, and am nobody and nothing." Whereas, however, Shakespeare's genius was of such a kind as to permit of an emotional approach even while this objectivity was retained intact, Shaw's power requires a complete sense of detachment

---

[1] Letter quoted in Frank Harris, *op. cit.* p. 224.

between the creative artist and his puppet creations. By thrusting himself into the person of Charteris he adopted a method false to his own spirit, and in the attempt to display emotion in the person of Julia he brought down his whole dramatic edifice in a mass of crumbling ruins about his head. Wilde might legitimately exploit himself; Shaw's secret strength lies in self-repression. That such is not the commonly accepted view of his work arises from the fact that there is a confusion between Shaw the man and Shaw the dramatist. The writer of the prefaces is not the writer of the plays; there may be propaganda and the enunciation of individually held opinions in the preface, say, to *Androcles and the Lion*, but in the drama itself Shaw is "nobody and nothing"; as each character speaks he gives himself to that character and of propaganda there is little or none.

Similar weaknesses are to be traced in *Mrs Warren's Profession*, which seems to have been projected for an Independent Theatre Society production of 1894 under the title of *Mrs Jarman's Profession*.[1] The construction is good, but the spirit appears at once too determined and too emotional for the free expression of his dramatic talents. *Arms and the Man*, on the other hand, and *The Devil's Disciple* are true Shaw. Technically, both of these show great theatrical progress. The element of surprise in both may thus be contrasted with the even monotony of *The Philanderer*. More important, however, is the harmonious retention of mood. All emotionalism has been banished; if Raina proposes to become passionate, she is promptly repressed by Captain Bluntschli and Dick performs the same office for Mrs Anderson. Fun rules in both; laughter holds his sides as the romantic Saranoff confronts the imperturbable Swiss officer, and any tendency to seriousness in *The Devil's Disciple* is immediately curbed by a situation of absolute merriment.

The Man of Destiny shows his progress along these lines. Again the technique is excellent; again constant surprise keeps our attention alert—no chance of boredom as we pass from the loss of the despatches and the Lieutenant's attitude

---

[1] See note in *The Theatre*, N.S. xxiv, Dec. 1894, 332.

to the discovery of the Strange Lady, from that to the duel between this Lady and Napoleon, to the question of Napoleon's honour, to the command concerning the despatches, to the revealing of the Lady, to the argument about the English and so to the unexpected close. The dramatist's extreme economy is evident here and his constant need of startling effect. In 1897 *The Theatre* reviewer might feel puzzled:

> *The Man of Destiny* is less a play than a simple medium for the airing of the author's well-known opinions relative to Socialism, political economy, the aggrandisement of England, and other cognate matters.... Seriously to criticise a piece of the kind would be consequently a waste of time and space.... That there is real cleverness to be found in the dialogue we do not deny, but it is a kind of cleverness ill-suited to the purposes of the stage—.[1]

but to-day we recognise in it those qualities which, in a more extended form, placed Shaw in the forefront of the embattled modern dramatists.

This consideration of Shaw's strength and weakness in his early work becomes of special importance when we attempt to evaluate his *Candida*. Unquestionably *Candida* relates itself to *Mrs Warren's Profession* rather than to *The Man of Destiny*. That it displays structural skill may not be denied; yet it may be questioned whether, in spite of the high critical esteem in which it is held, this play represents such a vitally effective contribution to the theatre as *Androcles* or *Arms and the Man*. There is perhaps more warmth in *Candida* than in most of Shaw's plays, but for his characteristic comedy Shaw does not need warmth—emotion is really as alien to his needs as it was to those of Etherege and his companions of the Restoration stage. *Candida* is a play which we might have imagined other dramatists writing; only Shaw could have conceived and wittily executed *The Man of Destiny* and *The Devil's Disciple*.

4. *Naturalism and Fantasy*

During the time that Wilde and Shaw were thus writing for the stage, the naturalistic movement became more assured

---

[1] *The Theatre*, N.S. xxx, Aug. 1897, 101–2.

and determined. All the antiquated devices had, it is true, not been abandoned, but the aim was that of reproducing contemporary life. Two playwrights of the decade may be selected as typical. C. Haddon Chambers had begun his career with *One of Them* (Margate, Sept. 1886) and *The Open Gate* (Com. March 1887), but great success arrived to him only with *The Tyranny of Tears* (Crit. April 1899). Based on the methods and ideals of Pinero and Jones, retaining the use of such ancient instruments as the soliloquy and the aside, this drama is yet deliberately domestic in execution and concept. It presents seriously what many farces had presented amusingly in earlier years[1]—a husband, Parbury, whose wife has forced him, by means of the "tyranny of tears", to abandon all his old friends. Finding his secretary, Miss Woodward, kissing his photograph, the wife orders her to be dismissed. He succeeds in summoning up some spirit and resolutely refuses, whereupon she leaves him. The plot demands a sad or indeterminate ending, but Chambers has seen fit to bring his final curtain down sentimentally—with the return of the wife and with the arrival of Parbury's friend, Gunning, who very conveniently makes a proposal of marriage to Miss Woodward. This treatment, with its mingling of sentiment and of would-be "realism", is thoroughly characteristic of the spirit of the drama during this decade.

Even more representative are the plays of one who, in his own time, moved with the theatrical vanguard—Sydney Grundy. Like Pinero and Jones, this author had begun writing for the stage in the seventies[2]—with *A Little Change* (H. July 1872), *All at Sea* (Manchester, Aug. 1873), *Reading for the Bar* (Str. Oct. 1876) and similar farces or comediettas. The first works which give him any claim to serious attention came in the following decade—*The Silver Shield* (Str. May 1885), *A Fool's Paradise* (P.W. Greenwich, Oct. 1887, as *The Mousetrap*; Gai. Feb. 1889), *The Dean's Daughter* (St J. Oct. 1888), written in association with F. C. Philips; these were

---

[1] See *supra*, pp. 152–3.
[2] Sir W. Watson, *Sydney Grundy and the Critics* (*The Theatre*, N.S. xxxiii, 1894).

followed by the famous *Pair of Spectacles* (Gar. Feb. 1890)[1] and *Sowing the Wind* (Com. Sept. 1893). Grundy possessed a perfectly good comic style which he constantly vitiated by attempting serious things beyond his reach. *The Silver Shield*, for example, has some excellent scenes in which, without eccentricity, laughter is won from domestic circumstance, but there is decided weakness in the handling of a situation in which the young wife, finding among her husband's papers a section of a play he is composing, imagines it to be an amatory epistle addressed to an actress. His tragedy, *Clito* (P'cess, May 1886), written in collaboration with W. Barrett, demonstrates clearly how ill-suited he was to deal with emotional problems seriously and profoundly. In his work as a whole appears a strange contradiction, well summed up by a reviewer of *The Late Mr Castello* (Com. Dec. 1895):

Mr Sydney Grundy presents the curious spectacle of a playwright whose method is as antiquated as his manner is distinctly modern. In the matter of construction he is half a century behind the times; in point of dialogue he is, if anything, rather in advance of them.[2]

In this he is not unrepresentative of his time. With Pinero and Jones the stage had at last reached adequate expression of realistic aims but the task of banishing the very last relics of the older conventional theatre was left to the playwrights of the first decade of our own century.

It is important to recognise that this adequate expression of realistic aims was the result of an age-long development; even at the risk of repeating what has already been emphasised, a final word must be said concerning this. One might almost treat the entirety of theatrical history from the sixteenth to the nineteenth centuries as one single movement in art, with a gradual approach being made towards an ultimate ideal. In making such a statement, one would not, of course, wish to deny the existence of a continuing tradition which linked the theatre, say, of 1750 with the theatre of 1600. Up

---

[1] See the biographical and critical notice in *The Theatre*, N.S. xvi, July 1890, 46–7.
[2] *The Theatre*, N.S. xxviii, Feb. 1896, 97.

to the end of the eighteenth century, actors were going about their tasks very much as Alleyn and Burbage might have done; dramatists were supplying their wares under the same conditions as had applied to Marlowe and Kyd; theatre management organised the repertoires in the same manner as Henslowe had done; and audiences still watched the performances taking place almost, if not quite, in their midst. This is true; but equally true is the fact that, with the introduction of the closed theatre and the consequent artificial lighting, with the rise of sentimental comedy and bourgeois tragedy, a definite movement was being made towards later naturalism. One great advance in this direction was being taken about 1770; another in 1810; still another in 1840; and a final one in 1870. By the end of the century little remained of the older stage save the wandering tent-playhouse. The last of these has now vanished, but even a few years ago one could find them, maintaining a precarious and doubtful vitality, in the Midland and Welsh circuits. Anyone who has been fortunate enough to have witnessed one of these shows may justifiably claim that here he has been in the presence of the last true descendants of the Elizabethan companies. A trifle melancholy is the reflection, akin to that we experience when, on some Highland roadway, we encounter a wretched group of poverty-stricken, diseased and emaciated tramps, last relics of a Stuart clan dispersed and rejected by advancing civilisation.

Realism, then, in the picture-frame stage, with the banishment of antiquated conventions, triumphed. In any art, when once virile conventions become stereotyped and hence bereft of meaning, only a return to realistic methods can produce sanity and fresh inspiration. It was Giotto's break-away from sterile, but once powerful, Byzantine models which opened up the path for the advance of Italian art during the Renaissance. Tom Robertson was the Giotto of the English theatre in the nineteenth century, and translated Ibsen was its Raphael.

Any dispassionate survey of this period convinces us that this realistic method was necessary, nay more, that it succeeded in producing a series of plays which, if not greater (as William Archer deemed) than the poetic Elizabethan dramas, are worthy of being placed alongside the masterpieces of any age. At the same time, we must recognise two things. The first is that realism can never be enough. To discuss the implications of this and show why that naturalism which was life and health and inspiration in 1900 cannot serve a later generation would take us far outside the confines of the late nineteenth century; but the second thing worthy of notice definitely belongs within these confines. It is the fact that, even in the midst of this naturalistic development, there were many attempts at escape. These must now occupy our attention.

The most obvious of the attempts is the cultivation of poetic drama, but it cannot be maintained that this age created more worthy examples of this kind than had been created in the preceding eras. During the forties Browning, encouraged by Macready, had sought to win theatrical success, but failed to secure a reasonably firm footing on the boards. He, in turn, was followed by the majestic solemnity of Tennyson. Much was hoped from Tennyson. Established as the most popular lyric writer of his day and a proven master in the realm of narrative verse, he was viewed by some as a man who might, if he desired, bring back the glories of Elizabeth's reign in the age of Victoria. Tennyson certainly desired it; of that there is no doubt, and "infinite trouble" he expended on his dramatic works. Not one of these, however, has any real theatric value. Partly the explanation for their failure may be sought in the prevailing didacticism which blunts their temper; Tennyson's patriotic orthodoxy at best is dull; but more perhaps is it to be traced to the lack of stage sense common to these poets. *Queen Mary* (Lyc. April 1876)[1] has a good theme and a wretched handling; *Harold* (printed 1877) seems to us monotonously pretentious; and *Becket* (Lyr. Feb.

[1] On the sources of Tennyson's plays see Werner Martin, *Die Quellen zu Tennysons erstem Drama "Queen Mary"* (Halle, 1912), Paul Jelling-haus, *Tennysons Drama "Harold"* (Borna-Leipzig, 1907) and Louis Grünert, *Tennysons Drama "Becket"* (Weimar, 1913).

1893) is fogged in Tennyson's most dignified gloom. True, he won a certain measure of success on the stage, but that was due, not to the inherent virtues of the plays but to a combination of the author's poetic fame and the equally popular acting of Irving and the Kendals.

After Tennyson came Stephen Phillips with his *Paolo and Francesca* (licensed 1899; St J. March 1902). *Paolo and Francesca* is a play which at once recalls the long, sorry series of its predecessors—poor ghosts revisiting the glimpses of an Elizabethan moon, and immediately differentiates itself from these. The Shakespearian plan Phillips has followed as a pattern, that is evident: Shakespeare's verse form becomes the model for his verse, and the characters are set forth in the manner of the great seventeenth-century tragedies. In so far, he shows himself a mere companion of the other poets of the time. When, however, we note that, at an early age, Phillips joined F. R. Benson's company and acted therein for a number of years, we realise that his training was not that of a lordly Byron, an eccentric Shelley or a lonely Keats. It is precisely this training on the part of the author that sets *Paolo and Francesca* apart from the other poetic plays of the nineteenth century. This drama is not a great masterpiece; there are weaknesses in it of structure, character-delineation and dialogue; but Phillips has honestly studied the technique of his craft and his tragedy is to be welcomed for its essentially dramatic qualities. Its main defect lies in its tendency towards elaborate lyricism and in its dependence upon ancient rhythmic patterns. In spite of his theatrical apprenticeship and in spite of the consequent endeavour to establish the poetic drama on a new foundation, Phillips did not succeed in breaking away from the vicious influences of the romantic style or in realising the true function of verse in the theatre. Lady Benson records that he "had a fine voice" but that he

would insist on rolling out his lines...making his diction unnatural and stilted. I asked him his reason for this, and he replied that he put a higher value on the beauty of the words than on their dramatic effect.[1]

---

[1] *Mainly Players: Bensonian Memories* (1926), pp. 65–6.

This is typical. Before a new poetic drama could arise, poets had to learn to forget Shakespeare and to remember that the theatre needs more than words sonorously rolled out. The virtue of *Murder in the Cathedral* and *The Ascent of F. 6* rests in the determined effort of their authors to find an entirely fresh foundation on which to work.

With these attempts to establish poetic drama on the stage must be related a certain romantic enthusiasm which, particularly in the nineties, surprisingly manifested itself among the audiences. Already attention has been drawn to the "Boom in Shakespeare" which even contemporaries had noticed.[1] Irving's great revivals were popular, mainly of course because of the actor-manager's personality, but partly at least because the surging throb of the Elizabethan drama created a mood different from and larger than that provided by Jones and Pinero. For the same reason there came a return of interest in flamboyantly adventuresome cloak-and-sword plays. *The Prisoner of Zenda* (St J. Jan. 1896), as adapted by Edward Rose from Anthony Hope's novel, started a fashion which usurped the earlier craze for Irish comedy-dramas. *The Three Musketeers* (Manchester, Aug. 1850), as adapted by Charles Rice, had hardly been a great success in 1850, but in the last years of the century plays on the same theme swept the boards. At the Imperial W. Heron Brown brought out one version (June 1898); H. A. Saintsbury's adaptation appeared at the Parkhurst (Sept. 1898); Henry Hamilton had his produced first at the Metropole, Camberwell (Sept. 1898) and later at the Globe (Oct. 1898); another version by Brian Daly and J. M. East appeared at the Lyric, Hammersmith (Nov. 1898); while Rice's independent version (originally produced at Manchester, Aug. 1850) was revived at the Britannia (Oct. 1898). The winter of '98 was decidedly a winter of the *Musketeers*. Nor did that theme stand alone; others of a like kind proved equally successful. Martin Harvey brought out Freeman Wills's *The Only Way* at the Lyceum in February 1899; L. B. Irving's *Robespierre* (Lyc. April 1899) belongs in the same category, as do Edward

---

[1] See *supra*, p. 38.

Rose's *In Days of Old* (St J. April 1899) and C. B. Fernald's *The Moonlight Blossom* (P.W. Sept. 1899).

All of these tell the same tale—a tale of unconscious dissatisfaction with the prevailing tendency towards realism. It is by no means strange that Gordon Craig was reared in the Irving tradition and that his first production, that of *Dido and Aeneas*, came in the spring of 1900.[1]

Even more significant is the restless deviation from realistic method already noted in the plays of Wilde and Shaw. The eccentric wit of the former and the fantastic fun of the latter lead them far from the dull imitation of life. And by their side stands J. M. Barrie.[2] Before the turn of the century Barrie had not accomplished much in the theatre, but what he had done proved that his was not a genius likely to be content with familiar description of easily observed natural forms. In some plays he sought escape in the world of romance—*Becky Sharp* (Terry's, June 1893), *Richard Savage* (Crit. April 1891), *The Little Minister* (H. Nov. 1897); elsewhere he applied older burlesque methods to newer idols, laughing at naturalism in *Ibsen's Ghost* (Toole's, May 1891); and in one other, *Walker, London* (Toole's, Feb. 1892), he displayed an individual quality which later was to blossom into richer bloom in *The Admirable Crichton* and *Peter Pan*. Barrie's true significance for the drama lies in his effort to substitute subjectivity for objectivity, artistic form and pattern for formal recording. His elfin humour, for which the epithet "pawky" is inevitable, releases him much in the same way as Shaw is released by his impish spirit of fun.

Nor were these men wholly without companions. One example of this will suffice. Robert Marshall has a play called *Shades of Night* (Lyc. March 1896) in which Captain Trivett and Winifred Yester are brought to a haunted room and there

---

[1] Enid Rose, *Gordon Craig and the Theatre* (n.d.) pp. 31–2.
[2] On his career see the studies by T. Moult (1928), F. J. H. Darton (1929) and J. A. Hammerton (1929). His writings are listed in B. D. Cutler, *Sir James M. Barrie: A Bibliography* (1931). H. M. Walbrook has an essay on *J. M. Barrie and the Theatre* (1922), Walter Eschenhauer another on *Sir James Barrie als Dramatiker: Ein Beitrag zum englischen Drama des zwanzigsten Jahrhunderts* (Halle, 1929).

confronted by the ghosts of their ancestors. The dialogue is not, maybe, very brilliant, but there is evident in its fantasy a wish to break away from current domestic realism. The ghosts of Lady Mildred and Sir Ludovic have made their appearance:

LADY MILDRED (*at back*). I believe, Captain Trivett, that your mother now rules the establishment here. That being so, might I ask you, as a favour, to request her to keep this room for the future aired and dusted?

CAPTAIN. Yes, yes,—of course—by all means.

LADY MILDRED. Thanks. This, you know, is my only gown.

SIR LUDOVIC. That's one of your hardships. We can only sport the togs we died in.

CAPTAIN. Then if you die in bed?

SIR LUDOVIC. You put an awkward question. A good deal would depend on the pattern. I think we had better go on with the business, Eh, Lady Mildred?

LADY MILDRED (*with great hauteur*). I certainly think so. I have no desire to pursue the present vein of the conversation....

SIR LUDOVIC (*crosses to* CAPTAIN *and* WINIFRED, LADY MILDRED *gets to table*). Your presence here to-night is a matter of great satisfaction to me. You'll now learn the true version of our story. But you mustn't laugh. You see we've never done it to an audience before, and no doubt we shall be a little awkward at first. Are you ready, Lady Mildred?

LADY MILDRED. Quite.

SIR LUDOVIC. Very well, then, (CAPTAIN *and* WINIFRED *go to the chair*, R. *corner*. WINIFRED *sits. To the others*). We begin with the declaration of my passion. The language may seem a little stilted, but you won't mind that?

CAPTAIN. Not at all.

SIR LUDOVIC. Thanks. Now then!

Throughout the scene that follows, the action of the Phantoms takes place at the back of the stage, C. *The tone of speech is hollow, the style melodramatic, but not extravagantly so. The ordinary mode of speech is adopted when the Phantoms stop the action at intervals to discuss it with* CAPTAIN TRIVETT *and* WINIFRED. LADY MILDRED *is seated at table*, SIR LUDOVIC *bending over her. A decanter and two glasses are on the table.*

"As evening looms from out the sundown and the burnished sword of daybreak smiles the raven wings of night, still do I protest, O LADY MILDRED, that but one thought draws from my soul!"

LADY MILDRED. "Lud! Sir Ludovic. Your ideas must be vastly limited!" I should like to point out, Miss Yester, that originally this gown was of a delicate shell pink brocade, lined with pale mauve velvet, and at the time my complexion was the talk of the country. (SIR LUDOVIC moves R. *up to window, much annoyed*.) In the astral world, you know, we become quite colourless.

WINIFRED. Yes, yes, I understand.

SIR LUDOVIC (*comes down*). However, to continue. "There is but one passion that dominates my soul, Lady Mildred. It is the burning love I bear you!"

LADY MILDRED. "You bear my fortune! Enough, Sir Ludovic, I will have none of you!"

SIR LUDOVIC (*starting back*). "Spurned?"

LADY MILDRED. "Aye, spurned! For I too love—my fortune!"

SIR LUDOVIC. "Am I then doomed to live—alas!—alone?"

LADY MILDRED. "Lud, Sir Ludovic! 'tis I who mean to live a lass alone!" (*Laughs and turns to the others*.) You see my play upon the words "alas! alone?"

SIR LUDOVIC. Isn't it good? I remember, though, I felt it terribly at the time.

CAPTAIN. It was a little heartless.

LADY MILDRED (*sharply*). Not at all. It was said quite artlessly.

CAPTAIN. Exactly—as I say—heartlessly.

LADY MILDRED. I said a-r-t artlessly—you supplied the *h*; not being my own I dropped it. (*Crosses L. a little*.) Besides, I knew he cared for nothing but my money.

SIR LUDOVIC. It's quite true; she saw through me.

CAPTAIN. Ah! You admit it?

SIR LUDOVIC. Oh, dear me, yes! I felt no love at all! It was all put on, like her complexion.

Quite clearly, such work as this indicates new scope for the theatre, and, even though we may not be prepared to reckon *Shades of Night* a great masterpiece, we may acclaim Marshall as one at least among a body of playwrights who, in the nineties, were striving to open up dramatic fields the frontiers of which were being narrowed by the stricter realists.

As we leave this century, however, we still find these stricter realists in control. This was their day and they made the most of it. Their works formed the characteristic expression of the time. The seeds planted by Lytton and Boucicault in the forties had now grown to sturdy plants bearing fruit, not juicily soft and providing only a moment's enjoyment, but hard and filled with the substance of good and evil. The last years of Victoria's reign closed with almost full realisation of that promise which her early patronage of the theatre had aroused. London now was displaying a dramatic vitality of which it had been innocent since the days of Queen Anne. In spite of her prudish temper and her bourgeois-like placidity, Victoria had succeeded in bringing to life once more a theatre acknowledged and supported by all classes among her subjects—a theatre which, despite all the restrictions imposed upon it by its clinging to realism, may not find a previous rival in England unless we travel in imagination back over four centuries to the Swan and the Globe and the Fortune, theatres which sheltered a Jonson and a Shakespeare, making still more glorious the glorious reign of an earlier queen.

APPENDIX A

THE THEATRES, 1850—1900

IN this list I have included (1) the theatres of London and its suburbs, (2) the London music-halls and (3) the chief provincial playhouses. Only for the first section is any attempt made to indicate precise dates. It should be noted that in the third section some of the theatres listed under varying titles were the same buildings successively renamed. Abbreviations used in the text and in Appendix B appear in square brackets immediately after the main title. Attention may be drawn to the fact that, in recording performances in the provinces, the use of T.R. for Theatre Royal has been dispensed with; thus record of a production at "Birmingham" on a certain date indicates the Theatre Royal, Birmingham. The earlier fortunes of some of the London playhouses will be found in *E.N.D.* i, 217–33. Invaluable comments regarding now vanished theatres are given by Errol Sherson in *London's Lost Theatres of the Nineteenth Century* (1925); many details regarding managements will be found in the files of *The Era*.

I. *London and Environs*

The Adelphi Theatre (Strand) [Adel.]. See *E.N.D.* i, 217. Rebuilt in 1858.

The Albert Palace (Shepherdess-walk, Britannia Fields, Hoxton) [Albert]. See *E.N.D.* i, 217.

The Albion Saloon (Poplar) [Albion]. Also known as *The Oriental Palace*.

The Alcazar Theatre [Alcazar]. See *The Connaught Theatre*.

The Alexandra Theatre (Highbury Barn, Newington) [Alex.]. Opened May 20, 1865, closed 1871. See Michael Williams, *Some London Theatres Past and Present* (1883), p. 43.

The Alexandra Theatre (Camden Town) [Alex.]. See *The Park Theatre*.

The Alexandra Theatre (Stoke Newington) [Alex.]. Opened on December 27, 1897. [It should be noted that between 1865 and 1871 the contraction "Alex." refers to the Highbury

Barn house, between 1873 and 1881 to that at Camden Town and between 1897 and 1900 to that at Stoke Newington.]

The Alexandra Palace (Muswell Hill) [Alex. Pal.]. Opened in 1889.

The Alfred Theatre [Alfred]. See *The Marylebone Theatre.*

The Alhambra Palace (Leicester-square) [Alh.]. Opened as a music-hall in 1858 and as a theatre in 1871. Destroyed by fire December 12, 1882; new building opened December 3, 1883.

The Aquarium Theatre [Aquar.]. See *The Imperial Theatre.*

Astley's Amphitheatre (Westminster Bridge-road) [Ast.]. See *E.N.D.* i, 224–5. Renamed *Sanger's Grand National Amphitheatre* in 1883. Destroyed in 1895.

The Athenaeum (Tottenham Court-road) [Athen.]. Plays were produced here between 1887 and 1889.

The Avenue Theatre (Northumberland-avenue, Charing Cross) [Aven.]. Opened March 10, 1882.

Barnard's Theatre Royal (Woolwich) [Barnard's].

The Bijou Theatre (Archer-street, Bayswater) [Bijou]. Opened in 1882 as *The Victoria Hall.* [Errol Sherson, *op. cit.* pp. 324–5, notes a Bijou Theatre in the Haymarket; my references seem to be all to the Bayswater house.]

The Borough Theatre, Stratford (Borough). Opened in 1896.

The Bower Operetta House (Stangate-street, Lambeth) [Bower]. See *E.N.D.* i, 218. Closed in 1878; sometimes known as *The Royal Stangate Theatre.*

The Britannia Theatre or *Saloon* (High-street, Hoxton) [Brit.]. See *E.N.D.* i, 218.

The Brixton Theatre (Lambeth) [Brixton]. Opened September 21, 1896.

The Broadway Theatre (New Cross) [Broadway]. Opened in 1896.

The Cabinet Theatre [Cab.]. See *The King's Cross Theatre.*

The Camborne Theatre [Camborne]. Of this house I have no record save that plays were produced there in 1889.

The Charing Cross Theatre (King William-street) [Ch. X.]. Opened in 1869, renamed *The Folly* in 1876 and *Toole's Theatre* in 1882. Demolished in 1895.

The City of London Theatre (near Bishopsgate Station, Norton Folgate) [C.L.]. See *E.N.D.* i, 225 and M. Williams, *op. cit.* pp. 47–9. Closed in 1868.

The Colosseum (Regent's Park) [Col.]. Originally opened in 1824; plays occasionally presented between 1850 and 1900.

The Comedy Theatre (Panton-street, Haymarket) [Com.]. Opened October 15, 1881.

The Connaught Theatre (Holborn) [Connaught]. Opened in November 1879; altered and renamed *The Alcazar Theatre* on December 26, 1882.

The Coronet Theatre (Notting Hill-gate). Opened on November 28, 1898.

The Court Theatre (Sloane-square, Chelsea) [Court]. Opened in 1871 as *The New Chelsea Theatre*. Demolished in 1887 and rebuilt the following year, opening on September 24, 1888. See Cecil Howard, *Dramatic Notes* (1889), p. 144.

Covent Garden Opera House (Covent Garden) [C.G.]. See *E.N.D.* i, 218–19. Burned May 6, 1856; new building opened on May 15, 1858.

Cremorne Gardens (Chelsea) [Cremorne]. Occasional plays were produced at this popular place of entertainment, which closed in April 1878.

The Criterion Theatre (Piccadilly) [Crit.]. Opened in 1874 and reconstructed in 1884.

The Crown Theatre (Camberwell) [Crown]. Opened on October 31, 1898.

The Crystal Palace (Sydenham) [C.P.]. Occasional plays and Christmas entertainments were produced here.

The Dalston Theatre (Hackney) [Dalston]. Opened September 25, 1898.

Daly's Theatre (Cranbourne-street, Leicester-square) [Daly's]. Opened in 1893.

The Theatre Royal, Drury Lane (Drury-lane) [D.L.]. See *E.N.D.* i, 219–20.

The Duchess Theatre (Balham) [Duchess]. Opened in 1899.

The Duke's Theatre [Duke's]. See *The Holborn Theatre*.

The Duke of York's Theatre (St Martin's-lane) [D.Y.]. Opened in 1892 as *The Trafalgar Square Theatre*; renamed *The Duke of York's* on September 26, 1895.

The Eastern Opera House, Pavilion Theatre. See *The Pavilion*.

The Eclectic Theatre. See *The Royalty Theatre*.

The Eden Theatre [Eden]. See *The Novelty Theatre*.

The Effingham Saloon (Whitechapel) [Eff.]. See *E.N.D.* i, 220.

The Elephant and Castle Theatre (New Kent-road, Elephant and Castle) [E.C.]. Opened in 1872; destroyed by fire in 1878; rebuilt 1879; reconstructed in 1882 and 1902.

The Empire Theatre of Varieties (Leicester-square) [Empire]. Opened as a music-hall on April 17, 1884.

The Empress Theatre (Lambeth) [Empress]. Opened in 1898.

The Folies Dramatiques [Folies Dramatiques]. See *The Novelty Theatre*.

The Folly Theatre [Folly]. See *The Charing Cross Theatre*.

The Gaiety Theatre (Strand) [Gai.]. Opened in 1868.

The Garrick Theatre (Charing Cross-road) [Gar.]. Opened in 1889.

The Globe Theatre (Newcastle-street, Strand) [Glo.]. Opened in November 1868. Destroyed in 1902.

The Grand Theatre (Islington) [Grand]. Opened in 1870 as *The Philharmonic Theatre*; burned on September 6, 1882; reopened August 4, 1883; burned December 28, 1887; reopened August 4, 1888 as *The Grand Theatre*.

The Grand Theatre (Fulham) [Grand, Fulham]. Opened on August 23, 1897.

The Great Queen Street Theatre [Great Queen Street]. See *The Novelty Theatre*.

The Grecian Saloon (Shepherdess-walk, Britannia Fields, Hoxton) [Grec.]. See *E.N.D.* i, 220.

The Royal Opera House, Haymarket [H.]. See *E.N.D.* i, 220–1. Also called *Her Majesty's Opera House*.

The Theatre Royal, Haymarket [H.]. See *E.N.D.* i, 221. Altered in 1872 and rebuilt in 1880. See E. L. Blanchard, *History of the Haymarket Theatre* (*Era Almanac*, 1873, pp. 1–16). [It should be noted that references to "H." in Appendix B are to this theatre.]

Hengler's Amphitheatre (Argyll-street, Oxford Circus) [Hengler's]. Occasional plays were produced here from 1889 onwards.

Her Majesty's Theatre (Haymarket) [H.M.]. Opened on April 28, 1897.

The Holborn Theatre (Holborn) [Holb.]. Opened on October 6, 1866 as *The Duke's Theatre*; renamed *The Mirror* in 1875 and *The Duke's* in 1879; destroyed by fire on July 4, 1880. Rebuilt and called *The International Theatre* from December 1883 to February 1884.

The Imperial Theatre (Westminster) [Imp.]. Opened in 1876 as *The Royal Aquarium and Winter Garden*; renamed *The Imperial Theatre* in 1879, with occasional later use of the original name. Reopened after alterations on April 11, 1898.

The International Theatre [Internat.]. See *The Holborn Theatre*.

The Jodrell Theatre [Jodrell]. See *The Novelty Theatre*.

The Theatre Royal, Kilburn [Kilburn]. Opened in 1886.

The King's Cross Theatre (King's Cross, New-road) [K.X.]. See *E.N.D.* i, 225 (under *The Royal Clarence Theatre*). After being known as *The Panharmonium*, it was renamed *The King's Cross Theatre* and *The Cabinet Theatre* (1852–67).

Ladbroke Hall (Bayswater) [Ladb. H.]. Opened in 1882.

The Lyceum Theatre (Wellington-street, Strand) [Lyc.]. See
   E.N.D. i, 221–2.
The Lyric Theatre (Shaftesbury-avenue) [Lyr.]. Opened on
   December 17, 1888.
The Lyric Hall (Ealing) [Lyr. Ealing]. Opened in 1889.
The Lyric Opera House (Hammersmith) [Lyr. Hammersmith].
   Opened in 1890.
The Manor Theatre (Hackney) [Manor]. Opened in 1896.
The Marionette Theatre [Marionette]. See *The Strand Theatre.*
The Marylebone Theatre (Church-street, Edgeware-road) [M'bone].
   See *E.N.D.* i, 222. Renamed *The Royal Alfred Theatre* on
   October 10, 1868; reverted to *The Marylebone* in 1872;
   renamed *The West London Theatre* on April 1, 1893. See
   M. Williams, *op. cit.* p. 80.
The Matinée Theatre [Mat.]. See *St George's Hall.*
The Metropole (Camberwell) [Metro.]. Opened in 1894.
The Mirror Theatre [Mirror]. See *The Holborn Theatre.*
Morton's Theatre (Greenwich) [Morton's, Greenwich]. Opened
   in 1896.
The New Chelsea Theatre [New Chelsea]. See *The Court Theatre.*
The New Queen's Theatre [New Qns.]. See *The Novelty Theatre.*
The New Theatre (Ealing) [New, Ealing]. Opened in 1898.
The New Victoria Palace. See *The Victoria Theatre.*
The North London Colosseum (Hackney) [N. London Col.].
   Opened about 1888; closed in 1890.
North Woolwich Gardens [N. Woolwich Gdns.].
The Novelty Theatre (Great Queen-street) [Nov.]. Opened on
   December 9, 1882; closed after two weeks and reopened as
   The Folies Dramatiques. Reopened in 1883 as *The Novelty.*
   Variously named as *The Joddrell Theatre* (1887–9), *The New
   Queen's Theatre* (1890), *The Eden Theatre* (1894) and *The
   Great Queen Street Theatre* (1900).
The Olympic Theatre (Wych-street, or Newcastle-street, Strand)
   [Olym.]. See *E.N.D.* i, 223.
The Opera Comique (Strand) [O.C.]. Opened in 1870; recon-
   structed in 1885; closed in 1899.
The Oriental Palace [Oriental]. See *The Albion Saloon.*
The Pandora Theatre [Pandora]. Of this house I have no record
   save that plays were being produced there in 1882–3.
The Park Theatre (Camden Town) [Park]. Opened in 1871;
   renamed *The Alexandra Theatre* on May 31, 1874; burned
   in 1881.
The Parkhurst Theatre (Camden-road, Holloway) [Parkhurst].
   Opened in 1890.

The Pavilion (Whitechapel-road, Mile End) [Pav.]. See *E.N.D.* i, 226. In 1860 known as *The Eastern Opera House Pavilion Theatre*.

The Pavilion or *London Pavilion* (Piccadilly) [Pav.]. Opened in 1861; reconstructed in 1885.

The Philharmonic Theatre (Islington) [Phil.]. See *The Grand Theatre*.

Portman Rooms (Baker-street) [Portman R.]. Used for the performance of plays from 1887.

The Prince of Wales's Theatre (Tottenham Court-road) [P.W.]. Opened in 1865 [formerly *The Queen's Theatre*, for which see *E.N.D.* i, 224].

The Prince's or *The Prince of Wales's Theatre* (Coventry-street) [P's]. Opened on January 18, 1884.

The Prince's Theatre (Kew) [P's, Kew].

The Princess's Theatre (Oxford-street) [P'cess]. See *E.N.D.* i, 224. Demolished in 1880 and reopened on November 11 of the same year.

The Princess of Wales's Theatre (Kennington) [P'cess of W.]. Opened in 1897.

Punch's Playhouse. See *The Strand Theatre*.

The Queen's Theatre [Qns.]. See *The Prince of Wales's Theatre*.

The Queen's Theatre (Longacre) [Qns.]. Opened in 1867; closed in 1878.

The Queen's Theatre (Queen's-road, Battersea) [Qns. Battersea]. Opened in 1892.

The Queen's Opera House (Crouch End) [Qns. O.H.]. Opened on July 27, 1897.

The Theatre Royal, Richmond [Richmond]. For the old theatre see *E.N.D.* i, 232-3. A new *Theatre Royal* was opened on September 16, 1899.

The Royal Alfred Theatre. See *The Alfred Theatre*.

The Royal Aquarium and Winter Garden. See *The Aquarium*.

The Royal Artillery Theatre (Woolwich) [R.A. Woolwich].

The Royal City of London Theatre. See *The City of London Theatre*.

The Royal County Theatre (Kingston) [County, Kingston]. Opened on October 4, 1897.

The Royal Court Theatre. See *The Court Theatre*.

The Royal Gallery of Illustration (Regent-street) [G.I.]. Opened in 1856.

The Royal Marylebone Theatre. See *The Marylebone Theatre*.

The Royal Stangate Theatre. See *The Stangate Theatre*.

The Royalty Theatre (Dean-street, Soho) [Roy.]. Originally opened in 1840; reconstructed in 1861 and 1883. Sometimes known as *The Soho Theatre* and as *The Eclectic Theatre, Soho.*

Sadler's Wells Theatre (Rosebury-avenue, Islington) [S.W.]. See *E.N.D.* i, 226–7.

St George's Hall (Langham-place) [St G.]. Opened in 1867; renamed *The Matinée Theatre* in 1897.

St James's Theatre (King-street, St James's) [St. J.]. See *E.N.D.* i, 227.

St Martin's Hall (Longacre) [St Martin's H.]. Opened in 1850. On its site *The Queen's Theatre* was built.

Salle Erard (Regent-street) [Salle Erard]. Opened in 1895.

Sanger's Grand National Amphitheatre [Sanger's]. See *Astley's Amphitheatre.*

The Savoy Theatre (Strand) [Sav.]. Opened on October 10, 1881.

The Shaftesbury Theatre (Shaftesbury-avenue) [Shaft.]. Opened on October 20, 1888.

The Shakespeare Theatre (Clapham Junction) [Shakespeare]. Opened on November 16, 1896.

The Soho Theatre [Soho]. See *The Royalty Theatre.*

The Standard Theatre (High-street, Shoreditch) [Stand.]. See *E.N.D.* i, 226. Destroyed by fire 1866; rebuilt 1867.

The Stangate Theatre [Stangate]. See *The Bower Operetta House.*

Steinway Hall (Lower Seymour-street) [Steinway H.]. Opened in 1887.

The Strand Theatre (Strand) [Str.]. See *E.N.D.* i, 227. Mss. was called *Punch's Playhouse* and *The Marionette Theatre* from May 1851 to May 1852. Reconstructed and enlarged during November 1865. See *A History of the Strand Theatre* (*Era Almanac*, 1872, pp. 6–10).

The Theatre Royal, Stratford [Stratford]. Opened in 1894.

The Surrey Theatre (Blackfriars-road) [Sur.]. See *E.N.D.* i, 227–8. Destroyed by fire in 1865 and rebuilt, opening on December 26 of that year.

The Terriss Theatre (Rotherhithe) [Terriss]. Opened on October 16, 1899.

Terry's Theatre (Strand) [Terry's]. Opened in 1888.

Toole's Theatre [Toole's]. See *The Charing Cross Theatre.*

The Trafalgar Square Theatre [Traf.]. See *The Duke of York's Theatre.*

The Vaudeville Theatre (Strand) [Vaud.]. Opened in 1870; reconstructed in 1891.

The Victoria Hall [Vic. H.]. See *The Bijou Theatre.*

The Victoria Hall (Ealing) [Vic. Ealing]. Opened in 1891.

The Victoria Theatre (Waterloo-road) [Vic.]. See *E.N.D.* i, 226.
    After reconstructions, opened on December 23, 1871 as *The
    New Victoria Palace*. See E. L. Blanchard, *The Victoria
    Theatre* (*Era Almanac*, 1873, pp. 7–12).
The West London Theatre [W.L.]. See *The Marylebone Theatre*.
The West Theatre, Albert Hall [West, Albert H.].
Wyndham's Theatre (Charing Cross-road) [Wyndham's]. Opened
    on November 16, 1899.

II. *Music Halls*

[Only the principal houses are here listed]

Albert	*Marylebone*
Alhambra	*Metropolitan*
Battersea Palace	*Middlesex*
Bedford	*Oxford*
Camberwell Palace of Varieties	*Palace of Varieties*
Cambridge	*Paragon*
Canterbury	*Parthenon, Greenwich*
Collins's	*People's, Peckham*
Deacon's	*Queen's, Poplar*
Eastern Empire	*Raglan*
Empire	*Royal*
Empress Palace, Brixton	*Sebright*
Foresters'	*South London*
Gatti's (Charing Cross)	*Standard*
Gatti's (Westminster Bridge Road)	*Star*
Grand Hall, Clapham	*Stratford Empire*
Granville	*Sun*
Hammersmith	*Tivoli*
Holloway Empire	*Varieties, Hoxton*
London	*Victoria Palace*
London Hippodrome	*Washington*
London Pavilion	*World's Fair*

III. *The Provinces, Scotland, Wales and Ireland*

Aberdare.   *The New* and *The Star.*
Aberdeen.   *Her Majesty's Opera House.*
Accrington.   *The Prince's.*

Aldershot.	Theatre Royal and The Victory.
Ashington.	Miner's.
Ashton.	Theatre Royal, Booth's, The People's Opera House and The Star.
Aston.	Theatre Royal.
Attercliffe.	Theatre Royal.
Barnsley.	Theatre Royal and The Queen's.
Barnstaple.	The New.
Barrow.	The Royalty.
Bath.	Theatre Royal.
Batley.	Theatre Royal.
Bedford.	The County.
Belfast.	Theatre Royal and Grand Opera House.
Bilston.	Theatre Royal.
Birkenhead.	Theatre Royal and The Metropole.
Birmingham.	Theatre Royal, The Adelphi, Coutt's, The Grand, The New, The Prince of Wales's and The Queen's.
Bishop Auckland.	The Eden.
Blackburn.	Theatre Royal, The Lyceum and The Prince's.
Blackpool.	The Grand, Her Majesty's Opera House, The Prince of Wales's and The Winter Gardens.
Blyth.	Theatre Royal and The Octagon.
Bolton.	Theatre Royal and The Grand.
Bootle.	Muncaster.
Bordesley.	The Imperial.
Boscombe.	The Grand.
Boston.	The Aquarium.
Bournemouth.	Theatre Royal.
Bradford.	Theatre Royal, Pullan's Theatre of Varieties and The Prince's.
Bridgend.	The Pavilion.
Bridlington.	The Spa and Victoria Rooms.
Brierley Hill.	Theatre Royal.
Brighton.	Theatre Royal, The Alhambra, The Aquarium, The Eden and The Gaiety.
Bristol.	Theatre Royal, The Prince's and The Queen's.
Bromley.	The Grand.
Burnley.	The Empire, The Gaiety and The Victoria Opera House.
Burton-on-Trent.	St George's.
Bury.	Theatre Royal and The Star.
Bury St Edmunds.	Theatre Royal.
Cambridge.	The New.

Canterbury.	*Theatre Royal.*
Cardiff.	*Theatre Royal, The Grand* and *The Philharmonic.*
Carlisle.	*Her Majesty's.*
Carmarthen.	*Warren's.*
Castleford.	*Theatre Royal.*
Chatham.	*Theatre Royal, The New* and *The Opera House.*
Chelmsford.	*Corn Exchange.*
Cheltenham.	*The Opera House.*
Chester.	*The Royalty.*
Chester-le-Street.	*The Queen's.*
Chesterfield.	*Theatre Royal.*
Chorley.	*The Grand.*
Clacton-on-Sea.	*The Operetta House.*
Coatbridge.	*Theatre Royal.*
Colchester.	*Theatre Royal.*
Consett.	*The New.*
Cork.	*The Opera House.*
Coventry.	*The Opera House.*
Crewe.	*The Albion* and *The Lyceum.*
Croydon.	*Theatre Royal* and *The Grand.*
Darlington.	*Theatre Royal.*
Darwen.	*Theatre Royal.*
Derby.	*The Grand.*
Devonport.	*The Metropole.*
Dewsbury.	*Theatre Royal.*
Doncaster.	*The Empire* and *The Royal Opera House.*
Douglas.	*The Grand.*
Dover.	*Theatre Royal* and *The Clarence.*
Dublin.	*Theatre Royal, The Gaiety* and *The Queen's.*
Dudley.	*The Opera House.*
Dundee.	*The Opera House (The People's).*
Durham.	*The Albany.*
Eastbourne.	*Theatre Royal, Devonshire Park* and *Floral Hall.*
Eccles.	*The Lyceum.*
Edinburgh.	*Theatre Royal, The Amphitheatre, The Grand, The Lyceum, The Operetta House, The Pavilion, The Princess's, The Southminster* and *The Waterloo Opera House.*
Evesham.	*The Victoria.*
Exeter.	*Theatre Royal, The New* and *The Victoria.*
Farnworth.	*The Queen's.*

Folkestone.	*The Pleasure Gardens.*
Gainsborough.	*The Royal Albert.*
Garston.	*Theatre Royal.*
Gateshead-on-Tyne.	*The Metropole.*
Glasgow.	*Theatre Royal, The Grand, Her Majesty's, The Lyceum, The Metropole, The Prince of Wales's, The Princess's, The Queen's* and *The Royalty.*
Gloucester.	*Theatre Royal.*
Goole.	*Theatre Royal.*
Great Yarmouth.	*Theatre Royal* and *The Aquarium.*
Greenock.	*Theatre Royal.*
Grimsby.	*Theatre Royal* and *The Prince of Wales's.*
Halifax.	*Theatre Royal* and *The Grand.*
Hanley.	*Theatre Royal* and *The Grand.*
Hartlepool, West.	*Theatre Royal, The Gaiety* and *The Grand.*
Hastings.	*The Gaiety.*
Hebburn.	*The Grand.*
Horwich.	*The New Prince's.*
Huddersfield.	*Theatre Royal* and *The Empire.*
Hull.	*Theatre Royal, The Alexandra* and *The Grand.*
Hyde.	*Theatre Royal.*
Ilkeston.	*The New.*
Inverness.	*Theatre Royal.*
Ipswich.	*The Lyceum.*
Jarrow-on-Tyne.	*Theatre Royal.*
Jersey.	*Theatre Royal.*
Keighley.	*The Queen's.*
Kidderminster.	*Theatre Royal.*
King's Lynn.	*Theatre Royal.*
Lancaster.	*The Athenaeum.*
Landport.	*The Prince's.*
Leamington.	*Theatre Royal* and *The Victoria Pavilion.*
Leeds.	*Theatre Royal, The Amphitheatre, The Grand, The Princess's* and *The Queen's.*
Leicester.	*Theatre Royal* and *The Royal Opera House.*
Leith.	*The Gaiety.*
Limerick.	*Theatre Royal.*
Lincoln.	*Theatre Royal.*
Lichfield.	*St James's Hall.*
Liverpool.	*The Adelphi, The Bijou, The Colosseum, The Court, The Empire, The Grand, The Lyric, The Prince of Wales's, The Rotunda, The Sefton, The Shakespeare* and *The Star.*

Llandudno.	*The Prince's.*
Llanelly.	*The Athenaeum Hall* and *The Royalty.*
Londonderry.	*The Opera House.*
Longton.	*The Queen's* and *The Victoria.*
Loughborough.	*The New.*
Lowestoft.	*The Marina.*
Luton.	*The Grand.*
Macclesfield.	*Theatre Royal.*
Maidenhead.	*Theatre Royal.*
Manchester.	*Theatre Royal, The Comedy, The Metropole, The Osborne, The Palace, The Prince's, The Queen's* and *The St James's.*
Margate.	*Theatre Royal* and *The Grand.*
Merthyr Tydvil.	*Theatre Royal, The Cambrian, The New, The Park* and *The Victoria.*
Mexborough.	*The Prince of Wales's.*
Middlesborough.	*Theatre Royal.*
Monmouth.	*The New.*
Morecambe.	*The Royalty.*
Neath.	*Assembly Rooms* and *The Bijou.*
New Brompton.	*The Public Hall.*
Newcastle-upon-Tyne.	*Theatre Royal, The Amphitheatre, The Empire, The Grainger, The Grand, The Palace, The Tyne* and *The Vaudeville.*
Newport.	*The Lyceum* and *The Prince of Wales's.*
Northampton.	*The Opera House.*
North Shields.	*Theatre Royal.*
Norwich.	*Theatre Royal.*
Nottingham.	*Theatre Royal* and *The Grand.*
Nuneaton.	*Theatre Royal.*
Oldham.	*Theatre Royal, The Adelphi, The Colosseum* and *The Empire.*
Openshaw.	*Harte's.*
Oxford.	*The New* and *The Victoria.*
Paignton.	*The Bijou* and *The Pier Pavilion.*
Paisley.	*The Paisley.*
Plymouth.	*Theatre Royal.*
Pontypridd.	*The Clarence.*
Portsmouth.	*Theatre Royal, The New* and *The Prince's.*
Preston.	*The Prince's.*
Radcliffe.	*The Grand.*
Ramsgate.	*The Amphitheatre* and *The Granville.*
Rawtenstall.	*The Grand.*
Reading.	*The County.*

Redditch.	*The Public Hall.*
Rochdale.	*Theatre Royal* and *The Prince of Wales's.*
Rochester.	*Corn Exchange.*
Rotherham.	*Theatre Royal.*
Runcorn.	*Theatre Royal.*
St Albans.	*The County.*
Salford.	*The Prince of Wales's* and *The Regent.*
Salisbury.	*The Queen's.*
Scarborough.	*Theatre Royal, The Aquarium* and *The Londes-borough.*
Seacombe.	*The Irving.*
Seaham Harbour.	*Theatre Royal.*
Sheffield.	*Theatre Royal, The Alexandra, The City* and *The Lyceum.*
Shrewsbury.	*Theatre Royal.*
Smethwick.	*Theatre Royal.*
Southampton.	*The Grand, The Prince of Wales's* and *The Royal Victoria Assembly Rooms.*
Southend-on-Sea.	*The Empire.*
Southport.	*The Bijou, The Opera House* and *The Winter Gardens.*
South Shields.	*Theatre Royal* and *The Grand.*
Spennymoor.	*The Cambridge.*
Stalybridge.	*The Grand.*
Stanley.	*The Victoria.*
Stockport.	*Theatre Royal, The New* and *The People's Opera House.*
Stockton-on-Tees.	*Theatre Royal.*
Stratford-on-Avon.	*The Memorial.*
Sudbury.	*The Victoria Hall.*
Sunderland.	*Theatre Royal, The Avenue* and *The Lyceum.*
Swansea.	*The Grand* and *The New.*
Swindon.	*The Queen's.*
Torquay.	*Theatre Royal* and *The Lyceum.*
Tunstall.	*The St James's.*
Wakefield.	*The Opera House.*
Wallsend.	*Theatre Royal.*
Walsall.	*The Alexandra Palace, The Grand, Her Majesty's, The Imperial* and *The St George's.*
Walsingham.	*The New.*
Walthamstow.	*The Victoria.*
Warrington.	*Theatre Royal* and *The Court.*
Wednesbury.	*Theatre Royal.*

West Bromwich.	*Theatre Royal.*
Wexford.	*Theatre Royal.*
Weymouth.	*The Jubilee Hall.*
Widnes.	*The Alexandra.*
Wigan.	*Theatre Royal* and *The Court.*
Wimbledon.	*The Drill Hall.*
Windsor.	*Theatre Royal.*
Wolverhampton.	*The Grand, The Prince of Wales's* and *The Star.*
Wombwell.	*The Gaiety.*
Worcester.	*Theatre Royal.*
Workington.	*The Queen's Opera House.*
Wrexham.	*The St James's.*
York.	*Theatre Royal.*

INDEX